Networking
for
Everyone

Connecting with People for Career and Job Success

By L. Michelle Tullier, Ph.D.

Networking for Everyone

Connecting with People for Career and Job Success

L. Michelle Tullier, Ph.D.
©1998 JIST Works, Inc.

Published by JIST Works, Inc.
720 N. Park Avenue
Indianapolis, IN 46202-3490
Phone: 317-264-3720   Fax: 317-264-3709
E-mail: jistworks@aol.com
World Wide Web Address: http://www.jist.com

See the back of this book for additional JIST titles and ordering information. Quantity discounts are available.
Library of Congress Cataloging-in-Publication Data

Printed in the United States of America

1 2 3 4 5 6 7 8 9   02 01 00 99 98

ISBN 1-56370-440-4

Dedication

To Susan W. Miller, M.A., for being a superb networking role model, friend, and window to a world of opportunities when I was getting my start.

Why Buy This Book?

Believe it or not, that's the first question we ask as publishers when we review a book: Would we buy it? In the case of *Networking for Everyone*, the answer was easy: a resounding YES!

Whether you're the office "ad hoc" counselor or the shy, introverted type, you'll find information in this book that will fit you to a tee. Although the book was written specifically to use networking to get a better job, the principles can apply to career development, and even to your personal life.

For example, you'll learn how to deal with sticky personal situations when you've put the proverbial foot in the mouth, how to make an action plan for networking, and how to be on the giving end of helping others in their networking endeavors.

If you read this book from front to back, we promise an endless array of tips and suggestions guaranteed to help you network successfully. However, the book is just as useful if you simply pick it up and find a place that pertains to your specific interest.

At any rate, be sure to check out the appendices at the back of the book, particularly the listing of Trade Associations. Michelle Tuillier spent almost as much time researching these extensive lists as she did writing the book, and they are useful!

And finally, enjoy! We know you will.

Table of Contents

Preface

Not long ago, I had an experience that reminded me just how important networking really is. It's not that I had forgotten about the power of networking. After all, I work with clients everyday who make tough decisions in their lives and careers, find satisfying jobs, and generally get their lives in order, all because they connect with other people who help them reach their goals. Also, as someone who is primarily self-employed, networking has to be an ongoing part of my life, or I won't stay in business. When it comes to my own networking, however, I sometimes find it hard to practice what I preach. Just as some of you might find networking to be a nuisance, aren't sure how to go about it, or even outright fear it, I too have my own love-hate relationship with this important—even vital—activity.

My networking skills were put to the test recently while I was in Florida attending a national conference for career counselors. One obvious reason for attending conferences is to learn something new from the informative workshops and speakers, but equally important is the chance to connect with the *people* there, not just the *information*. Therefore, before setting foot in any conference room, I usually have to psych myself up to intro-duce myself to strangers and revisit old acquaintances. This is difficult for me because I'm not a natural-born networker. You could even say that I'm a loner at heart and even a little bit shy. Now, don't get me wrong—I put up a good front, so people don't see me as a shrinking violet. I can shake hands, strike up conversations, and schmooze with the best of 'em, but it's a real effort for me. Each time I succeed, though, I am reminded that networking is a skill that can be learned.

At this particular conference, I was only one-and-a-half days into the four-day meeting and was already feeling drained from all the network-ing. I had gone to the hotel dining room for lunch and was looking forward to a little quiet time alone. As I waited for the hostess to seat me, the thought crossed my mind that other people from the conference might see me standing in line by myself and ask me to join them. I secretly hoped that this wouldn't happen and even wished that I had some kind of serious work to do over lunch so that I could legitimately and politely turn down an invitation. Just as these schemes were running through my mind, I heard a voice say, "Are you with the conference? Would you like to join me for lunch?" Feeling I had no alternative, I meekly said, "Yes, sure, thank you."

Well, that half-hearted acceptance ended up leading to a most enjoyable and fortuitous encounter. Gina, my lunch companion, was a bright, personable graduate student working on her doctorate in the same field in which I had received mine. Not only were our professional interests similar, but we even clicked in some silly, but fun, ways. It turned out that we both happen to be only children, share an intense dislike of mayonnaise, and both love big band music from the thirties and forties. And, best of all, we have a similar taste for adventure. By the end of the lunch, Gina had invited me (or actually, I kind of invited myself) to join her on an hour-long drive to Cape Canaveral to watch the launch of the space shuttle Atlantis at 4:27 a.m. on the Sunday morning after the conference ended.

When that day arrived, we met in the hotel lobby at 3:00 a.m., groggy but giddy, and made the drive to NASA's launch pad. Before we knew it, the launch countdown had begun, and we found ourselves shouting out the final seconds as we stood on the banks of the intracoastal waterway, shoulder-to-shoulder with a cross-section of American society. Though shuttle missions have become almost routine, everyone nonetheless breathed a collective sigh of relief and awe as that miraculous tribute to American courage and brilliance took off into outer space to meet up with Russian cosmonauts at the Mir space station. Witnessing this ultimate example of networking on the part of the U.S. and Russians (not just international but practically intergalactic networking!), I thought how ironic it was that a simple little networking over soup and salad had led me to this opportunity of a lifetime.

What if I had said "no" to the lunch invitation? We both would have missed out on what turned out to be a mutually rewarding experience. Gina took me on an outing I'll never forget, and I, in turn, was able to offer her some advice about career counseling, writing dissertations, and careers in psychology. We've kept in touch with each other since then, exchanging photos from our adventure and communicating by e-mail to share professional information or just to say hello. So, I made a friend and established a mutually beneficial professional relationship all because Gina took the initiative to ask me to join her for lunch and because I stretched beyond my comfort zone and said "Yes."

I consider myself lucky to have had this experience, because it reminded me that networking can be not only professionally rewarding, but also plain old fun—two things I hope this book will be for you.

Michelle Tullier
New York City
May 1997

About the Author

As a career counselor in universities and private practice for more than a decade, Michelle Tullier has witnessed countless networking success stories—people of all ages reaching their professional goals by connecting with others. Her own success as an entrepreneur is testament to the fact that her networking strategies work. Michelle's private practice in career counseling attracts clients from across the U.S. and abroad, and she has been a consultant to Fortune 500 companies on networking, time management, and other professional issues. She is also on the faculty of New York University's School of Continuing Education where she teaches beginning and experienced career consultants. Michelle's prior experience includes positions in the career centers of Barnard College at Columbia University and UCLA. She is also the author of books on job hunting and cover letters. Michelle holds a Ph.D. in counseling psychology from UCLA and a bachelor's degree from Wellesley College. She and her husband, Michael, live in the heart of New York City where networking opportunities abound.

Acknowledgments

This book's existence is testament to the fact that networking works. It would not have come into being without the countless resources, ideas, and support that came from so many people.

I am enormously grateful to LaVerne Ludden and Mike Farr of JIST for having been receptive to the initial networking efforts that launched this project—especially to LaVerne for a topic suggestion that was right on target. Many thanks also to Jim Irizarry and Sara Hall for sharing my enthusiasm for this book and for being such a pleasure to work with. A great deal of credit and thanks goes also to Brad Miser, Dr. David Noble, and Marta Partington, for their attentive, skilled, and caring approach to the editing of this book.

Once this project was under way, I could not have completed it without the assistance of my dedicated and resourceful intern Dori Zuravicky. Her ability to handle seemingly endless loose ends, all with a smiling face, was astounding and appreciated more than she could ever know. My gratitude goes also to the many colleagues, clients, and students who shared their knowledge, insight, and that most precious commodity of all—their time. They include Sara Bauman, Ellis Chase, Georgia Donati, Kathi Elster, Nancy Friedberg, Matthew Haas, Tim Haft, Scott Heinz, Erica Hertz, Jeanne Krier, Boyd Leake, Lauren LeVeen, David Rizzotto, Sheryl Spanier, Marci Taub, Kate Weil, and Gina Zanardelli.

As always, I am forever indebted to Michelle Raftery, "M.R.," for the wise counsel and friendship that saw me through this project from contract to completion. This book also would never have made it to completion without the comic relief provided through the welcome exchange of e-mails, faxes, and "Free Friday" calls with Tracy Calhoun,

Joanna Morris Hurley, Millie Kim, Molly Minnear, and Bob Morrell (and extra special thanks to Bob for teaching me how to write way back when). I also want to acknowledge Kathleen Mathews Hohlstein for her uncanny talent at keeping track of, and in touch with, people in far-flung lands. Her efforts were a true inspiration as I wrote this book.

And the biggest thanks of all goes to Michael Gazelle for being the most patient man on Earth.

Introduction

A book on networking needs almost no introduction. If you've ever looked for a job, tried to change careers, or contemplated starting your own business, chances are that someone has said to you, "You'll only get what you want through networking." Even students who haven't yet entered the working world have usually heard about this little thing called *networking,* which is so touted in the "real world." You've probably picked up this book because you've already been introduced to the idea that networking is an important element in professional and personal success. Therefore, I probably don't have to sell you on the basic virtues of networking. However, I would like to tell you something that you may not already know:

Networking

Networking is fast becoming not just a helpful tool for career success, but also an essential skill for career survival.

With the dramatic changes that took place in the work world during the early and mid-1990s, more and more people realize that they need to take charge of their careers rather than wait passively for companies and other organizations to move them up the ladder of success. With massive layoffs—also known as downsizing—and reshuffling of jobs, people have had to seek new opportunities in ways they never did before. These changes have not affected just mid-career and senior-level workers either; college grads in the '90s have had to be more proactive and self-sufficient in finding jobs than their 1980s counterparts were. While the economy and job market seem to be turning around as we approach the 21st century, the old ideas of job security and career stability are nevertheless still on shaky ground—there's no room for career complacency these days. This new focus on self-reliance only increases the need to cultivate connections and gain visibility—that is, network—in order to find jobs, get ahead, or even just to obtain job security.

There is no security in life, only opportunity.

—Mark Twain

Then there are the 60 million people—nearly half of all working Americans—whom trend analysts predict will be part of the contingency workforce by the year 2000. Working as a freelancer, consultant, temporary employee, or entrepreneur means entering a life of continual self-promotion to survive and thrive. It's no question that, for the self-employed, networking skills are even more essential for survival.

In addition to this, advances in technology are making it possible to connect (network) with others on a broader scale and with greater frequency than ever before. You probably already see these changes in your daily life. Are there people with whom you are corresponding more than you did in the past because e-mail makes it much more convenient and inexpensive to do so? Are you more likely to share information with colleagues because it's easy to pop the information in the fax machine or send it by modem with the click of a mouse button? Are you more inclined to call people the minute you think of something that pertains to them, because you can leave a message any time of the day or night on voice mail without disturbing them? Do you have new friends or business associates all around the world because of the Internet?

Some might argue that technology is generating only impersonal communication, but at least it's communication of some sort. You'll see in this book that networking consists of much more than face-to-face encounters. Documents sailing across fax lines, voice messages on answering machines, and e-mail messages on computer screens are valuable forms of communication. As the world moves further into the Information Age, connecting with others in this fashion is becoming a way of life.

Your Work Will Connect You with Others

"Work does not exist in a vacuum. It is deeply embedded in a political-economic-societal context that nudges and constrains the translation of technology into work activities and people's participation in them."

Ann Howard (*The Changing Nature of Work,* Jossey-Bass, Inc., 1995, p. 3)

"A person's identity does not occur in a vacuum. It is a social product, the result of repeated exchanges with others significant in one's world. It is through relationships (and feedback and help and caring) that we discover who we are, what we do best, and how to be better."

Douglas T. Hall (*The Career is Dead: Long Live the Career,* Jossey-Bass, Inc., 1996, p. 4)

What This Book Will Do for You

The objective of *Networking for Everyone* is to teach you strategies for networking that will help you reach your career or business goals and to give you access to print, electronic, and people resources to support and enable your networking efforts. Whether you've been cultivating contacts for years or find yourself starting from scratch, whether you're a born schmoozer or an avowed loner, this book is for you. Having guided many people through the networking process, I've found that the key to success in networking is to approach it in a way that's right for you and your unique personality.

Some people don't even try to develop contacts because they just don't see themselves as being "outgoing." For some, networking can feel downright uncomfortable, unnatural, or unsettling. Others might not hesitate to pick up the phone and make a cold call or shake the hand of a stranger, but they often lack knowledge of the best strategies for making good on those contacts (sometimes that gregariousness needs to be reined in a bit so that more in-depth relationships can develop). One of the main goals of this book is to show you how networking can work *with* your personal style, not against it.

Networking Is a Skill You Can Learn

There's no question that some people seem to have more of a natural gift for networking than others. Some just find it second nature to develop meaningful connections with large numbers of people. These are the ones who might introduce themselves to others at parties, volunteer to head up committees, rarely get nervous when meeting someone new, and just generally seem to have the "gift of gab." In short, they tend to be more extroverted and more relationship-oriented. If you feel that at least some of this description suits you, then congratulations, you've won half the battle toward becoming a successful networker. Now you can complement your innate gifts with the practical tools and techniques this book offers.

What about those of you I didn't just describe—those who cringe at the thought of mingling at gatherings, have little interest in small talk, and feel like you're bugging people if you ask them for help? Well, I have a pleasant surprise for you. You, too, have won half the battle toward being a savvy networker.

Networking is not just about collecting contacts like trophies; it's about quality connections and meaningful relationships. So, those natural tendencies that lead you to say, "Why can't I just do my job and not have to network to get ahead?" are the same personality characteristics that make you especially well suited for the "quality-over-quantity" approach that this book advocates.

Do you tend to have a few close friendships rather than a wide circle of acquaintances? Can you express yourself more powerfully in writing than on the phone? As a more introverted type—whether you're just a bit independent or an all-out wallflower—you possess many valuable traits that, surprising as it may seem, make you well equipped for successful networking.

In addition to showing how networking can fit into your own communication and work styles, *Networking for Everyone* also shows you ways to stretch past your comfort zone and develop skills that can complement your innate tendencies. That doesn't mean that the aim is to turn introverts into extroverts, or vice versa. That wouldn't be right and, besides, is pretty much impossible. No, the goal is simply to nurture those less-developed sides of you.

For introverts, that might mean learning the value of picking up the phone to call a contact instead of taking the more comfortable route of writing a note. For extroverts, that might mean sitting back and carefully planning a networking strategy before diving into the fray and meeting as many people as possible. Whether you're naturally inclined to take the quantity or the quality route when cultivating a personal network, there's always something new to learn about truly strategic, effective networking. By learning tried-and-true techniques and putting them into practice, I guarantee that you can become a skilled networker.

Who This Book Is For: All Things to All People

Trying to be all things to all people is usually a bad idea. The nice thing about networking strategies, though, is that advice for a college grad looking for a first job is not that different from the advice I would give an experienced executive leaving the corporate world to start a consulting business. While the specifics of their circumstances and experience levels differ, the basic principles of smart networking don't. That's why just about anybody should be able to apply the techniques in this book to most situations. Unlike many networking guides that gear advice exclusively toward experienced readers, this book has information and examples that should appeal both to those of you who already have a fairly sophisticated command of networking, as well as to those who don't even know how or where to begin.

Regardless of your age or experience level, there are common situations where networking can help you. These include the following:

⟹ Choosing a direction for your career

⟹ Looking for a job

⟹ Getting ahead or being more productive in your current position

⟹ Establishing or expanding your own business

How to Get the Most Out of This Book

Networking for Everyone is designed as a comprehensive guide. I've tried to address just about every issue related to the networking process, and in the appendixes I refer you to additional resources for further guidance and support. In addition, instead of just giving advice and tips on networking, I walk you through the steps of the process. These steps include:

⟹ Identifying who is in your network

⟹ Expanding that network

⟹ Planning a strategy for making and improving connections

⟹ Making contact with your contacts

⟹ Keeping your network going and growing

⟹ Dealing with special situations like those faced by students or those who are shy

⟹ Handling the sometimes sticky issues that arise when dealing with difficult people or situations

Worksheets, checklists, and other activities are interspersed throughout the book to help you take action. You'll also find summaries at the end of each chapter so that you don't lose sight of the big picture. The Action Plan in chapter 15 will keep you on track long after you've closed the book.

Because this is a "do it" book and not just a "how to" book, it's best to read *Networking for Everyone* from cover to cover. That way, you'll have a clear idea of the process of networking and can get a feel for all the steps involved. If you're pressed for time, though, you might turn to the sections that deal with the skills you most need to develop immediately and read those in depth, catching up on the rest of the book after your "networking crisis" has passed. Whichever way you approach it, I hope you'll find this guide to be a trusted handbook that sees you through many fulfilling and rewarding encounters with people, whether in person, online, over the phone, or through the good old U.S. mail.

The Whats, Whens, Wheres, and Hows of Networking

I use not only all the brains I have, but all I can borrow.

—WOODROW WILSON

Imagine you've been transported into the future to a time when the first resort hotel has just been built on Mars. You find yourself perusing the establishment's glossy brochure, which boasts of cool evening breezes and rock-climbing fun for the whole family, and decide to make Mars your vacation destination this year. So, you set out to make the necessary arrangements as you would for any trip. Ah, but this particular vacation is not exactly to familiar territory, is it? It's not a pack-up-the-car-and-head-for-Disney-World kind of vacation.

How will you ever plan this trip? Your questions probably range from "Should I pack a tennis racket, and do I need a voltage adapter for my blow dryer and electric shaver?" to "How will I breathe, will there be water to drink, and do I have to dress up for dinner?" You'll also probably want to do some reading about the history of the planet, the terrain, the weather, and the local customs. And, you'll want to find the best shuttle fare and rent a four-wheel drive sojourner to do some sight-seeing once you get to the Red Planet. How will you ever find all this information?

Well, the methods you'd use to plan a journey to such uncharted territory as Mars are likely to be fairly familiar territory. You can ask family and friends to find people who've already been there (remember, this is a future fantasy!) or to see if anybody knows someone connected with NASA. You can search the Internet for Web sites with information about Mars or join newsgroups filled with informative Mars aficionados. You might also look up old science teachers or professors to see what they know. You can browse the travel section of bookstores to see if anyone has written about travel to Mars, or you can enlist the services of a expert travel agent. The list could go on and on.

So, what do we call this process of gathering information and connecting with people to make your vacation safe and enjoyable? It's networking. And, if you think about it, these are the same methods you would use to make sure that your career or business is secure, satisfying, and successful. To find a job, for example, you might ask your family and friends to get leads. To choose a career direction, you might try to find someone who knows anyone in the field you're interested in to get more information, just as the folks at NASA might have information about travel to Mars. To be more successful in your current job, you might add a career management coach to your network of contacts, just as a vacation-planner turns to a travel professional. To start or expand your own business, you could look up former bosses and colleagues who've become consultants or entrepreneurs to learn the ropes from them, much like getting in touch with former teachers who could help with your trip to Mars.

The point here is that networking is a natural, common sense process made up of activities that are probably not all that unfamiliar to you. Chances are that you already cultivate contacts and seek out information daily. Have you ever mentioned to a couple of friends that you were looking for a new place to live, deciding on which type of car to buy, or trying to choose a new doctor? In no time at all, you probably had more suggestions than you knew what to do with, and other people you'd never even met started coming out of the woodwork to put in their two cents.

Experienced networkers know that the same thing happens when they start spreading the word that they're looking for a new job, trying to build up a business, or deciding on a new career direction. People who actively network find that they actually know more people, or at least have access to more people and more sources of information, than they realized and that those people and information sources provide all sorts of valuable suggestions and leads.

The key is to take these everyday experiences of connecting with people and information and see them as part of a cohesive networking strategy. This book will help you do just that. First, though, it's important to develop a good working definition of networking and to get a basic understanding of when you do it and generally how to go about it. That's the focus of this chapter.

A New Definition of Networking

To develop a good, working definition of networking that reflects the times in which we live and work, first look at what networking is not. Networking is not about bothering, pestering, or using people. It's not about being pushy, and it's not a contest to see who can collect the most business cards or shake the most hands. It's not a one-sided, selfish, flash-in-the-pan activity.

Truly effective networking is based on relationships that are cultivated and nurtured so that a mutual exchange of information, advice, and support is given and received. If this is the definition of networking that you live and work by, you should never feel as if you're begging, being demanding, or bothering the other person. When you take the time to develop mutually beneficial relationships, networking takes on a new and better meaning. You can comfortably turn to people in your network when you need help with a career or business decision or transition, and the people in your network know that they can turn to you when they need assistance.

Redefining the Networking Cliché

When defining networking, many people think of the popular cliché, "It's not what you know, it's who you know." Well, in keeping with the definition of networking offered in the preceding section, I propose a few new twists on that familiar saying.

The New Networking

Networking is not about superficial connections and brief encounters. It's about cultivating relationships with others in a meaningful way so that you have people to turn to when you need information and support, and people you can help when they need someone to turn to.

It's who you know....

Without a doubt, the "who you know" part of the cliché is still the cornerstone of networking. Knowing people in high places, low places, and everywhere in-between is a key to career success. Networking is something of a numbers game. The more people you know, the easier it is to get ahead in your career or business. Quantity cannot come at the expense of quality, however, which leads us to the next point.

It's who knows what you need to know....

That's a bit of a tongue twister, but it's meant to be that way to make you think more carefully about networking. As mentioned earlier, networking is not a contest to see who can collect the most business cards. In other words, effective networking is not simply a matter of getting as many people as possible into your Rolodex or database. While having a large circle of contacts is a real plus, networking is not simply a numbers game. Quality is just as important as quantity, if not more so. That's where "It's who knows what you need to know" comes in. When you set out to meet people, it is important to zero in on people who have the information, knowledge, or expertise that you need. Instead of meeting huge numbers of people randomly, find a balance between quantity and quality and develop relationships with those who know what you need to know.

It's what you know....

According to conventional wisdom, "*what* you know doesn't count; it's *who* you know that matters." Well, that way of thinking just doesn't cut it in today's world, and there are two reasons why. First, many relationships these days develop and thrive because people share information with each other. For example, if someone posts a question on a Web site message board and you are knowledgeable about that particular topic, you can make a valuable contact if you reply. Being well informed can clearly open doors for you not just online but in life in general.

The second reason that "what you know" counts is that employers are more interested than ever before in your skills and knowledge rather than the job titles you've had. So, if you're looking for a new job or just to get ahead in your career, "what you know" is as important as "who you know."

It's who knows that you know what you know....

Here's another tongue twister to get you thinking more strategically about how you network. Simply put, it's a question of how visible you are or how many others know that you exist and that you have a certain area of expertise or knowledge base. Anyone who's ever tried to sell a product—whether it's lemonade at a neighborhood stand or high-ticket items in a multi-million-dollar business—knows that it's better to have customers coming to you than to have to chase after customers yourself. Well, the same principle is at work in networking. Sure, you have to make overtures to develop relationships with others, but wouldn't it be nice to have people occasionally calling you for a change? If you're looking for a job, trying to manage your career more effectively, or seeking clients or customers for your own business, the more visible you are, the more likely it is that they'll do that. Speaking in public, publishing magazine, journal, or newsletter articles, getting quoted in the paper, having a leadership role in a professional association, and having your own Web site are just some of the many ways to gain visibility. (These are all discussed in more detail throughout this book.)

So, to get off to the right start in networking, you should forget you ever heard "It's not what you know, it's who you know." Instead, have "It's both what you know and who you know that count" as your guiding force when you network to connect with people and information.

The Psychology of Networking

One nice phenomenon people experience when they actively network is that most people genuinely want to help. Not only do I hear reports all the time from clients in my private practice who are pleasantly surprised to find their networking efforts well received, but I frequently witness this good side of human nature myself. For example, as a part-time professor in a university's continuing education program, I often have to ask career counseling colleagues to volunteer their time as guest speakers in my evening classes. No matter how much I remind myself that these are nice, generous people who will be happy to help if their schedules allow, I still get a bit nervous when I pick up the phone to make the request. I find, though, that 99.9 percent of the time that I ask these busy people to extend their workday by a few hours, travel to a campus in a part of town far from where they live and work, and share the "tricks of their trade," all for no compensation, they accept with pleasure. This experience is always a refreshing and reassuring glimpse into human nature.

In addition to reflecting generosity of spirit and basic kindness, positive results like these may reflect also the idea of "what goes around comes around." Almost all the people you'll make contact with in your networking efforts are likely to have gotten where they are in their careers or businesses because someone else helped them along the way. As this happens, it creates a feeling of obligation in people and a desire to pay back a debt of sorts. This obligation can often be satisfied by helping others advance in their careers or grow their businesses.

Now, hear me out before the cynic in you says, "Wait a minute. You can't tell me that everyone on this planet is kindhearted and willing to go out on a limb for the next person." While I am saying that a frequent phenomenon in the networking process is that people do want to help, I'm not claiming that everyone you encounter will do so out of a sense of altruism. Some people just like the power-trip aspect of giving others advice, voicing opinions, or helping them find jobs. Others like to talk about themselves so much that they're willing to meet with anybody and everybody just to have someone else hear them talk.

What Have You Done for Me Lately?

Social psychologists who study helping behavior have identified several phenomena that may be working in your favor when you set out to network. They have found that while some people may seem to be motivated to help others out of sheer altruism, they are actually doing so because of the potential benefits to themselves. Research has confirmed the existence of a concept that psychologists call "self-reward," which is the idea that helping others can reinforce in our own minds the notion that we are good people. It's the idea that we are motivated to lend a hand because we get an ego-boost from being able to pat ourselves on the back for our good deeds. Helping can also keep us from feeling the shame and guilt that would result from not assisting others in need. As Abraham Lincoln once said when he stopped his carriage on a road to save some baby pigs from danger, "I should have had no peace of mind all day had I gone on and left that suffering old sow worrying over those pigs. I did it to get peace of mind."

Source: Reuben M. Baron and William G. Graziano, *Social Psychology* (Holt, Rinehart, Winston, Inc., Chicago, 1991), pp. 354-356.

When to Network

You're never too young—or too old—to network. Each stage of adult life brings professional challenges that inevitably require the assistance of others to overcome and goals that can be achieved only if you connect with the right people and information. Regardless of your age or stage in your career, you might be working toward any of the following four goals, which networking can help you achieve:

→ **Career Choice.** Throughout this book, a goal of "career choice" refers to an effort to make a satisfying and appropriate decision about your career direction. For you, that might mean choosing a first career field out of high school or college, or moving to a new career field after any number of years in the work world. You might be making a choice between several career options or have one specific career field in mind and need to confirm that it's the right direction for you.

➤ **Job Search.** If "job search" is your goal, then for the purposes of this book, this means that you are simply seeking employment—whether full-time or part-time, permanent or temporary. This category also includes internships and apprenticeships in addition to paid jobs. Whether you're hunting for your first job or looking to change jobs after many years of experience, networking is one of the most effective job search methods.

➤ **Career Management.** Having a goal of networking for "career management" purposes means that you want to be more productive and successful in your current job or in your career in general. What this might mean for you specifically is that you're hoping to get a promotion or a raise, to be more efficient and effective in doing your job, to plot a course for where your career path is heading, or any of a number of other career management goals unique to you and your situation.

➤ **Business Development.** This goal describes those who are self-employed or are contemplating self-employment as consultants, freelancers, business owners, or professionals in private practice. Your goal might be to decide if self-employment is right for you, in which case networking can provide the information and guidance you need to make such a big decision. If you are already working on your own, your goal might be to network so that you can expand your business or maintain a successful one.

These four goals are themes carried throughout *Networking for Everyone*, so when the terms "career choice," "job search," "career management," and "business development" are mentioned again, in most cases they are the goals defined here. Throughout the book also are case studies of actual people who have networked successfully toward each of the four goals. The next several sections of this chapter introduce you to four people—John, Ana, Sam, and Monica—and show you where and how networking came in handy for them.

Networking in Choosing a Career

Many people think of networking as useful primarily for job searching, not realizing how useful—and essential—networking is when you are identifying the field in which you want to work. Whether you're choosing your first career fresh out of school or changing careers in midlife, networking can help you uncover possibilities, evaluate each career option, and make a good decision.

To illustrate the power of networking in choosing a career, we present the case of John, a high school science teacher who was looking to make a transition into the health care field. He had read a career guidebook that described health care occupations, and as a result of that reading, decided that nursing, physical therapy, and becoming a physician's assistant were options he wanted to look into further. To get this research started, he set up a meeting with a nurse whom a friend had put him in touch with. (The meeting he had with her is called a Fact-Finding Mission— something you can read about in more detail in chapter 7.) This first attempt at networking not only helped him learn more about one of his career options—nursing—but also made him aware of a profession he hadn't even thought about—genetic counseling. To see how that happened, notice how networking comes into play in the career-choice process and how it helped John specifically.

Generating Career Options

Meeting with people in fact-finding missions and attending professional conferences or other events can help you identify career options that you hadn't been aware of previously. Thinking of career options off the top of your head, asking friends for career ideas, or reading about various careers in guidebooks is a good starting point but is often not sufficient for uncovering the full range of options open to you. The world of work is a big place, so you want to use all possible methods to navigate around it. Talking to people who are knowledgeable about a given field or industry is a great way to do that.

For example, when John met with that nurse to discuss her profession, she happened to mention genetic counselors as a particular type of medical professional whom she sometimes comes into contact with on her job. The nurse's specialty was oncology (working with cancer patients), and some genetic counselors specialize in advising people about their predisposition for cancer, so oncology nurses and genetic counselors can have frequent contact with each other on the job. John had heard of genetic counseling but didn't really know much about it. He was intrigued by the thought of that type of work, though, so he added it to his list of careers to research and set about getting more information. John's case is a typical example of how networking can generate interesting new career options.

Obtaining Career Information

Researching a particular career or occupation is an essential step in deciding whether to enter that field. As John found, reading guidebooks is one way to learn about the nature of the work in a given career, as well as typical salaries, qualifications needed to get into the field, and projected employment outlook for that career field. Other sources he could have used include Web sites that profile career fields (many of these are listed in Appendix C) and literature from professional associations. These and other research methods are described in more detail in the "How to Prepare for a Fact-Finding Mission" section of chapter 7.

Network contacts, however, often turn out to be the best source of information. People who work in a field you're considering entering can share the trials and tribulations of their jobs, tell you what types of people tend to be satisfied and successful in that career field, and provide other useful information that you often can't get in a book or pamphlet.

John, for example, found out all sorts of valuable information about the field of genetic counseling when he met with a genetic counselor whom his nurse friend arranged for him to meet. Before the appointment with the counselor, John learned a bit about the field from the Web site of the genetic counseling professional association. This preliminary research enabled him to come to the meeting armed with focused questions. (Examples of questions to ask in a fact-finding mission are provided in chapter 7.) John left the meeting not only with thorough answers to his questions, but also with suggestions for more people to talk to, professional journals to read, and a list of graduate programs he could investigate.

Making a Career Decision

Your network contacts not only provide information about careers but also serve as surrogate career counselors of sorts, helping you understand how your own interests, skills, experiences, and goals might mesh with a career field you're considering.

Networking proved helpful to John at the decision-making stage because he found that, after two months of researching his options for a career change, he had narrowed the choice to nursing or genetic counseling but couldn't decide between the two. The pros and cons of each seemed to balance out each other. So, in a career counseling session he had with me, I helped him sort out his priorities so that he could know which pros were really important to him and which cons he especially wanted to avoid. By discussing his interests, strengths, and values with me, he was able to come to some conclusions. He realized that, while he had both an interest in science and a desire to help other people, the academic interest in science and research had a slight edge. He then had phone conversations with nurses and genetic counselors he had met with earlier to ask them which option they thought would be a better match for him based on those priorities. From those talks, he got a sense that genetic counseling might be the better way to go because he found the possibility of research jobs in genetics to be particularly intriguing. He still wasn't 100 percent sure about his decision, though. The next section will help you see what he did to get out of this quandary.

Opening Up Opportunities to "Try Out" a Career

Networking can help you uncover useful opportunities to "try out" career fields, such as internships, volunteer or pro bono work, temporary projects, classes, and others. As John found, just reading about career options is rarely, if ever, sufficient for making an informed decision, and even talking with people for further information is often not enough to determine which direction is best for you. After all, you spend a lot of time on a job, so it helps to go in knowing what to expect.

You may also need to gain some practical experience in a new field before you can be fully employed in it. Experience can also enable you to enter a field in a higher position or get into a degree program.

So, short-term, hands-on experiences are one way to be sure that the career choice you make is right for you, and this experience also increases your chances of making a smooth transition into it.

While there are many good directories available that list internship and volunteer opportunities, and college career centers can often direct you to such experiences, networking is one of the most effective ways to uncover the best opportunities. This is especially true if you're several years or more into your career and do not have the luxury of taking time off from paid work to be an unpaid intern or volunteer. Networking can be a way to find out about project-based work or other short-term activities you may be able to engage in during your spare time (assuming you have some!) to get your foot in the door of a new career area.

In John's case, networking came in handy in that one of his contacts let him know about a particular genetics research study in progress that might need lab technicians for the coming summer. Since John had basic laboratory skills, having been a biology major in college, and since he had the summer off from teaching, the opportunity was perfect. With the help of his contacts, he did get a job with the project and also enrolled in an introductory nursing course in summer school so that he would be trying out both fields at once. Those experiences led to a happy ending to John's story. He was able to decide that genetic counseling and research were the directions he wanted to head, so he stayed in his high school teaching job for one more academic year while applying to graduate programs in human genetics. One year later, he was successfully ensconced in an accredited master's degree program taking classes part-time, working part-time in the lab again, volunteering at a hospital to get experience interacting with patients, and doing occasional science tutoring with students to make some extra money. All in all, he was pleased with his decision and on the road to a satisfying career.

Networking in the Job Search Process

Networking as a way to generate job leads has long been one of the most popular and effective of all job search methods. You might answer classified ads every day, send out hundreds of unsolicited resumes to places you'd like to work, post your resume on the Internet, and sign up with employment agencies or executive recruiters, but you're likely to find that word of mouth is the way you hear about the job you eventually land.

The Power of Word of Mouth

Depending on whose numbers you choose to believe, the percentage of jobs found through networking is about 60 to 80 percent or even higher, according to studies conducted by outplacement firms, executive search firms, and the U.S. Department of Labor.

Although many savvy job seekers realize that networking is the name of the game, too often they think of networking in overly narrow terms. They often see networking in a job search as simply telling your immediate circle of friends, family, and colleagues to keep an eye out for jobs for you. While it can be tempting to look at friends and family as "people who can get me a job," the reality is that this narrow approach to networking inevitably leads to a lot of dead ends. Even if they would love to do so, most people do not have the power to snap their fingers and "get you a job." Networking in a job search involves more than simply asking people if they know of any openings or to be on the lookout for openings for you. Networking for a job requires that you be more resourceful in the way that you utilize your contacts. It also requires that you expand your efforts beyond your inner circle of family, close friends, and colleagues.

Our second case study, Ana, is an example of someone who used networking effectively to get a job after some false starts in her search. Ana was a corporate attorney hoping to get a job in finance. Since her search involved not only a change of jobs but also a career field change, it was a particularly challenging one. After spending a couple of months applying for jobs listed in the paper and contacting headhunters (executive search firms) and reaching only dead ends, she decided to turn to networking. Ana called everyone in her immediate network—about 40 people—to tell them that she was looking for a job. She also attended a few events for finance professionals where she met several new people to whom she gave her resume. She called those new contacts a few days later to follow up and found that they didn't know of any openings at that time. So, she asked them to let her know if they heard of anything.

After several weeks and just a couple of leads that didn't pan out, Ana realized she had reached another dead end. What else could she have done? The following are examples of ways that networking can take on a broader role in a search—ways that ended up paying off for Ana.

Planning Strategy

Instead of just asking your contacts to keep an eye out for jobs for you as Ana did, why not sit down with them for advice on your search strategy? In doing so, you're developing a relationship and showing them that there is a way they can help you whether or not they are aware of actual job openings. And most importantly, you're keeping the door open with your contacts because you've given them a more open-ended project—your ever-evolving search strategy—not one that has built-in limits, such as asking, "Do you know of any jobs?" (In chapter 8, you'll read about the "strategy session," which is a meeting in which you have your contacts help you plan a strategy for your job search.)

Ana conducted several strategy sessions that helped her see what she could be doing to make her job search more effective. She got a list from her college of alumni working in finance and also recontacted a few of the people she had met at that early networking event she had attended. Ana then met with these contacts—some in-person and others by phone—to get some ideas for rejuvenating her search. From these meetings, she learned that she should be attending meetings of the local chapter of a particular professional association for women in finance; taking a class in Microsoft Excel, a program many financial analysts need to know; and describing her work experience in a significantly different manner to sound less "lawyerly." In other words, she needed to go back to the drawing board to make herself a more desirable candidate.

Preparing the Tools of Your Search

When you develop your resume, cover letters, and thank-you letters and prepare for interviews, it's helpful to have input from others. You can get help from not only career counselors, job search coaches, and guidebooks, but also people who work in the field in which you want to get a job. Who is better able to tell you what they would want to see in your resume, or to conduct a mock interview with you, than people who work in your target field?

Ana, for example, identified the two people who had been most helpful and generous with their time during her round of strategy sessions and asked them for another hour of their time. After first taking some of the action they had suggested in those sessions, she came back to them with a revised version of her resume and cover letters, as well as with a list of questions that she had found difficult to answer in the few job interviews she had had. By doing so, she received helpful critiques of her written materials, plus suggestions of ways to tackle the tough interview questions.

Uncovering Job Leads

Here's where networking most often comes into the job search process—asking others for information about jobs that are, or might be, available. This is what's really meant by the proverbial "hidden job market." Instead of just sitting at home and answering ads or mailing unsolicited resumes, you talk to people and hear about jobs that haven't yet been advertised.

In the course of her strategy sessions, Ana did find out about job openings that she was able to interview for. So, even though she was meeting with her contacts primarily for advice about her search strategy, she did learn about actual jobs too.

Enlisting "Go-Betweens" in Your Search

One notch up on the involvement scale for a contact is a person who acts on your behalf as you search for a job. Some people in your network will take the extra step of not only telling you about an opening but actively intervening on your behalf. They might hand-deliver your resume and recommend you as a candidate to the person who has the power to hire you.

> *The go-between wears out a thousand sandals.*
>
> —JAPANESE PROVERB

Ana, for example, found that one particular contact she had been meeting with took Ana under her wing and got very involved in acting on her behalf. The contact not only told Ana about openings, but also hand-delivered Ana's resume to a number of people in her company and spoke to them at length about Ana's qualifications. One of these efforts led to Ana's being interviewed and subsequently hired, so developing a relationship with that contact certainly paid off.

Helping You Evaluate Offers

When you do start to get job offers, it's useful to get advice from the more helpful and knowledgeable members of your network to help you decide whether you should accept or decline an offer. They can walk you through the process of evaluating the offer based on the terms of the deal, the nature of the job, the goals you had originally expressed to them, and their knowledge of what is considered to be a "good job" in their field.

This benefit of networking also came in handy for Ana. In addition to the offer she received through one of her contacts, she also got an offer as a result of a newspaper ad she had answered. Both were for financial analyst positions with comparable job responsibilities, but they differed in that one had a higher salary whereas the other was at a more prestigious company. She didn't know which job to take. By consulting with several people in her network, she was able to determine which job would be the better opportunity for her, both in the short term and for reaching her long-range goals.

Emotional Support During the Ups and Downs

A less tangible, but equally important, function of networking in a job search is to attend to your emotional needs during the often frustrating and demoralizing process of trying to get a job. Any transition in life requires a support system, and the job search is no exception. A strong network can provide this support system for you.

It sure did in Ana's case. Her search took ten months to reach a successful conclusion, a wait that seemed like an eternity to her. Though she was generally confident in her abilities and knew she would eventually get a job, her spirits certainly did flag at times. The reassurance and empathy she received not only from family and close friends but also from some of the new contacts she developed in the world of finance helped her get past the rough spots.

Networking and the Career Management Process

Once you've obtained a job, you might think that you can stop networking and just concentrate on doing your work. Wrong! People who are the most successful tend to be those who continually cultivate and maintain rewarding relationships within and outside their workplace.

Sam, our third case study, is an excellent example of effective career management through networking. As an art director for an advertising agency, Sam produces, or oversees the production of, artwork for ads that go into magazines and newspapers. He also sometimes gets involved in the creative direction of television commercials. Sam rose from a junior position at his company to management level in only a year because of his talent as an illustrator, proficiency in graphic design computer applications, and seemingly endless creativity. He knows, though, that in a competitive business like advertising, he has to nurture his talent and keep producing increasingly innovative work to keep his job secure. He also realizes that talent alone is not enough to rise to the higher levels of management that he hopes to reach.

The following are some of the ways that networking can enhance your own career management, and some examples of how Sam has used them to his benefit.

Being More Productive and Successful on the Job

If you have a job where productivity and success rely on generating sales or referrals of clients or customers, networking is essential. But what if your work doesn't involve selling per se? Networking is still important in that it can help you find ways to solve problems, improve efficiency, and stay fresh and innovative. Good networking can also help you keep an eye on what the competition is up to.

Sam, for example, makes a point of having lunch at least once a week with "creative types"—illustrators, painters, graphic designers, photographers, and so on—who work outside the advertising field. He finds that viewing their work and talking with them help to inject a new vitality into his own work. Direct involvement also helps him maintain a pool of top-notch freelancers he can bring in to work in his agency when needed. Sam also meets periodically with art directors from other ad agencies, particularly from those firms that specialize in the types of clients his agency doesn't service and are thus not competitors. Doing so helps bring a fresh perspective to the way he approaches his own ad campaigns.

Advancing in Your Job

Promotions, raises, and plum assignments do not always go to the people who are most deserving based on merit. They frequently go to the employees who are the most visible—that is, those whose strengths and accomplishments are well known to the people who have the power to advance others' careers. Given this reality, networking is likely to be a key element in your own advancement. Do you remember that tongue twister from earlier in this chapter—"who knows that you know what you know"? Well, here it is in action. Just doing your job well is not enough to get ahead; you have to be visible as well.

To make sure he doesn't become invisible in his large agency, Sam takes the initiative to meet frequently with his bosses to discuss what's happening in his department and to find out what objectives they want him to meet. On the surface, these discussions are simply standard strategy or check-in meetings between a mid-level manager and senior managers. Beneath the surface, however, these meetings are critical opportunities for Sam to ensure that upper management is aware of his successes as well as his dedication to continual improvement. In other words, he stays visible.

Advancing in Your Career

In addition to getting ahead at your current job, you might also be concerned about getting ahead in your career in general. Are there long-range goals you're striving for? Do you hope to have reached a certain level in your field five, ten, or fifteen years from now? Do you want to be making a certain amount of money by a particular age? Do you hope to transition into a new career field or a different industry in a few years? Developing professional relationships with people who can steer you in the right direction toward your goals is essential for successful career management. Networking helps secretaries move into nonclerical positions, enables salespeople to move into management, catapults company vice-presidents to presidents, and facilitates just about any other transition you might want to make—either with your current employer or elsewhere.

To take a proactive stance in directing his own career, Sam meets a few times a year with a retired advertising executive who had headed up the creative departments of two of the country's top agencies. Serving as a mentor of sorts, this experienced person advises Sam about how to conduct a successful career in advertising based on his years of experience. Sam also participates actively in professional associations so that he is well known among his colleagues. As a result, he often hears of job openings before they're advertised. He chooses not to pursue most of them, but at least he knows that when he *is* ready to make a move, he has a well-developed network to turn to. After all, an important element in career management is cultivating contacts now, even if you might not need them until later.

Networking in the Business Development Process

Whether you are operating a booming enterprise or are still employed by someone else and just daydreaming about being your own boss, networking is essential to your success. Seeking the advice and guidance of people who are already self-employed (as consultants, freelancers, business owners, or professionals in private practice) can help you make good decisions about how to start, expand, or maintain a successful business.

Networking certainly helped Monica, a Web site producer for the electronic division of a magazine publishing conglomerate. Monica was getting tired of the bureaucracy and politics where she was working and began to think that maybe she could strike out on her own as a freelance Web site designer/producer. She often designed home pages for friends in her spare time, so she had some idea of what it might be like to freelance but wasn't sure how to get started. Monica knew her skills lay in technical and creative areas, not in business, so she was at a loss as to how to develop a successful business of her own. As the fourth case study that you'll be following throughout this book, Monica's story is a superb example of how connecting with the right people and information can turn a vague idea into a successful reality.

Following are some of the ways that networking can facilitate the process of starting, growing, and maintaining your own business.

Deciding to Go into Business for Yourself

The thought of being your own boss can be exciting but can also bring up a host of concerns. Can I make enough money to survive? Do I really know how to run a business? Is there a market for my product or service?

If you're thinking of becoming self-employed as a small business owner, consultant, freelancer, or professional in private practice, networking can help you answer those questions and make the right decision. Turning to knowledgeable people and valuable sources of information (the "who you know and what you know" idea) can help you survey the demand for your product or service, identify what you really need to know about running a business, and carefully assess the financial risk involved.

Monica, for example, embarked on a thorough research process to find out everything she could about running a business. She read all the latest books on small business operation, consulting, and freelancing. (Many of these are listed in Appendix D.) She became a regular visitor to Web sites devoted to self-employment and home-based business (see Appendix C for a list of sites), and she spoke with several computer consultants to learn about the ups and downs of their work. After a few months of research, Monica felt she was equipped with enough information to make a good decision. She decided that she definitely would strike out on her own but also decided that she would do so only after carefully planning a strategy for how she would start and build her business.

Building a Business

You've probably heard all the dismal statistics about how many businesses fail in the first year (usually about 80 percent of them, according to the U.S. Department of Labor). Why the poor success rate? It's because most people dive into self-employment on a wing and a prayer without the careful planning and budgeting that's necessary to survive and thrive. Launching a business—whether it's a small freelance operation run out of your home, or a full-fledged corporation with employees and a suite of offices—requires that you first map out a detailed business plan to guide your every step.

After all her research at the decision-making stage, Monica knew that quitting her job on an impulse and setting up shop as a consultant with nothing more than a business card and a phone line would be a recipe for disaster. Therefore, she created a rough draft of a business plan, using some do-it-yourself business plan software, and then took it to the advisors at SCORE, a branch of the U.S. Small Business Administration that provides advice free of charge (see Appendix C for ways to locate a SCORE office near you). They reviewed her business plan and pointed out some areas that she needed to work on. She also went back to a couple of the computer consultants she had spoken with earlier to get input on her plan from the perspective of people actively working in her field. With all of this help, she was able to put together a solid business plan that was even professional enough to impress a bank to lend her some start-up capital for equipment she needed to purchase.

Expanding a Business

In *Field of Dreams*, the voice said "If you build it, they will come." Well, anyone who's self-employed knows that just building a business isn't enough. You have to build it, spread the word about it, and then "they" will come. That, of course, is where networking comes in handy. To grow a business, you have to make people aware of what you have to offer. In a previous section, you saw that in the career management process, you can't just do your job well, you have to be visible too. The same holds true for running a business or being a consultant.

I know that when I started my private practice in career counseling, I hoped that if I just provided high-quality service to my clients, word would spread and my practice would grow exponentially. Well, word of mouth among clients did help, but it wasn't enough. I also had to get involved in professional associations, take the initiative to get out and meet people who could refer clients to me, and just generally be as visible as possible. The same was true for Monica after she launched her consulting business. While satisfied clients did refer business to her, she soon learned that she had to find the time to cultivate a wider circle of referral sources. So, she became active in her local Chamber of Commerce and also joined two professional associations made up of people from a wide variety of businesses. Doing so made greater numbers of people aware of what she had to offer, and she soon became a household name in her community.

Maintaining a Business

Working on your own can be enormously rewarding. You have considerable, if not total, control over when and how you work. Your income potential is not limited to the salary an employer has granted you. You have the satisfaction of seeing your visions become realities. All in all, self-employment can be very gratifying. There is, however, a downside. Successful businesses inevitably have seemingly inexplicable dry spells. The pressure of being solely responsible for your own paycheck, or for meeting a payroll if you have employees, can become overwhelming. The long hours you have to put in can be exhausting. The constant need not only to do your job but also to bring in business can be stressful. Maintaining a business takes perseverance, hard work, and a little faith that it's all worth it in the long run.

Monica reached this point only one year into her consulting business. She was exhausted by the long hours she had been keeping and felt that she was just barely keeping her head above water financially. She could see that the business was growing. Momentum was building steadily, but she hadn't yet reached the point where she could relax for even a moment. To get over this rough patch, Monica consulted two people who had been serving as mentors for her. One was an experienced consultant who had nothing to do with the computer industry but was an excellent source of advice, inspiration, and moral support. The other was actually a paid mentor—a business strategy coach she met with for hourly sessions (such coaches are discussed in more detail in the Allied Forces section of chapter 3). These advisors helped her find ways to focus her efforts and redefine her business goals so that she could be more streamlined in the way she worked. Doing so enabled her to see greater rewards for less output of time and energy. Her meetings with the advisors also helped her realize that every business has rough patches and that it just takes a little patience and perseverance to get past them.

As you can see from the cases of John, Ana, Sam, and Monica, connecting with people and information is a crucial part of any career or business endeavor. Whether your goal is career choice, job search, career management, or business development, networking helps you reach that goal. I'll be telling you more about these four cases in later chapters and will discuss in more detail some of the specific networking methods that they used. The remainder of this chapter will now round out your overview of networking by discussing where people network and the basic methods they use to do so.

Where to Network

Networking opportunities can be as impromptu as small talk with the person sitting next to you on a plane to a formal, scheduled appointment in someone's office. Chapter 10 discusses many places and occasions for networking, but as a way of introduction, here's a brief overview of the categories of networking avenues:

- **One-to-One Meetings**. One-to-one meetings with network contacts can range from an informal chat with a coworker to an exchange of e-mail with an online contact to a formal appointment. Chapters 7, 8, and 9 focus on the various types of one-to-one meetings you might have depending on your needs and goals and offer tips on protocol and strategy for requesting, scheduling, and conducting such meetings.

- **Conferences and Conventions**. Large, structured events like conferences or conventions in a given profession or industry (or ones which encompass a number of industries or career fields) are often excellent opportunities to expand your network. Chapter 10 tells you how to make the most of these events.

- **Career or Job Fairs**. As with conferences and conventions, attending career fairs or job fairs (the names are used somewhat interchangeably) can be a valuable way to expand your network. They are not only an obvious source of job openings and business opportunities, but also a convenient way to meet a lot of new people under one roof. Fairs are also described in chapter 10.

➡ **Academic/Training Settings.** You can also network while taking classes through a continuing education program or full degree program as well as in short-term seminars, lectures, and workshops. (This type of networking is also covered in chapter 10.) Your classmates, instructors, and guest speakers can often expand your network significantly.

➡ **Networking Meetings.** Across the country, there are many informal groups formed for the express purpose of networking. These might be called "breakfast clubs," "happy hour groups," or "lead or tip groups." While some are quite large and may be under the umbrella of an international networking organization, many are informal, independent groups formed by a few people with common interests. Some groups have members who are all in the same industry, while others cross over industries, but have a common function like sales or management. Others are for entrepreneurs, while yet others are for women or people of the same ethnic group. (See chapter 3 for more details.)

➡ **The Internet.** In a sense, the Internet shouldn't even be a separate category, because it can simply be the vehicle for communicating in many of the other forums. You can, for example, conduct one-to-one meetings online, participate in gatherings of like-minded people through chat rooms and newsgroups, or attend seminars in Web site auditoriums. Ways to network on the Web and Internet are discussed in more detail in chapter 10, and many useful Web site addresses are provided in Appendix C.

➡ **Social/Recreational/Community Settings.** Valuable contacts are made and relationships nurtured in such ordinary settings as health clubs, cocktail parties, neighborhood meetings, and many other gatherings. These opportunities are also addressed in chapter 10.

Networking Methods

In addition to thinking of places where you can network, it's useful to have an overview of *how* to network. While most of this book is devoted to this topic, here's a quick look at the basic methods you can use to connect with your contacts:

Neanderthal Networking?

Networking may have its origins in the self-preservation instinct that has led human beings since prehistoric times to band together to fend off enemy aggression.

⮕ Face-to-face

⮕ By letter or note

⮕ Over the telephone

⮕ Via e-mail and other online communication

⮕ Through public speaking opportunities

The methods you choose from this list depends on a number of factors including your preferred communication style, your networking time frame, your goals and needs, and your resources. In most cases, a thorough networking effort involves a combination of all these approaches. Chapter 2 provides ideas for developing a networking strategy incorporating these approaches, while chapter 6 offers tips on how to handle specific encounters, including techniques for oral and written communication.

Quick Summary

What Networking Is Not

⮕ Bothering, pestering, or using people

⮕ A contest to see who can collect the most contacts

⮕ A one-sided, one-shot deal

What Networking Is

Networking is a process of cultivating and maintaining relationships in which a mutual exchange of information, advice, and support facilitates the growth, success, and happiness of all involved.

When to Network

- To choose a career direction

- To generate career options

- To obtain information about careers

- To make career decisions

- To find opportunities for "trying out" career options

- To obtain a job

- For help planning your job search strategy

- For help preparing the tools of your job search

- To uncover leads

- To find people to act as agents for you

- To find people to interview or hire you

- For guidance as you evaluate job offers

- For emotional support

- To help you manage your career

- To be more productive and successful on the job

- To make decisions about going into business for yourself

⟹ To develop and grow a business, consulting practice, or other self-employment enterprise

Where to Network

⟹ One-to-one meetings

⟹ Conferences and conventions

⟹ Career or job fairs

⟹ Academic/Training settings

⟹ Networking clubs/groups

⟹ The Internet

⟹ Social/Recreational/Community settings

Networking Methods

⟹ In person

⟹ Via e-mail and other online communications

⟹ By writing letters and notes

⟹ Through public speaking opportunities

⟹ Over the telephone

Planning Your Networking Strategy

All rising to great places is by a winding stair.

—Francis Bacon

Now that you've learned what networking is generally all about and have seen how effective it can be through the examples of John, Ana, Sam, and Monica, you might feel ready to dive right into the networking process. When you have decisions to make about your career or business or when you need a new job, it feels good to take action. After all, you won't reach your goals by sitting home and not connecting with anyone. But think about whether you're really prepared to embark on an active networking campaign or to expand your current networking efforts. Like any endeavor in life, it's important to have a plan when you are preparing to network. Otherwise, there's no telling where you'll end up or how long it will take to get there.

This doesn't mean you have to put off actual networking for an indefinite period of time while you labor preparing an elaborate strategy. Planning strategy can be as simple as pausing for five minutes to plan a pitch before making a phone call or as thorough as spending a few months plotting your course toward a major goal. This chapter introduces you to the big picture of networking strategy. Then in chapter 2 you learn how to identify the right people to help you implement that strategy.

Three main steps are involved in planning a networking strategy, regardless of whether you are networking for a career choice, a job search, career management, or business development. These are the steps:

➠ Establishing well-defined goals

➠ Setting objectives to reach those goals

➠ Creating a plan to meet those objectives

Let's look at each of these steps in more detail.

Establishing Well-Defined Goals

The first step in networking is to know why you're doing it. Without a goal in mind, networking is aimless and a poor use of your time. Of course, there is some value in cultivating random ongoing relationships since you never know which of them will turn out to be fruitful. Doing so ensures that you're addressing the "quantity" aspect of networking discussed in chapter 1. Strategic networking, however, is quality networking. Strategic networking is based on getting to know the right people—those who can enrich your professional life in a meaningful way, and whose lives you can, in turn, influence positively. Having clearly defined goals is one way to make your networking strategic.

What Is a Goal?

You can think of a goal as the result you hope to attain. You might also see it as a vision, a dream, or a point in the near or distant future when you will feel as if you've accomplished something. The only thing a goal is not is a fantasy. A fantasy is too remote, too unattainable. A goal might seem like a fantasy at times in that it may feel beyond your reach—a job search that drags on and on, a career choice that seems impossible to make, a hoped-for promotion or raise that keeps slipping from your grasp, a business that just won't get off the ground. If your goal seems impossible to reach, the problem may lie not with the goal itself (as long as it's a realistic goal) but with the means you're using to reach that end—that is, the objectives, the plan, or the people. (Later sections of this chapter show you how to handle the objectives and the plan, whereas chapter 3 addresses the people part.)

A goal should also be a reflection of who you are and what you really want. That may sound kind of obvious. After all, who would go after a goal they really don't want? Well, you'd be surprised how many people do. Some people go after a particular type of job because it's what their spouse or their parents want them to do. Some people think they should start a business or become a consultant just because it seems to be the thing to do these days, when in fact they're really not entrepreneurial types. So, make sure that the goals you set are based on what truly interests you and is important to you.

Be Careful What You Wish For

The case of Nicole, a television producer I worked with recently, is a good example of striving for an unwanted goal. Nicole was a senior producer on a prime-time show for a major network. She was known for doing outstanding work and was well liked by her bosses, so when she heard about an exciting new program in development, she thought she was a shoe-in for becoming one of its producers. Much to her dismay, when she approached her boss about transferring to the new show, she found out she wasn't a shoe-in. The fact that she was doing such a great job with her current program (its ratings had gone way up since she came on board) meant that her boss couldn't risk taking her off that show. She pushed and pushed, using every tactic she could think of to persuade him and other senior managers to move her, but they wouldn't budge.

Nicole came to see me at that point, hoping to get some new thoughts on how to change their minds. Instead, I had her start by telling me why she wanted the transfer in the first place. As she tried to articulate her reasons to me, she realized that she had actually never articulated them to herself. She had sort of been on autopilot, hearing about the new show, then impulsively assuming she wanted to work on it because it would be more prestigious than her current one and would present fresh challenges. As she talked, though, she realized that those weren't necessarily valid reasons.

I then asked what her priorities were at that point in her life—basically what she would like to change or keep the same in her life. She had no difficulty answering that question. Her priority was to have more of a balance between her work and personal life. She wanted more time with her friends, maybe the time to develop a lasting romantic relationship, more time to go to the gym, and more time for some freelance projects she had been doing. Her current job had just started to allow her to do that. Now that she had pulled that show up from its ratings hole, her job had become less demanding—almost routine. After years of working eighty-hour weeks to get to this high level of her profession, she was enjoying having a more relaxing pace to her life. As she talked about all this, the prestige and fresh challenges of the new show seemed less and less appealing to her.

I did ask her to make sure that she wasn't just rationalizing—talking herself out of wanting the transfer because she couldn't have it. She assured me she wasn't, and I could tell she wasn't. She had realized that she was at a major turning point in her life and that, with her priorities changing, her goals needed to change, too.

What Are Your Goals?

As you know by now, the four broad categories of goals addressed in this book are career choice, job search, career management, and business development. You probably don't have any problem deciding which of those areas is the goal you want to work toward (and you might be working toward more than one at once, which is fine). What might not come as easily, though, is defining your goal more precisely than those broad categories. The following are some specific goals you might hold.

Career Choice Goals

➠ Choosing an entirely new career field (for example, transitioning from being a police officer to a businessperson, or from being a marketing executive to a physical therapist)

➠ Choosing a new specialization within your field (for example, going from being a police officer to a private investigator, or from being a physical therapist to an occupational therapist)

➠ Choosing a new industry or sector (for example, a lawyer moving from government work to a corporate firm, or a salesperson in the insurance industry moving into sales in the computer industry)

➠ Choosing your first career (for example, a student transitioning into the work world for the first time, or someone who has been a full-time parent choosing a first career outside the home)

You may find it difficult to choose one of these four choices as your goal. You might, for example, know that you're dissatisfied with the career field you're currently in and want to make a change, but you don't know if you just need to change industries or make a slight shift in your field or if you need a whole new career. If so, there's no need to feel that you must define your goal as precisely as the ones listed above. Those are provided to serve as examples and to show that it can be helpful to think about what you really mean when you say, "I need a new career."

John's Goal

To choose within the health care profession a satisfying career that will build on my science background and interest in medicine.

Ana's Goal

To obtain in an investment bank or other financial institution an analyst position that builds on my research experience, quantitative abilities, and knowledge of corporate financial transactions, but does not involve legal work per se.

Job Search Goals

⟾ To obtain a new job in your same field and industry (for example, a loan officer in a commercial bank who wants the same kind of job in a different bank because she's concerned that her bank is having financial troubles; or a graphic designer who would like a job in a larger design firm where there is more opportunity for advancement)

⟾ To obtain the same type of job but in a different field or industry (for example, a customer service representative for a phone company who wants to work as a customer service rep for a mail-order retail company; or a museum administrator who wants to work on the business side of a theater company)

⟾ To obtain your first job (as a student entering the world of work for the first time, or anyone who has not worked before)

These are just a few of the many types of goals one might have related to a job search. Your situation may fit one of these scenarios or be slightly different from these. The important point here is that to find a job, you have to know what you're looking for. So, be sure to define your job search goals as carefully as possible.

Career Management Goals

⟾ To be more productive and successful in your job (that is, to be more efficient, make more sales, be more creative, be a better manager, be a better communicator, and so on)

⟾ To get ahead at your job (that is, to get a promotion, a raise, increased responsibility, or more satisfying assignments/projects)

→ To get ahead in your career in general (that is, to reach a particular level in your career track, to make more money by a certain time, to achieve a certain level of stature in your professional community)

If career management is the category you're most concerned about, you're likely to have multiple goals in this area. Often people have short-term goals related to doing their current job better, but also have long-range goals concerning where they would like their careers to head in the coming years.

Business Development Goals

→ To decide if you should go into business for yourself

→ To establish a new business

→ To grow or expand an existing business

→ To maintain a mature business

Business development goals are fairly straightforward and usually easy to identify based on where you are in the business development process. The important thing to remember is to base your goals on what you really want.

For example, in my own business, a career counseling private practice, I have been tempted over the years to set goals that I soon found out I didn't want to strive for. I have considered taking on partners or employees, expanding the range of services I offer, moving into larger office space, and once was even enticed by someone's suggestion of opening up satellite offices of my practice around the country—in a sense, franchising. Before acting on these ideas, however, I have always come to the realization that I prefer to keep my practice small (in structure, not in volume of clients), where I am the sole

Sam's Goals

To continue to generate fresh, highly creative and effective artwork for advertisements; to become a more skilled manager; and to be head of a creative department of an ad agency within five years.

Monica's Goal

To make a careful decision about whether to start a Web site development business, and if so, to plan an effective strategy for launching a successful business.

counselor. I prefer to operate within the model that physicians and psychologists have typically followed, that of a true professional practice, not a business. I realized that I would prefer to grow in other ways, namely writing, teaching, and some organizational consulting, while seeing clients a few days a week. If I took on partners or tried to become a large-scale enterprise with offices around the country, I would have to spend much more time as a manager and less time doing the actual counseling and in the professional activities that enrich my counseling. I offer this story as an example of how easy it is to be tempted by what you might think it means to be "a successful entrepreneur" when, in fact, the way one defines that term can vary greatly.

My Goals

Now that you've learned what goals are all about and have seen some examples of specific goals, try writing your goal (or goals) in the space provided below. You'll also have a chance to state your goals in chapter 15 when you put together your action plan. For now, just write down your goal(s) as you think it is now; later you can revise it if necessary when you get to chapter 15.

_____

_____

_____

_____

_____

Setting Objectives to Reach Your Goals

The next task in developing a networking strategy is to set objectives that will help you reach your goals.

What Are Objectives?

Objectives can be viewed as steps—or milestones, in business parlance—along the way to your ultimate destination. As with any major project, it is helpful to break down your networking goals into smaller, achievable, and measurable steps. That's what the objectives are.

Different goals, of course, call for different objectives. If your goal is to get a job in eight weeks, your objective might be to go on a certain number of interviews per week. If your goal is to be promoted at work in a year, you might have weekly or monthly objectives related to gaining visibility, taking on new responsibilities, or developing skills.

What Are Your Objectives?

In thinking about how you can break down your goals into measurable objectives, it might be helpful for you to see the objectives that our four case studies set for themselves. While your own objectives will differ from theirs, you may nevertheless be able to model yours after theirs somewhat.

John's Objectives

➤ To gain an overview of all the different types of jobs in the health care professions

➤ To select from all of those choices a manageable number of professions that interest me enough to explore them further

➤ To learn everything I can about these professions from which I will be making a selection

➤ To narrow my choices down to the one profession that I would like to train for and enter

As you can see, John's list of objectives is a logical, step-by-step way to reach his ultimate goal of choosing the right career. In the "Creating a

Plan to Meet Your Objectives" section of this chapter, you'll see what action he took to reach each of these objectives.

Ana's Objectives

➠ To learn how I can most effectively and smoothly make the transition from law to finance

➠ To prepare powerful self-marketing materials (resume, portfolio, and cover letters)

➠ To go on at least five job interviews per week until I land a job

Ana's objectives follow a logical progression from plotting a course for her job transition to putting together the written materials she'll need to get a job, to having enough interviews to increase her odds of getting job offers. What you don't see in this list of objectives is how she'll actually accomplish these steps. That's where the plan comes in. Her plan, as you'll see in the "Creating a Plan to Meet Your Objectives" section of this chapter, includes the networking activities that will help her meet each objective.

Sam's Objectives

➠ To keep on top of the latest technological developments and creative trends in graphic arts through classes and networking

➠ To learn management techniques, specifically delegating, reprimanding, and morale-boosting, through formal training and mentoring

➠ To learn the best strategies for working my way into a creative services department head position

Notice how each of Sam's objectives matches the goals you saw listed a few pages back. To meet the goals of keeping his artwork fresh and innovative and becoming a better manager, he set objectives that broke those goals down into more specific things he needs to learn. For his long-range career goal, he set an objective of plotting a course toward becoming a department head. Later you'll see how his plan assigns specific activities to reach each objective.

Monica's Objectives

⟹ To assess the market demand for Web site services

⟹ To survey the competition in the Web site consulting business

⟹ To assess my own priorities for my life—for example, desired income, lifestyle, and geographic location

⟹ To learn the best approach to starting a business

Monica's first three objectives are mini-goals on the road to her ultimate goal of making a decision about whether she should go into business for herself. Each objective will help her make that decision. Her last objective is a good example of the subtle difference between a goal and an objective. Her goal is to plan an effective strategy for starting her business. Her objective is to learn what will make that strategy an effective one, so the objective enables her to reach the goal.

My Objectives

Now that you've read some examples of how goals can be broken down into objectives, think about what some of your objectives might be for reaching your own goals. Remember, you'll have another chance to list your objectives when you get to the action plan in chapter 15. For now, just jot down any ideas you have at this point.

_____

_____

_____

_____

_____

_____

_____

Creating a Plan to Meet Your Objectives

After identifying your goals and objectives, the next step is to map out a plan that will help you meet your objectives, which in turn will enable you to reach your goals. A "plan" can be defined as a list of networking activities (connecting with people *and* information) that will lead to successful completion of your objectives. For examples, look at the following plans for John, Ana, Sam, and Monica.

John's Networking Plan

Goal: To choose within the health care profession a satisfying career that will build on my science background and interest in medicine

Objective: To gain an overview of all the different types of jobs in the health care professions

Plan:

➡ Go to my local public library and to bookstores and read career guidebooks that describe careers in health care

➡ Do an Internet search for information on careers in health care

➡ Ask my friends and colleagues about who they know who works in health care to get an idea of different types of jobs people hold (and to start to develop a network of people I can talk to about their work)

Objective: To select from all of those choices a manageable number of professions that interest me enough to explore them further

Plan:

➡ Think about what aspects of science and medicine interest me, what I want out of a career, and how much training I'm willing to undergo. Come up with a list of criteria for this career transition—for example, characteristics I want my new career to have, or needs of mine that it must meet.

- Compare those criteria to what I've learned about the various careers I've read about. Choose a maximum of five health care careers that seem to meet my criteria, and put those on my final list of careers to research further.

Objective: To learn everything I can about the professions from which I will be choosing one

Plan:

- Contact the professional associations for the fields I'm exploring and request that they send me written information on careers in their field. Also find out what journals and newsletters they publish that might give me valuable information.

- Meet with people who work in the fields I'm considering to learn more about the nature of the work and what they like and don't like about their jobs. (These meetings would be fact-finding missions as described in chapter 7.)

Objective: To narrow my choices down to the one profession that I would like to train for and enter

Plan:

- Review the criteria I established earlier and see which of my choices best fits what I really want out of my next career.

- Go back to the people I spoke with before and ask for their opinions about which of my choices best fits my criteria.

- If I have trouble narrowing my options to the one field I want to enter, find ways to "test out" each choice. Testing the choices might include taking classes, doing volunteer work, or getting a summer job in one or more of the options.

Ana's Networking Plan

Goal: To obtain in an investment bank an analyst position that builds on my research experience, quantitative abilities, and knowledge of corporate financial transactions, but does not involve legal work per se.

Objective: To learn how I can most effectively and smoothly make the transition from law to finance

Plan:
- ➠ Talk with people in finance to get their suggestions on the best way to break into their field. (Ways to find people to talk to are suggested in chapter 2.)

- ➠ Meet with a career counselor to learn strategies for making a career transition. (Career counselors and job search coaches are discussed in chapter 2, and ways to find them are provided in Appendix C.)

Objective: To prepare powerful self-marketing materials (resume, portfolio, and cover letters)

Plan:
- ➠ Read guidebooks on writing resumes and cover letters and preparing portfolios. (Many of these are listed in Appendix D.)

- ➠ Prepare a rough draft of these materials and show them to my contacts in finance to get their input on how to make them more effective.

- ➠ Meet with a job search coach to have my written materials critiqued.

Objective: To go on at least five job interviews per week until I land a job

Plan:
- ➠ Make at least ten calls and send out at least ten targeted cover letters and resumes a day.

- ➠ Post my resume on the Internet and also search employment Web sites for job listings I can reply to. (Many such Web sites are listed in Appendix C.)

➡ Attend as many meetings and conferences as possible where I can meet people who work in finance.

Sam's Networking Plan

Goal: To continue to generate fresh, highly creative and effective artwork for advertisements; to become a more skilled manager; to be head of a creative department of an ad agency within five years.

Objective: To keep on top of the latest technological developments and creative trends in the graphic arts through classes and networking

Plan: ➡ Attend continuing education seminars offered by advertising and graphic design professional associations

➡ Meet regularly (as often as once a week for lunch or drinks after work, if possible) with other "creative types"—for example, illustrators and photographers—to talk about and view their work

Objective: To learn management techniques, specifically delegating, reprimanding, and morale-boosting, through formal training and mentoring

Plan: ➡ Ask my boss to send me occasionally to seminars on management techniques

➡ Check out the management section of bookstores to find books to read on managing people effectively

➡ Meet periodically (once every one or two months) with experienced managers from various industries who can advise me about what works and doesn't work when it comes to managing people

Objective: To learn the best strategies for working my way into a creative services department head position

Plan: ⇒ Meet periodically (once every two or three months) with a "mentor," someone with considerable experience in advertising who can help me manage my career toward my goal of being a creative services department head.

⇒ Meet with a career management coach to learn strategies for reaching my long-term goals. (Career management coaches, or executive coaches, are discussed in chapter 3, and Appendix C lists sources for finding a coach.)

⇒ Attend professional association meetings and conferences as often as possible to stay visible.

Monica's Networking Plan

Goal: To make a careful decision about whether to start a Web site development business, and if so, to plan an effective strategy for launching a successful business

Objective: To assess the market demand for Web site services

Plan: ⇒ Search the Internet and contact professional associations for computer consultants to find data on the number of freelance Web site designers/producers in this country

⇒ Do a search of past issues of business and computer magazines to find articles on Internet consulting businesses

⇒ Conduct an informal survey (by phone and in person) of businesses and individuals in my area to get a sense of how much demand there may be for my services

Objective: To learn more about my competitors in the Web site consulting business

Plan: ⇒ Make anonymous calls (or have a friend do it) to local Web site designers to find out about their services, prices, and professional credentials

Objective: To assess my own priorities for my life—for example, desired income, lifestyle, and geographic location

Plan: ⟶ Meet with a business strategy advisor or career counselor for help in identifying my interests, strengths, and priorities and to learn if I am well-suited to being an entrepreneur. (Ways to find such professionals are provided in Appendix C.)

Objective: To learn the best approach to starting a business

Plan: ⟶ Read every book I can find at my local library and bookstores about starting a small business or becoming a consultant. (Books like these are listed in Appendix D.)

⟶ Browse Web sites that focus on consulting, small business, and home-based business. (Many of these are listed in Appendix C.)

⟶ Meet with experienced entrepreneurs from a variety of fields to get their input on my business strategy and for help in constructing a business plan. (I call meetings like these "strategy sessions" and discuss them in chapter 8.)

Characteristics of an Effective Networking Plan

⟶ **It's systematic.** Networking activities are listed and planned for, not just jotted down as vague ideas, so that you have a clear plan you can stick to.

⟶ **It balances quantity and quality.** An effective strategy enables you to meet large numbers of people and develop quality relationships.

⟶ **It fits your personal style.** An effective strategy does not require you to do too many things that you're not comfortable doing and maximizes activities that take advantage of your strengths.

➡ **It fits your goals.** You need to know that the steps you're taking to reach your goals are the ones that will actually get you there. No wild goose chases, please!

➡ **It's based on thorough preparation.** Even the best networking plan will fail if you haven't done your homework—that is, researching a career field or business idea before talking to people about it, perfecting your communication skills, and so on.

Now that you've read several examples of plans that were devised to meet various objectives and goals, you might be getting some ideas of things you can do to reach your own goals. At the end of this book in chapter 15, you'll have a chance to create a detailed action plan where you can record these ideas. Rather than create your plan now, it's probably best that you wait until you've read the rest of the book so you'll have a more complete awareness of the many different types of networking activities that you might want to include in your plan.

The Serendipity Factor

In addition to a carefully orchestrated networking strategy, don't overlook the power of the serendipity factor. Impromptu encounters with people can become rewarding networking opportunities in ways you never could have anticipated.

I once struck up a conversation with a woman sitting next to me on a train headed into New York City from a Long Island beach town. It turned out that Martha (not her real name) worked on Wall Street and was thinking of·making a job change as well as a transition into a different specialty area within finance. After talking with her about her career situation and also having a pleasant conversation on other topics, we arrived at our destination. Before departing, we exchanged business cards and promised to keep in touch. Shortly after that encounter, I received a phone call from Martha requesting an official career counseling session with me to continue the discussion we had had on the train. Just acquiring Martha as a client would have been sufficient reward for that chance encounter on the train, but there were other benefits as well. One of my clients benefited in that I was able to refer him to a "headhunter" (an executive recruiter) whom Martha knew well. This headhunter typically deals only with experienced candidates, but as a favor to Martha, he made the effort to find an excellent entry-level job for my client—a recent graduate who had been trying for months to break into finance at the height of the recession in the early '90s. And, to top it all off, that executive recruiter ended up referring several clients to me over the months and years that followed. The serendipity factor certainly paid off in this case!

So, the next time you hesitate to start up a conversation with the friendly looking person next to you or to accept an invitation to go somewhere, think twice. You never know what good things might happen if you deviate a bit from your carefully crafted plan. These chance encounters are just as important in the networking process as your carefully planned strategies are. (In chapter 10, you'll find more examples of places that chance encounters are likely to occur and tips for handling them effectively.)

Quick Summary

Having a well-crafted networking strategy is essential for reaching your goals.

A Networking Strategy Consists of....

⮕ establishing well-defined goals.

⮕ setting objectives to reach those goals.

⮕ creating a plan to meet those objectives.

A goal is an end you are striving to reach by various means.

Goals Should....

➧ reflect your own values and wishes, not those of other people or society-at-large.

➧ be realistic and attainable, not fantasies.

Objectives are the "mini-goals" along the way to a goal.

Objectives Should Be....

➧ measurable.

➧ realistic.

➧ logical means to a desired end—that is, to the goal.

A plan in networking is a to-do list of sorts. It consists of actions that will lead to objectives being met.

A Plan Should....

➧ be systematic.

➧ balance quantity and quality.

➧ fit your personal style.

➧ fit your goals.

➧ be based on thorough preparation.

Take advantage of the "serendipity factor" in networking. You never know where a valuable contact or useful bit of information may come from.

3

Developing Your Network

I read somewhere that everybody on this planet is separated by only six other people. Six degrees of separation. Between us and everybody else on this planet. The President of the United States. A gondolier in Venice. Fill in the names.

—OUISA IN *SIX DEGREES OF SEPARATION* BY JOHN GUARE

As you saw in the sample networking plans of chapter 2, a key to reaching your career or business objectives and goals is to enlist the help of knowledgeable, supportive people. You read, for example, that John needs to talk to people who work in health care for help with his career decision. Ana needs people to critique her resume before she starts sending it out. Sam needs a mentor to help him steer his career in the right direction. And, Monica needs people to fill her in on the ups and downs of life as a consultant. Where will they find all these people?

Well, John, Ana, Sam, and Monica can probably find some people to help right in their immediate circle of family, friends, and professional colleagues. From there, they might need to branch out to friends-of-friends and more distant professional acquaintances. Then, they'll need to cultivate completely new contacts through the many means suggested later in this chapter.

You, too, probably have the makings of a network of helpful people among your immediate contacts (as well as people whom you in turn could help). Whether your network consists of nothing more than the ten names programmed into speed-dialing on your telephone, or whether you have a Rolodex stuffed to the gills with hundreds of names, it never hurts to identify more people who might be instrumental in your quest for your career or business goals. In this chapter, you'll search your memory banks and go through records and files in your office or home to take stock of those whom you know already. You will also learn about ways to cultivate new contacts and expand your network well beyond the people you already know or have known in the past.

You'll learn, too, about the "STARS" system for taking a closer look at who makes up your network. This system involves classifying people as strategists, targets, allied forces, role models, or supporters, based on the role each person plays in helping you reach your goals.

Taking Stock of Your Network and Potential Network

When you take stock of the people you know or could have access to, it's helpful to think of categories of contacts. The following pages walk you through several broad categories. These include personal, work, education, professional groups, career services, personal and professional services, and multimedia. Each of the categories is explained in detail, and worksheets follow each category description so that you can start writing down the names of people you know (or could get to know) in each category. Doing so enables you to have the makings of an inventory of sorts—a comprehensive listing of your network.

(Chapter 4 shows you how to set up a contact management system on your computer or on index cards, so you might choose to leave the worksheets in this chapter blank and wait until chapter 4 to record your network inventory. Nevertheless, it's a good idea to jot down at least some names on the worksheets here as a foundation for the more permanent contact management system you will establish in chapter 4.)

Supplies You'll Need to Expand Your Network

To compile an inventory of your contacts, you'll need a few things. First, think of all the places—besides your brain—where you'll find names and contact information for people you already know or at least know of. You should gather all of the contact information that you can lay your hands on. You'll probably find it in:

⫸ Address books (your current one as well as old ones)

⫸ Rolodex or business card file

⫸ Holiday card and birthday lists

⫸ Computer databases of contacts

⫸ Company directories (current and past jobs)

⫸ A directory for your school or college (current students or alumni)

⫸ Files of clients, customers, or other professional contacts

⫸ Membership rosters of professional or community groups you belong to

As you fill in the worksheets that follow each of the contact categories, be open to including anyone or any group that comes to mind. Now is not the time to say things like, "I don't know if they could really be of any help." Don't start censoring your list! It's very likely that people you haven't kept in touch with or are just barely acquainted with can be a valuable part of your network. And people who you think don't have much information or many resources may have more than you expect. So include them all—at least for now.

Personal Contacts

This category includes family, friends, acquaintances, and neighbors, as well as people you come across through involvement in clubs, community activities, sports, religious organizations, and other affiliations.

Some people hesitate to call on family and friends for help in reaching their own career or business goals. While it is important not to rely too heavily on people close to you, there is nothing wrong with enlisting their help on a basic level. Say you're looking for a job in accounting and your uncle is a big shot at a major accounting firm. It's understandable that you might feel uncomfortable if he were simply to get you a job, but could you at least let him give you some advice or put you in touch with some of his colleagues? That way, any job you do obtain, you know you got because of your own efforts and qualifications. He just helped steer you in the right direction. In competitive situations, it's essential that you utilize all possible sources of leads, advice, and contacts, so you might need to stretch past your comfort zone when dealing with family and friends who could help.

You might also need to stretch a bit if you are uncomfortable contacting people you don't know all that well, such as friends-of-friends or acquaintances you know of through some organization like your church or a community sports league to which you belong. If you approach them with tact and courtesy and don't expect the world, most people will be happy to help out, even if they don't know you very well.

Take a look at the categories of personal contacts on the worksheet that follows and make note of people you know in each category. (In the case of clubs or other groups, it may not be practical to list all members in this small space, so just list the name of the organization. Also, for categories like "Friends & Acquaintances" in which you may have a lot of names to list, you might just want to list several key people and then write something like "See address book" to refer you to the rest.)

In addition to writing down names of people you know in each category, think about how you could expand your network by getting involved with some of the organizations, activities, or people mentioned in these categories.

Personal Contacts Worksheet

Family:

_____

_____

_____

_____

_____

Friends & Acquaintances:

_____

_____

_____

_____

_____

Clubs & Organizations (include social clubs, country clubs, book clubs, parents' groups, sports teams, gyms/health clubs, fraternities/sororities, and other such groups):

_____

_____

_____

_____

_____

Community Groups (fund-raising or other services for charities; advisory or governing bodies of organizations, such as Boards of Trustees; neighborhood associations and other civic groups; foundations and other philanthropic groups; cultural organizations; or parent-teacher groups):

_____

_____

_____

_____

_____

_____

Religious Organizations (churches, mosques, temples, religious study groups, social groups, or youth groups):

_____

_____

_____

_____

_____

_____

Work Contacts

Your current and past work experiences are excellent sources of network contacts. Bosses, coworkers, clients, and customers should all be considered as potential network members. This category is not limited to paid jobs, either. It also includes volunteer work, internships, and other professional assignments.

Work contacts proved useful for Sam, for example, in that one of his former bosses became his mentor. After the boss retired from an illustrious career in advertising, Sam stayed in touch with him, and they gradually developed a mentor-protégé relationship.

Pull out your current resume as well as old ones, along with any company directories you've saved from past jobs, and think about who you know from all your jobs, internships, and other work-related projects. Write as many people as you can think of on the worksheet that follows.

Work Contacts Worksheet

Coworkers (current and former):

_____

_____

_____

_____

_____

Supervisors (current and former):

_____

_____

_____

_____

_____

Colleagues (clients, customers, project team members, freelancers, consultants, temps, people at other organizations in your industry, investors, and shareholders):

_____

_____

_____

_____

_____

_____

Volunteer Work Colleagues & Supervisors:

_____

_____

_____

_____

_____

_____

_____

_____

Education Contacts

Whether you are a current student or an alumnus, educational institutions offer ready-made networks. Your classmates from high school, college, or graduate school are often very willing to help you reach your career goals.

Don't forget about other educational settings as well. If you've taken any continuing education or other part-time, nondegree classes or have been through vocational training programs on your own or through an employer, you've undoubtedly met people (classmates, instructors, and guest speakers) who could be valuable members of your network.

Monica, for example, expanded her network greatly through the business strategy seminar she took over several weeks. Not only were her fellow participants good sources of future clients for her consulting business, but the instructor and guest speakers were as well.

Think about the people you know (or used to know) through educational settings and list them on the Education Contacts Worksheet. (Here's a worksheet where you may not be able to list individual names but can refer to an alumni directory or class roster.)

Education Contacts Worksheet

Alumni (high school, college, or graduate school):

_____

_____

_____

_____

_____

Teachers & Professors (high school, college, or graduate school):

_____

_____

_____

_____

_____

Advisors, Deans, & Coaches (high school, college, or graduate school):

_____

_____

_____

_____

_____

Continuing Education Courses/Seminars/Workshops (classmates, instructors, or guest speakers):

_____

_____

_____

_____

_____

Job Training Programs (classmates, instructors, or guest speakers):

_____

_____

_____

_____

_____

Professional Groups Contacts

If you don't already belong to professional or trade associations, consider joining any of the organizations for your career field or industry. Attending meetings, conferences, seminars, and social events sponsored by such groups is an excellent way to expand your network. (See Appendix B for a sampling of associations if you need to find ones to join.)

You might also want to join organizations whose sole focus is networking. These are groups of people who get together out of some common interest or background, such as gender, race, or functional area. Examples of groups formed around a functional area are an organization for people in sales across many different industries; or an organization whose members are all writers from various settings, including newspapers, magazines, advertising copywriters, and others.

These groups are sometimes referred to as "breakfast clubs" or might just be called "networking groups." For salespeople and entrepreneurs, they are often referred to as "lead" or "tip" groups since a main focus of their meetings is to share leads to customers or clients. One such group came in handy for Marvin, a client of mine who worked in a printing business but wanted to start his own dating service. For help in getting his business going, he joined a group of African-American entrepreneurs who met for breakfast once a month. Most of them were older and more experienced than Marvin, so he learned a great deal about how to launch and run a successful business. The group consisted of only about fifteen people and wasn't listed in any kind of directory; he just heard about it through word of mouth.

If you don't already belong to some sort of networking group—either a small, informal one or one of the large, formal ones (see the "Ready-Made Networks" window)—but think one could be useful to you, ask your friends and colleagues to see if anyone knows of any such groups.`

Professional Groups Contacts Worksheet

Professional or Trade Associations:

_____

_____

_____

_____

Networking Groups, Breakfast Clubs, Tip or Lead Groups:

_____

_____

_____

_____

Career Services Contacts

If you are working with a career consultant or job placement professional, or have in the past, be sure to count the individual as part of your network. This group includes career counselors in private practice as well as ones who work in college or community-based career development or employment centers. Also consider recruiters in employment agencies and executive search firms, as well as outplacement consultants. Some public libraries are also staffed with career resource experts. (The various types of career services professionals are also discussed and defined later in this chapter in the Allied Forces section.)

Ready-Made Networks

Three major networking and referral organizations that can point you to a chapter near you are Ali Lassen's Leads Clubs, Inc. at (800) 783-3761 and www.leadsclub.com; Business Networking Int'l, Inc. at (800) 825-8286 and www.BNI.com; and LeTip International, Inc. at (800) 25-LETIP and www.letip.com.

Think about any career services professionals you have ever worked with in the past or are dealing with currently and add them to the worksheet that follows. If you don't know of anyone to list, consider asking your friends and professional colleagues for referrals to people they have worked with.

Career Services Contacts Worksheet

Employment Agencies & Executive Recruiters:

_____

_____

_____

_____

Outplacement Firms:

_____

_____

_____

_____

Career Counseling Centers or Employment Offices:

_____

_____

_____

_____

Career Counselors or Consultants in Private Practice:

_____

_____

_____

_____

Career Resource Librarians:

_____

_____

_____

_____

Personal and Professional Services Contacts

People who provide personal and professional services are excellent sources of leads, resources, and information. People like your physician, dentist, accountant, hairdresser, or fitness trainer might be just the link you need to the right people or information since they come across a large number of people daily.

Don't forget, too, about stockbrokers and financial planners, insurance agents, realtors, pharmacists, mechanics, doormen and landlords, dry cleaners, tailors, housekeepers, and many others. You never know who might turn out to be a wealth of leads and information.

I never cease to be amazed by the stories I hear from clients and friends who tell me how these types of people have helped them. There was the recent college graduate, for example, who got his first job in marketing because one of the trainers at his gym passed his resume on to a high-level marketing executive who happened to be one of the trainer's best private clients.

Then there were the two public relations executives who didn't know each other but happened to use the same stockbroker. They both talked to the broker about their interest in leaving their jobs and starting their own firm, so he put the two of them in touch with each other, and they ended up becoming partners.

Even more amazing was the young woman who went to a tailor to have her interviewing suit altered. Being a chatty type, she talked to the tailor while standing there having her hem pinned up, telling him she hoped this new suit would bring her luck, particularly with one company she had been trying to get an interview with. He said, "What a coincidence, a customer was here this morning who works for that company." The savvy job seeker then left a copy of her resume with the tailor, with a note attached, and asked the tailor to give it to the customer when he came back to pick up his clothes. He did, and the effort resulted in an interview for the job seeker. So, it clearly just takes a little luck and chutzpah, plus a lot of initiative, to make the most of situations like these.

Now think about the people you come across in your daily life or occasionally who provide personal or professional services, not just to you, but to many others as well. List their names on the following worksheet.

Personal and Professional Services Contacts Worksheet

Physicians:

_____

_____

_____

_____

Dentists:

_____

_____

_____

_____

Attorneys:

_____

_____

_____

_____

Accountants:

_____

_____

_____

_____

Stockbrokers & Financial Planners:

_____

_____

_____

_____

Bankers:

_____

_____

_____

_____

Insurance Agents:

_____

_____

_____

_____

Realtors:

_____

_____

_____

_____

Hairdressers or Barbers:

_____
_____
_____
_____

Manicurists:

_____
_____
_____
_____

Fitness Trainers:

_____
_____
_____
_____

Pharmacists:

_____
_____
_____
_____

Mechanics:

_____
_____
_____
_____

Dry Cleaners:

_____

_____

_____

_____

Tailors:

_____

_____

_____

_____

Landlords:

_____

_____

_____

_____

Doormen:

_____

_____

_____

_____

Housekeepers:

_____

_____

_____

_____

Multimedia Contacts

An often overlooked source of network contacts is all around us every day—media and technology. The Internet is clearly revolutionizing the way people network with e-mail, bulletin boards, newsgroups, and chat rooms. (Networking on the Internet and the World Wide Web is discussed in more detail in chapter 10.)

Besides the Internet, though, less obvious networking opportunities exist through books, newspapers, magazines, television, and radio. Reading or hearing about people whose work interests you or whose career paths you admire is a great source of people to contact who might be willing to help you. You can also use information presented in the media to contact companies and organizations that may be good sources of information and help.

John, for example, read about a particular genetics research study in a professional journal. He noticed that the author of the article, who was also the director of the research project, happened to be on the faculty of a university in his town. So, he wrote to the author, expressing his interest in learning more about the field of genetics research and possible interest in a part-time lab technician job. The director was too busy to reply, but he asked the project's associate director to get back to John and call him in for an interview, which led to a great part-time job for John.

Ana put the things she read to similar good use. A regular part of her job search was to write to companies mentioned or profiled in newspaper articles. She did not end up getting her job that way, but did get several interviews. The companies were impressed that she had taken the initiative to contact them based on the media coverage. Doing so set her apart from the many job seekers who send out mass mailings of generic cover letters to companies listed in business directories they find in the library. Whether you are networking for a job search or for another pursuit, contacting people or places you read about is generally more effective than the less targeted approach of mass mailings to random lists of people or organizations.

Multimedia Contacts Worksheet

Internet

Newsgroups:

_____

_____

_____

_____

_____

Web Sites:

_____

_____

_____

_____

_____

My Personal E-mail Address List:

_____

_____

_____

_____

_____

Newspapers, Magazines, and Journals

Editors:

_____

_____

_____

_____

_____

Reporters:

_____
_____
_____
_____

Writers:

_____
_____
_____
_____

People & Organizations Profiled or Quoted in Articles:

_____
_____
_____
_____

Books

Authors:

_____
_____
_____
_____

Editors:

_____
_____
_____
_____

Agents:

_____

_____

_____

_____

Radio and Television

Producers & Directors:

_____

_____

_____

_____

Reporters & Anchors:

_____

_____

_____

_____

Guests or People Profiled or Mentioned:

_____

_____

_____

_____

Network Strengths and Weaknesses Checklist

Now that you have identified sources of people for your networking base, take stock of where you stand in each sphere. Use the following checklist to see how you stand in each area.

Personal Contacts	✓ Strength	✓ Weakness
Family		
Friends and acquaintances		
Clubs and social organizations		
Community groups		
Neighbors		
Sports		
Religious organizations		
Work Contacts		
Coworkers (current and past)		
Supervisors (current and past)		
Volunteer work		
Career Services Contacts		
Employment agencies and executive recruiters		
Outplacement firms		
Career counseling and employment offices		
Career counselors and consultants		
Librarians		
Education Contacts		
Alumni (high school, college, graduate school)		
Continuing education course classmates, instructors, and guest speakers		

Education, cont.	✔ Strength	✔ Weakness
Job training program classmates, instructors, and guest speakers		
Teachers and professors		
Advisors, deans, and coaches		
Professional Groups Contacts		
Professional and trade associations		
Networking groups		
Multimedia Contacts		
Internet		
Newsgroups		
Web sites e-mail lists		
Newspapers and magazines		
Editors		
Reporters and writers		
People and organizations profiled in articles		
Books		
Authors		
Editors		
Agents		
Radio and Television		
Producers and directors		
Reporters and anchors		
Guests or people profiled		

Taking a Closer Look at Your Network— The STARS System

When you take stock of your network, there is a danger in simply having a random list of names on paper or in a computer database. Sure, you can look at your list with pride and say, "Look how many people I know!" but can you say with certainty that you know the right people to help with your objectives and goals?

Think about how this idea plays out in your personal life. Is there a particular person you vent your frustrations to when you have a rough day at work? Do you have others you rely on for advice about your finances or problems in your marriage or relationships? You might also have people you can call on to talk you through a computer difficulty or to recommend a good book on a particular topic. And there are always those who can be counted on to recommend the perfect restaurant or for a reliable review of the latest movies.

The people in your personal network fill a variety of roles. Some provide emotional support, some give information, and others help with strategy. Some might just set a good example, serving as role models. Others are friends, family, and coworkers. Still others might be professionals like a psychotherapist or a financial advisor.

Well, the same thing happens with your professional network. Some people are the ones you turn to for help in solving problems on the job, others provide inspiration or emotional support as you make transitions, and some give you concrete leads or strategy tips for obtaining jobs, customers, or clients. Many people will provide more than one of these "services," while others might be best equipped to meet just one specific need.

To examine the roles played by the people in your network, you might use a system I've developed called "STARS." The STARS system involves seeing your contacts as fitting into five basic categories: Strategists, Targets, Allied forces, Role models, and Supporters. Sorting your network into these five categories can be a great way to keep your contacts organized, and it will help you be clear about which people you should turn to in specific situations.

On the following pages, you will find descriptions of each of the STARS categories, followed by worksheets where you can list the members of your network who might fit into each category. (Remember that some people will fill more than one role, so feel free to list some of the same people on more than one worksheet.) Completing the worksheets will help you make sure that you have enough people in each of the STARS categories, which, in turn, will bring you closer to reaching your career or business goals.

Strategists

Strategists are key members of your network. They are the people who will sit down with you, roll up their sleeves, and help you hammer out a strategy for reaching your goals. They might help you devise a business plan or job search strategy, or may act as surrogate career counselors helping you decide on a career focus. They can be from within the field in which you work (or in which you want to work) or might be from the outside. A salesperson in tele-communications, for example, might learn new sales techniques from a strategist who is in sales in another industry.

Strategists generally provide advice, information, resources, and leads. In

Your Network STARS

Strategists. The people who help you plot a course toward your goals.

Targets. The people most closely linked to your career or business goals—for example, prospective employers, customers, or clients.

Allied forces. The professionals who provide expertise to strengthen your networking efforts.

Role models. The mentors or sages of your search who set a good example and offer advice and wisdom.

Supporters. The people who provide emotional support along the way to reaching your goals.

doing so, they help you solve problems, become innovative in the way you work, plan a job hunting strategy, reach your goals, and get access to needed information. In most cases, strategists should make up the majority of your network since they provide the broadest range of support.

Who Are Your Strategists?

Now that you're familiar with the concept of a strategist, think about who might serve that function for you. Who could help you plan a strategy for making a career decision, getting a job, managing your career, or developing a business? Write their names below.

_____

_____

_____

_____

_____

_____

_____

_____

_____

_____

_____

_____

Targets

The targets in your network are those people who you think are the ones most closely linked to your goals. If you're a job seeker, for example, targets are the prospective employers who you hope will interview you and eventually hire you. If you're trying to be more successful on your job or in your own business, targets may be potential customers or clients. Targets are obviously an essential part of any network and are often the hardest to come by of all the categories. In fact, you're probably networking primarily to get to your targets.

Hitting the Target

To identify the targets in her network, Ana relied on alumni from her alma maters. She started by contacting the career development offices of the college and law school she had attended and requesting that they send her a list of alumni working in finance. I suggested to Ana that she ask the career offices to include both alumni working in the city where she wanted to work (Chicago) and in other cities around the country that are known as financial centers (New York, San Francisco, Atlanta, and others). By doing so, she would gain access to a network that would include both strategists and targets. Here's why: she was able to contact the people in the cities where she didn't want to work and ask them for advice about her strategy, using them as guinea pigs of sorts. She could discuss her concerns about making the transition from law to finance and was able to show them rough drafts of her resume for their suggestions. Since she knew that she didn't want to work in their offices, she was able to be more candid with them and let them see her as a "diamond in the rough"—something she couldn't do if they were actual targets—that is, people she wanted to work for. She was then able to turn to her targets—alumni working in Chicago—presenting herself as a polished job candidate.

Now Think of Who Your Targets Are

Your list of targets is likely to be the longest of all the STARS lists, so I don't suggest you try to list your targets here in the book. Instead, you should make lists of all prospective employers or clients in your computer or on paper.

Allied Forces

If you've ever been behind the scenes in a modeling agency or movie set, you've seen the "army" of people it takes to get someone ready for the camera. Make-up artists, wardrobe consultants, voice and diction coaches, physical fitness trainers, cosmetic dentists, and a host of other professionals all play a part in getting someone in "camera ready" condition. While you don't need to go to such lengths to network effectively (and movie-star physical appearance is not a prerequisite for successful networking!), you may need to call in some outside experts for certain aspects of the process. These "allied forces" are people who can ensure that your networking efforts are not wasted because of some flaw in your personal presentation.

For example, you don't want to go to the trouble of making ten cold calls a day only to find that your voice isn't conveying the right degree of professionalism or enthusiasm. Or, you might agonize over writing a letter to request a networking meeting, only to find that your letter could have been stronger if you had consulted a business writing expert or a job search coach. Similarly, an image consultant or public speaking seminar could come in handy if you have to represent your company at a speaking engagement.

Depending on your networking objectives and the areas where you could use some improvement, your allied forces might include:

➤ **Image Consultants.** Image consultants help you make a good first, and lasting, impression. They advise clients on wardrobe, hair, and make-up as well as on other aspects of their personal presentation, such as voice, diction, and etiquette. Some also specialize in media consulting, helping people convey the right image on television or radio appearances.

➤ **Voice Coaches.** Voice coaches help you improve your speaking voice in such areas as diction, tone, rate of speech, and energy level. Some can help correct regional or foreign accents, and some with higher levels of training can work with speech impairments or impediments. They can help you project a more confident, professional, and engaging self on the phone, in person, or when speaking in public.

➠ **Career Development Professionals.** Within the career development profession, you'll find many different titles used, reflecting the range of services these experts offer. *Career counselors*, for example, typically have an advanced degree (master's or doctorate) in counseling or psychology and may counsel clients on career choices, job search, and career management, or just on one or two of those areas. There are also professionals who provide the same services but call themselves *career consultants, career strategists,* or similar titles. They may or may not have degrees in counseling but often have experience in human resources or other areas in which they have helped people develop and manage their careers. Then there are the *executive coaches,* also known as *career management consultants.* They usually don't work with people who are choosing careers or job hunting but instead help people be more successful, satisfied, and productive on their current jobs. (You'll find more information about executive coaches in chapter 8.) Whatever their title, and whichever specific services they offer, career development professionals are often excellent sources of advice and guidance in the networking process.

➠ **Business Strategy Consultants**. Like a career counselor for the self-employed, business strategy consultants help you make decisions about going into business for yourself and also advise you on how to make your business successful once you get it started. Some work with you one-on-one in hourly sessions, while others offer group workshops or seminars. Business strategy consultants either work independently or offer seminars through business schools and other community education centers.

➠ **Professional Organizers.** I often talk with people who are fed up with the mess of papers and files on their desk or the disaster area that is their closet and find they are thrilled to learn that professional organizers exist. These are people who will come to your home or office and show you how to get rid of clutter, set up organizational systems, and stay organized. It's difficult to be an effective networker when your home and office are in disarray, so a professional organizer may be a key member of your network's allied forces.

➠ **Publicists.** For the serious networkers, or for those who are self-employed, a publicist may be just what you need. Publicists can make you or your business more visible by planning and implementing a public relations campaign that might get you on television or radio or featured in a magazine or newspaper. Remember, that much of networking is about being visible—getting someone to know that you know what you know. If you're willing to spend a few bucks, publicists are a surefire way to gain that visibility and spread the word about what you know and have to offer.

➧ **Psychotherapists.** Some people consider a psychotherapist to be an essential member of their network for on-going support and reflection on their daily lives. Others find that they benefit from short-term counseling as help to them get through a tough time. Making a career decision or managing your career, for example, can bring up all sorts of difficult questions about what you want out of life. Psychotherapy may be the right arena in which to explore such lofty issues as your values, hopes, and dreams, thus enabling you to make the more mundane decisions about your daily work life.

A job search, too, can bring about the need for some professional mental health treatment. I have worked with many job seekers who, unfortunately, find themselves in a true depression over the trials and tribulations of job hunting, particularly if they are unemployed. Seeking the help of a psychotherapist (either a therapist with a master's degree in counseling or social work or a psychologist with a Ph.D.) is often just what they need to bounce back and keep going with their job searches.

Let Your Fingers Do the Walking

In addition to the referral sources listed in Appendix C, don't forget about your local *Yellow Pages* telephone directory as a handy source of allied forces.

Finding Allied Forces

Are you interested in adding some of the professionals described above to your own "allied forces" but don't know where to find them? You can turn to Appendix C for suggestions. In that appendix, you'll find listings of places and people who can refer you to any of these experts. Many of the listings are for professional associations that can also provide you with guidelines for choosing a member of their field, so that you know what to look for in a so-called expert before you hand over your money and time.

Taking Stock of Your Allied Forces

The following chart lists most of the typical allied forces that are useful in networking, and also provides spaces labeled "Other" where you can list additional experts. To use this chart, put check marks in the "Already Utilize" column next to the experts who are already a part of your network. For those who might be able to help you, but whom you don't have in your network, place check marks in the "Need to Find" column.

Professional	Already Utilize	Need to Find
Career Counselor	_____	_____
Executive Coach	_____	_____
Business Strategy Consultant	_____	_____
Voice Coach	_____	_____
Image Consultant	_____	_____
Professional Organizer	_____	_____
Publicist	_____	_____
Psychotherapist	_____	_____
Other:	_____	_____
Other:	_____	_____
Other:	_____	_____

Finding Your Allied Forces in the Not-So-Ivory Tower

Involving professional consultants in your networking efforts doesn't have to be expensive and time-consuming. Seminars and classes offered in centers of adult learning or universities' continuing education departments can be an excellent way to refine your networking techniques in a group setting without the expense of a private coach or consultant. These courses are usually taught by people who are not ivory tower academics but real-world consultants and experts in communications, business strategy, public relations, and many other areas. Many colleges and universities have divisions or departments with names like Adult Learning, University Extension, Adult Education, or Continuing Education. These departments typically offer an interesting array of courses that are not part of a degree program and therefore don't require a big investment of time or money and usually do not have competitive admissions.

Also be on the lookout for learning centers in your area that have names such as "The Learning Annex," "The Learning Alliance," "The Discovery Center," or many others. These kinds of private or nonprofit organizations offer many practical career development and life skills courses.

Here's a taste of what adult learning has to offer. The following course titles represent a sampling of seminars and workshops offered at just one school during recent semesters:

- Becoming Assertive
- Building Self-Esteem
- Making Plans That Work
- Letting Go of Clutter
- Getting Results from Using the Telephone in Your Job Search
- The Online Job Search
- Effective Networking Techniques
- Essential Networking Skills for Shy Networkers
- Speaking Without Fear
- Speaking Effectively
- Good Humor: The Uses of Wit, Laughter, & Humor in Everyday Life
- Developing Your Voice
- Professional Writing with Style
- Overcoming Stage Fright
- Marketing Your Small Business Product or Service

Source: *New York University School of Continuing Education Bulletin,* Spring 1997 and Summer 1997 editions.

Role Models

These are the sages of your search—the people who serve as wise counsel for any of your professional endeavors. You might think of them as mentors or teachers who guide you through the steps of your professional development. While they are likely to be considerably more experienced than you are, they don't necessarily have to be older than you.

How to Find a Mentor

It is becoming increasingly common for large companies to have in-house mentoring programs in which junior employees are paired with more senior ones. Ask your human resources department if you're not already aware of such a program. If you are not employed in a large company, or if your company does not offer mentoring, then contact local civic organizations like the Chamber of Commerce or a Kiwanis Club to see if they can help. Also, two helpful Web sites that focus on mentoring are Don Clark's Mentor Page at www.nwlink.com/~donclark/hrd/mentor.html; and the International Mentoring Association at www.indiana.edu/~rugsdev/genrinf. If you're a business owner or consultant, you might find a mentor through your local office of the Small Business Administration or on the Web at The Entrepreneurship Centre Mentoring Program (www.entrepreneurship.com).

In addition to being people whom you get to know well and meet with frequently or periodically, role models can also be people you don't actually know, but whose work you respect and admire. You can choose all sorts of people as your role models, including prominent people in your field, celebrities, or historical figures, even though they're not people you are likely to pick up the phone and call. They can, nevertheless, serve as "remote role models." First Lady Hillary Clinton was subjected to a lot of ribbing by the press when they got wind of her imaginary conversations with Eleanor Roosevelt. Well, regardless of the controversy surrounding that news, the late Mrs. Roosevelt is a good example of a remote role model—someone who provides inspiration because of her accomplishments—and even offers guidance indirectly by having modeled certain behavior in the past. Of course, you do want to be sure that you have some living, breathing role models to turn to for an interactive relationship as well!

Who Are Your Role Models?

Think of the people who serve as role models for you or who could serve as role models if you had a chance to develop a mentoring relationship with them. Also think of remote role models—historical figures or famous contemporary people whose careers have set good examples for you. List everyone you can think of in the spaces that follow.

An Easy Way to Find Remote Role Models

Check your local bookstore or library for biographies of people whose careers and lives could serve as role models for your own.

Supporters

Unlike remote role models, supporters are people you know well and who are very much accessible, maybe even under your own roof. They are the ones who provide emotional support when the going gets tough, encouragement when you're on the way up, and a kick in the pants when you're slacking off. They are likely to be family members or close friends, but might also be that coworker or classmate who's always there for you.

A supporter can be someone who fits into one of the other STARS categories as well, like a strategist who can dish out not only advice but also empathy and sympathy. The allied forces are also good sources of supporters. Having a therapist or counselor in your network or being part of a support group like a job hunting club or business strategy workshop can provide valuable emotional support and the "cheerleading" you need to keep going. Even if you're tough as nails and highly resilient, it helps to have a few supporters in your network.

Ana, for example, found that out of all her friends, two people turned out to be the most supportive through the long process of her job search. They were the ones she could call for encouragement when she hit a dry spell in her search and was ready to throw in the towel and go back to the practice of law. They were also the ones who would give her a quick pep talk before interviews.

Supporters also came in handy for John over the months that he was trying to make a career decision and, ultimately, a career transition. While friends were helpful to him in this process, he found that his best supporters were the participants in an eight-week career change workshop that he took through a local university. Since his fellow participants were all going through a similar decision-making and transition process, they were particularly sensitive to what he was going through. He also found that the structure of the workshop—meeting with the same people regularly over a two-month period—provided support in and of itself.

Who Are Your Supporters?

Use the spaces that follow to make a list of the supporters in your network. The supporters might be people who have helped you out in the past during difficult periods of time or challenging situations. They may also be people whose supportive nature has not been "tested" yet but who you believe have the qualities of a supporter.

_____

_____

_____

_____

_____

_____

_____

_____

_____

_____

Quick Summary

Having a sufficient number of the right people in your network is essential for reaching your career or business objectives and goals. In this chapter, you learned that potential contacts can be found in seven main categories:

➠ Personal

➠ Work

➠ Education

➠ Professional groups

⟫ Career services

⟫ Personal and professional services

⟫ Multimedia

This chapter also introduced the concept of the STARS system, a process of classifying your contacts as strategists, targets, allied forces, role models, or supporters according to the roles each person plays in your network:

⟫ **Strategists.** The people who help you plot a course toward your goals

⟫ **Targets.** The people most closely linked to your career or business goals—for example, prospective employers, customers, or clients

⟫ **Allied forces.** The professionals who provide expertise to strengthen your networking efforts

⟫ **Role models.** The mentors or sages of your search who set a good example and offer advice and wisdom

⟫ **Supporters.** The people who provide emotional support along the way to reaching your goals

Preparing to Be an Organized and a Time-Wise Networker

Out of intense complexities intense simplicities emerge.

—WINSTON CHURCHILL

Where did I put that phone number? What did I do with that article I wanted to send Nancy? When did I last talk to Dodge, and what did I say? How will I ever find time to get to that meeting tonight? If your organizational system consists of piles of paper on your desk, Post-it® notes on your computer monitor, and a bulletin board with so many layers it would keep an archaeologist happy for a few months, you probably ask yourself a lot of these questions. If the answers are not readily forthcoming, it may be time to put some better organizational and time management systems in place. Being organized with your papers, computer files, and time is critical to success in networking. This chapter offers tips and techniques for keeping track of who you know and what you know and for finding the time to keep up with all those people and all that information.

You'll find four main sections in this chapter. The first three address organizational systems, and the final section offers tips for managing your time more effectively. The following are the four sections:

1. Keeping Track of Who You Know

2. Keeping Track of What You Know

3. Keeping Track of Your Networking Activities

4. Finding the Time to Network

In chapter 3 you began to take an inventory of your network by jotting down names of people in various networking categories on the worksheets provided in that chapter. The first section of this chapter focuses on developing a more permanent, detailed system for keeping track of who you know. You learn about contact management systems—databases that keep records of your contacts. I also guide you through the process of setting up "to be entered" files and "key people" files—two additional handy organizational tools for keeping track of who you know.

Keeping Track of Who You Know

Keeping accurate and organized records of the people you know (or could get to know) is essential to successful networking. The first step in that process is to develop a contact management system (CMS)—an easily accessible, detailed database of the people you know or hope to know.

Setting Up a Contact Management System

You have two basic choices for your contact management system: keeping it on paper or in your computer. The most efficient way to compile and access your network is to have it as a database on your computer. This need not be a complex, sophisticated marvel of computer programming. There are many software packages easily found at your neighborhood computer store that help you set up a simple but powerful CMS. Several of the more popular contact management software programs are listed in Appendix D.

If you don't have access to a computer, or would prefer not to keep your contacts that way, your other option is to put them on paper. I recommend an index card system instead of listing people in notebooks or folders. Using index cards simulates a computer database. You can file the data on your contacts in various sections of an index card box, depending on the category in which the contact falls. You can also add a fairly substantial amount of information to the cards (compared to a list on one large sheet of paper on which you have limited space to record information on each person).

Whether you use old fashioned paper or a "high-tech" computer data-base, you'll want to list various data for each of your contacts. These data include the following:

➠ First Name

➠ Nickname (if applicable)

➠ Last Name

➠ Title

➠ Job Title

➠ Employer

➠ Address (office, home, or both)

Working in the Fields

Each of these data elements is called a field in computer database language.

⟹ Telephone (office, home, or both)

⟹ Fax

⟹ E-mail Address

⟹ Career Field

⟹ STARS Category(ies)

⟹ Referred By

⟹ When and Where You Met

⟹ Birth date

⟹ Other Personal Information (for example, names of spouse or children, personal interests, hobbies, and so forth)

⟹ Notes (for miscellaneous information that doesn't fall into the other data types)

Whichever type of contact management system you use—computer or index card method—make sure it works well for you. You aren't likely to make use of a system that is cumbersome or difficult, so make sure your system matches your personality and work style. Some criteria to consider when purchasing or setting up a CMS are the following:

⟹ Is it accessible?

⟹ Is it easy to use?

⟹ Is it manageable?

⟹ Is it expandable?

⟹ Is it portable?

What Can I Do with All Those Business Cards and Random Slips of Paper I Collect?

Linda Rothschild, President of ~~CROSS IT OFF YOUR LIST~~, a New York-based professional organizing and concierge service, has a helpful system to distinguish between people she classifies as resources versus actual members of your network. She says, for example, "You might have names of ten people who can repair your computer, but when it comes time to need a computer repaired, you'll choose one person, and that's the name that goes into your central database. All the rest stay in what I call your resource file, a box of index cards sorted according to the type of resource. You can staple business cards to the index cards or just write directly on the card and then file it under the category for that type of resource." According to Linda, "Your database should be clean, containing only the names of people you actually have some contact with or plan to contact in the near future. Everyone else goes in the resource file. Otherwise, you'll have thousands of entries cluttering up your system."

Keeping a "To Be Entered" File

As you collect business cards or names of new contacts on little slips of paper, you don't always have time to enter them in your CMS right away. As a result, valuable information can easily get lost—cards forgotten in the pockets of jackets sent to the cleaners, Post-it notes that slip through that crack between your desk and the wall, and so on. The way to solve this problem is to have one place where you keep this kind of information temporarily until you can enter it into your CMS. Take an accordion file folder (the kind that's like a regular file folder but is closed on the sides and expands to half an inch or an inch in depth) and keep it in an easily accessible spot on or near your desk. Every time you write down a name or receive a business card, brochure, or other piece of paper, drop it in your to-be-entered file.

This also works well when you receive a change-of-address notice. While it's best to update your CMS immediately when you learn of an address change, new phone number, etc., it's not always possible to do so. The to-be-entered file is at least a safe resting place until you have time to enter the new information.

The Value of To-Be-Entered Files—Learning the Hard Way

During her job search, Ana learned the hard way that she needed to keep better track of all the names she was collecting during her networking activities. Midway through her search, she attended a particular meeting of women in finance and met about fifteen people who said they would be happy to help her out in any way they could. She collected business cards from all of those potential strategists and targets; and on the back of each card she wrote some notes to herself, indicating how she should follow up with each person. When Ana got home, she took the cards out of her pocket and dropped them on a table on top of a stack of newspapers. She thought to herself that she should probably enter the names and addresses right away in her computer so she could get the follow-up letters out promptly the next morning, but she was too tired to do so. Well, a couple of days passed before she got around to writing the letters, and in the meantime, more newspapers had been piled on top of the cards. You can probably imagine what happened at this point! Yes, she decided to throw out the stack of newspapers, forgetting that the cards were buried within them. By the time she realized what she'd done, the papers—and the valuable business cards—were on their way to recycling heaven. If only she had had a to-be-entered file, she could have come home from the meeting and taken two seconds to drop the cards in that file where they would have been safe and ready to retrieve when she got around to writing the follow-up letters.

Setting Up Key People Files

As you interact with various people during your networking, you'll probably find that there are some people or organizations you have frequent contact with and others you rarely deal with. It's helpful to identify the key people whom you talk to, meet with, or correspond with, and to set up "key people" (KP) files for these contacts. A KP file is simply a manila file folder labeled with the person's name (or an accordion file or pocket folder if you expect to collect a lot of papers related to that person). As you communicate with key people, you can file copies of letters, e-mail, faxes, and notes from phone calls to keep a running record of your communication with that person.

In my business, my key people files are one of the most important elements of my organizational system. There are times when I need to contact someone I haven't spoken with in several months, and I need to remember exactly when our last communication was and what its nature was. Often that person is someone who refers clients to me, so it is particularly important that I know if I thanked him or her for the last client referred to me. With key people files, I can quickly find copies of the last referral thank-you notes I sent or perhaps a slip of paper where I made notes from the last phone conversation I had with someone.

Keeping Track of What You Know

Networking for any purpose, whether for career choice, job search, career advancement, or business promotion, inevitably involves a lot of research. Magazine articles, information from Web sites, and notes you take when speaking to people all have to have a place to go. There are also the materials that you haven't gotten to yet—journals to peruse, newspaper clippings to read, Web sites to browse, and so on. It can seem as if you'll never catch up. Keeping up with information relevant to your field is important so that you are informed and knowledgeable as you interact with others. Remember, it's not just who you know, it's what you know that counts as well.

Networking on the Big Screen

Film buffs might recall a good example of the key people files in action in *The Year of Living Dangerously* in which Mel Gibson's character discovers the secret cache of files that Linda Hunt's character keeps on people in her life.

Keeping close track of what you know is also important for remaining true to the notion of networking as a two-way street. If you are able to serve as a sort of "information clearinghouse," you are keeping tabs on information not only for yourself but for others as well. Imagine that someone calls and says, "Do you know of a good book on…?" or "Have you ever come across a service that does…?" If you've kept track of such resources, you'll have an answer without a lot of fuss, and your networking becomes a give-and-take process, not just a one-sided, selfish activity. To be able to do that, you should consider setting up "topic files" and "resource files" as described in the following section.

Setting Up Topic Files and Resource Files

Next to rocket science and brain surgery, setting up a decent filing system has got to be one of life's greatest challenges. They're always too complicated or not complex enough, hard to maintain or never even used at all. The art and science of filing is beyond the scope of this book, so you're better off turning to some of the excellent books on organizing listed in Appendix D or contacting the National Association of Professional Organizers listed in Appendix C.

For now, I'll offer one simple piece of advice that can help you get started managing all the information you collect: think of files as topic files or resource files. Topic files are the places you keep articles, handouts from seminars, and any other materials that inform you about a topic that's of interest to you. For example, in my career counseling practice, I have files on such topics as Gender Issues and Careers, Careers and Disabilities, Entrepreneurial Issues, Psychological Issues and Careers, and many others. Examine the articles or other papers you have lying around in piles and see how you can sort them into topic files.

Resource files are slightly different in that they are arranged more around a function than a topic. This is where you might keep brochures, flyers, or other information on people or places that provide services or products of use to you. For example, my resource files include Other Career Counselors, Psychotherapists, Tutors, and others to whom I might need to refer clients. Some of the people whose materials are in the resource files might also be listed in your CMS.

Organization Pays

Matthew Haas, a project manager with an urban planning and preservation organization, is a great example of organized networking in action. Matthew is always on the lookout for articles in newspapers, magazines, and professional journals that are of interest to him, whether relevant to his current job or just related to his other interests. He immediately clips the article, tracks down the telephone number of the person or organization featured or quoted in the article, and attaches the contact information to the article. He then files it in the appropriate topic or key person file.

Doing this provides him with continuous reference files to turn to whenever he needs them. The organization has paid off. Once he had to write a cover letter for a job and found that he had kept several articles on the person he was writing. This showed the prospective employer that he had been following that person's work and was serious about working for him. His advanced planning came in handy: he got the job. "Networking is something you carry with you all throughout your life, not just something you do when you need a job," Matthew says.

Keeping Track of Your Networking Activities

As you've learned by now, effective networking is based more on quality than on quantity. There is some value, however, to keeping track of how much networking you've done. When you're networking in connection with one particular project—like a job search, for example, it's important to keep a running record of all your networking efforts. The Project Progress Log described later in this section is one way to keep that record as it serves as a log of meetings you have attended, people you've spoken with, and so on.

You might also want to keep a record of your networking activities with one particular person, not one whole project. The Record of Contact Log described in the following section is one of the best ways to keep tabs on your interactions with one person.

Using Record-of-Contact Logs

Record-of-contact logs are for use primarily with the key people files described earlier in this chapter. In addition to keeping a paper trail of communication in each KP file—for example, copies of letters, faxes, e-mail, and so on—it is also helpful to have one sheet of paper in the file that shows a record of communication with that person. That sheet of paper is a record-of-contact log—a form you can easily create using the sample below as your guide. The sample log provided here shows a record of John's networking activity with one person during his career decision-making process.

Contact Name: Veronica Martin, M.S., C.G.C., Certified Genetic Counselor

Address: Dept. of Genetics, Hope Hospital 3535 City Blvd., Richmond, VA 11111

Phone: (555) 222-2222

Fax: (555) 222-2223

E-mail: vmartin@hope.com

Date	Type of Communication (phone, e-mail, mtg., etc.)	Summary of Communication	Follow-through Needed?
3/14/97	Phone	Introduced myself. Told her of my interest in g.c. Set up meeting for 3/19 at 4:00.	Call 3/18 to confirm mtg.
3/18	Left voice mail	Confirmed that I will meet her tomorrow at 4:00.	

| 3/19 | Meeting | Very helpful mtg. See notes in file. | Send thank-you ASAP |
| 3/21 | Letter | Mailed thank-you letter. | Copy on file. |

Using Project Progress Logs

If you need to keep track of networking related to one project—such as a job search or promoting a new development in your business—you need a log that lists all of your networking efforts related to that particular project. This enables you to have one running list of people you've contacted, events you have attended, mailings you have sent out, and so on. The project progress log is not as detailed as the record-of-contact log in that the former does not include summaries of communication or follow-up notes. That information should be kept only on the record-of-contact logs in the key people files.

The project progress log is instead intended only as a basic record sheet that you can glance at quickly to get a sense of your overall networking progress. For example, each time John contacted Veronica as indicated on the record-of-contact sheet in the preceding section, he would then make a brief note of each contact with her on his project progress log. He would also list anyone else he spoke to as well. Then, at the end of a week or a month when he wanted to take stock of how much networking he had been doing, he could look at his project progress log and see how many people he had contacted to date.

You can develop a form similar to the following sample to suit your own purpose. The sample here shows entries that Ana made during a few days of her job search.

Date	Name	Type of Communication
9/10/97	Joe Adams	Phone conversation
9/10	Ann Richardson	Phone conversation

9/10	Sue Mullin	Phone conversation
9/10	Bob Taft	Left him message
9/12	Bob Taft	Left second message

Finding the Time to Network

You've now read about ways to keep track of who know you, what you know, and what you've done; and I wouldn't be surprised if you're saying, "Nice systems, but I want to know HOW AM I GOING TO GET IT ALL DONE?!" That's a normal concern because there *is* a lot to do in networking. It requires not only time spent meeting with people and attending events, but also lots of preparation and follow-through. All of these activities can be quite time-consuming. This can be especially difficult if you work full-time or have other significant demands on your time.

One of the best ways to solve this time dilemma between adequate networking and an already full life is to realize that you don't have to get it *all* done. You just have to do the things that are important to you, are critical for your job security or success, and will help you reach your goals.

So, how do you do even just those things? Well, like filing systems, the overall issue of dealing with time is a *biiiiiggg* topic, best left to the time management books recommended in Appendix D and the experts found in Appendix C. That said, though, there are a few simple things you can do to start being more productive. In the following sections are some suggestions that you can use to make sure that you network as efficiently and effectively as possible.

Use a Frequency-of-Contact System

It's easy to fall into the trap of calling or having lunch with the same people over and over, but what about all those other names buried deep in your contact management system? Are there people you've forgotten about whom you'd do well to get in touch with? To make sure that you're not forgetting anyone important, and to ensure that you spend the right amount of time with the right people, it is helpful to use a system of prioritizing that I call the frequency-of-contact system.

This system involves sorting your contacts into four basic categories—frequent, moderate, occasional, and periodic—based on how often you need to be in touch with them. Exactly how you define each of these terms will vary according to the nature of your work and the size of your network. If you're in public relations, for example, frequent contact might mean checking in with a particular media source or a client every other day. If you're a student, frequent could mean once a semester.

Frequent contacts are those people you should speak to regularly (for you that might mean every day, once a week, or twice a month) because they are an active part of your professional life as strategists, targets, referrals sources, resources, or perhaps just friends you enjoy speaking with. *Moderate* and *occasional* contacts are, of course, those people you need to stay in touch with a little less than the frequent category. The *periodic* category includes those people you have no reason to communicate with regularly, but don't want to forget about or be forgotten by. They might be on a mailing list you keep so that you can update them periodically (every six months, once a year, or even less frequently) about events or happenings in your professional life or your business.

If you have your contacts in a computer database, consider adding a field for the four categories and label each person as either frequent, moderate, occasional, or periodic. Then you can easily sort people according to their priority. For example, say you designate the first Thursday of every month as your "occasional follow-up day." (Fridays, by the way, are often a difficult day to reach people since it's the day of the week they're most likely to take off. Mondays aren't so hot either since people are likely to be extra busy then or just kind of grouchy.) When one of those Thursdays arrives, you simply type "occasional" into the appropriate search field of your database, click "find" or "search" (depending on how your system works), and you'll get a list of the people you need to call, write, or e-mail that day. If you're using an index card method of keeping your contacts, simply arrange them in the card box by dividers labeled with each of the four categories, or keep a separate list of the people in each category.

Establish a "To Be Contacted" System

The frequency-of-contact system described in the preceding section is primarily useful for long-range networking in that it enables you to keep track of people over time. There are often times, though, when you need to get in touch with someone within the next few days, regardless of whether that person is a "frequent," "moderate," "occasional," or "periodic" contact. Say you're talking on the phone to someone we'll call Tim to request some information and Tim suggests that you contact Brad, a mutual acquaintance, to get the information you need. You agree to do so but know that you won't have time to call Brad in the next few days, and it's not really an urgent matter anyway. In that case, you just need some way to make a note to yourself to give Brad a call some time in the near future. That's where the to-be-contacted system comes in.

If your CMS is on your computer, it might include a feature that links contacts to your calendar, alerting you of people to call or write on certain days. If so, you already have a built-in, to-be-contacted system. If not, you can easily develop your own. One way is simply to keep a running list of people to contact. I start with a sheet of paper on a clipboard and make three columns which I label "To Call," "To Write," and "To E-mail." It's a primitive system in this hi-tech age, but it works, and it doesn't require that I turn on my computer to see it. Then, at the start of each day, I pull some names off my list and write them on the daily "To Do" pages of my appointment book. That way, they don't just languish on a list but actually get done because they're scheduled on the calendar. Of course, you can often just put a name directly in your appointment book if you need to contact the person in the next day or so. No need to put it on the list first. The list is most useful for people you don't need to contact right away, but should contact in the near future. If they're on the to-be-contacted list, you're less likely to forget about them.

Keep a "Research to Do" List

As you go about your daily routine, you might think of information you need on a particular topic or hear of a book or Web site you want to look up. It's easy to forget about these things if they're not written down. Invariably, you'll be online sending e-mail or visiting a site and then sign off, only to find that you forgot to look up that neat Web site you read about in a magazine the day before. Or, you find yourself stopping in a bookstore to pass some time between appointments and can't remember what book it was that you'd been wanting to get. To keep this from happening, start a research-to-do list.

You can use the paper-on-a-clipboard method, or you might want to use a page in an appointment book so you have the list with you while you're out. I divide the page into categories such as "WWW" for Web sites I want to look up next time I'm online, "Books" for books to skim through or buy next time I'm in a bookstore, and "Info needed" for miscellaneous topics I need to find out about. You should use whichever headings make sense for your needs. However you do it, keeping handy a list like this can make it much easier to keep on top of information that can enrich your professional

The Eyes Have It

A great way to stay on top of new books that would interest you is through a convenient service at Amazon.com Books, the online bookstore (at www.amazon.com). You can indicate topics that interest you, and Amazon's system called "Eyes" will send you an e-mail every time a new book becomes available on those topics. It lists the book title, author, publisher, and price. You can then go to the site and order it online, or you can make a note of it on your research-to-do list for future purchase or perusing.

life. This system also puts you one step closer to being the information clearinghouse that makes you valuable to members of your network.

Schedule Daily, Weekly, and Monthly Tasks

Scheduling things in your appointment book is a very simple, but enormously powerful action. We tend to schedule things like meetings, classes, project deadlines, social dates, and significant days like birthdays or anniversaries. What we don't often schedule are things like the day each month that I check in with my Occasional Contacts, the week each year that I take a "working vacation" at my job or in my business to concentrate on reorganizing my office and work life in general, or the time of day every Tuesday and Thursday that I make calls to the Frequent Contacts listed in my CMS.

Think about the things you need to be doing to make networking an integral part of your life, and block out time for them. If you don't think that you have the time, think again. Do you really not have the time, or are you just not placing priority on these tasks so you're not finding the time? Time is a stand-alone entity. It's there no matter what. We're all allotted the same amount of time every day, every month, every year. What you decide to do with your time makes the difference.

Maximize the Return on Your Efforts

Have you ever had a day go by when you felt as if you had done a lot, but had nothing to show for it? Sometimes you get this feeling about not just a day but a month or even a whole year that seemed busy but unproductive. This feeling often results from doing too many things that don't get you any closer to where you want to be. As you learned in chapter 2, setting clear goals and breaking them down into manageable objectives, or steps, is essential for making career decisions, finding jobs, managing your career, or developing a business.

From a time management perspective, defining your goals and objectives is the key to answering such questions as, "What should I do next today?"

"Should I call this person or that one?" "Should I go to that meeting next week?" "Should I head my business in this direction or that one this year?" "Should I take this promotion at work or look for a new job elsewhere?" If you've defined what you want out of life in general and then set some specific goals for the coming months and years, you can answer these questions more easily. So, in addition to the more specific, tangible time management systems recommended on previous pages, also keep in mind that one of the best ways to be a time-wise networker is simply to keep your goals in the forefront of your mind.

Keeping the End in Sight

"Each part of your life—today's behavior, tomorrow's behavior, next week's behavior, next month's behavior—can be examined in the context of the whole, of what really matters most to you. By keeping that end clearly in mind, you can make certain that whatever you do on any particular day does not violate criteria you have defined as supremely important, and that each day of your life contributes in a meaningful way to the vision you have of your life as a whole."

Source: *The Seven Habits of Highly Effective People* by Stephen Covey (Simon & Schuster, 1989).

Quick Summary

Putting organizational and time management systems in place is an important step toward becoming an effective and efficient networker. This chapter described systems for keeping track of people, information, and networking activities and offered tips on finding the time to network.

To help you keep track of who you know, three systems were discussed:

⟹ **Contact Management Systems (CMS).** A CMS is a database of people in your network kept on index cards or in your computer.

⟹ **To-Be-Entered Files.** These are accordion folders in which you can quickly drop business cards or slips of papers with names for safekeeping until you have time to enter them in your contact management system.

➤ **Key People Files.** These are file folders in which you keep records of communication with people you interact with frequently or periodically. They contain copies of letters, faxes, e-mail, and notes from phone conversations.

To help you keep track of what you know, two types of files were suggested:

➤ **Topic Files.** These contain information (for example, newspaper and magazine articles, and printouts from Web sites) on topics of interest to you or related to your career or business.

➤ **Resource Files.** These contain information (for example, business cards, brochures, and flyers) on people and organizations that provide products or services you need to know about.

To help you keep track of your networking activities, two types of forms were suggested:

➤ **Record-of-Contact Logs.** These are forms on which you keep a record of all communication with a particular person. The logs include the name of the contact, nature of the contact (phone, in-person, etc.), results of the communication, and follow-up needed.

➤ **Project Progress Logs.** These are forms on which you keep a running list of people you talk to or meet with and events you attend. These logs help you keep track of the volume of networking you have done.

To help you find the time to network, five systems were suggested:

➤ **Frequency-of-Contact System.** Classifying the priority of people in your network as frequent, moderate, occasional, or periodic helps you keep track of how often you should be in touch with people.

➤ **To-be-Contacted System.** To keep from losing track of people you need to get in touch with, use a to-be-contacted system. This is either a running list of people or a system in your computer that alerts you to which people you need to contact on which days.

➠ **Research-To-Do List.** To keep you from losing track of information you need to obtain, this list enables you to list in one place all research needed to be done.

➠ **Schedule Tasks.** This tip discussed the importance of your scheduling specific times or blocks of time when you will get things done, instead of just keeping a list of things to do.

➠ **Keep Your Goals in Sight.** A final suggestion for making effective use of time was to keep your goals in sight at all times. Remembering the goals and objectives you established in chapter 2 helps you make decisions about how to spend your time day to day or minute to minute.

Preparing Your Self-Marketing Tools

Never to talk of oneself is a form of hypocrisy.

—FRIEDRICH NIETZSCHE

The networking process invariably requires that you talk about yourself a great deal. Even though true networking is a give-and-take, relationship-based process, it nonetheless involves considerable discussion of what *you* need, who *you* are, and what you want others to do for *you*. Subtle, but effective, self-marketing or self-promotion is an inevitable component of networking.

If you are networking as part of a job search, this focus on self-marketing should come as no surprise. Our case study Ana, for example, found that even when she was speaking with people who were functioning purely as strategists, she still had to make sure that she was impressing them with her qualifications just in case they should happen to become targets—that is, people who could hire her.

Self-promotion is not just for job hunting, however. If you want people to help you make a career decision, get ahead in your career, or develop your business, you have to show them that you're worth the trouble. John, for example, had to make sure people knew that he had a basic aptitude for science and a genuine commitment to helping others so that the nurses and genetic counselors he contacted would give him the time of day. Sam, too, had to make sure that the role models who were serving as mentors to him were aware of his talents and accomplishments. That way, they would know he was deserving of promotions and would consider it worth their while to help him plot a course for getting ahead in his career. The same was true for Monica, who had to let people know that she had sufficient experience with Web site development to start her own business.

In this chapter, you learn how to prepare self-marketing materials—resumes, bios, references, portfolios, and business promotional literature. You learn also how to construct a personal pitch, which is the cornerstone of those materials. We'll begin, though, with a few preparatory steps outlined in the following section.

Preparatory Steps to Effective Self-Marketing

In order to make a good impression and get your point across when networking, you should take a few preparatory steps: Know yourself and know what you want. Taking these two steps will make it much easier to pick up the phone and make a cold call; converse with a stranger at a conference; or write resumes, bios, and other written tools.

Know Who You Are

Knowing who you are—your interests, strengths, values, and personality type—is the essential foundation for all networking communication. Knowing yourself ensures that you can clearly convey to others what you're all about and what you're looking for.

Networking for a job search or career advancement, for example, requires that you "sell" other people on your strengths and capabilities. Knowing your strengths is a first step in having a convincing self-marketing campaign. Networking to help you make a career decision also requires that you have a solid handle on who you are and what your priorities are so that, as you learn about various career options, you can rule out options that don't fit and rule in the ones that do. Self-awareness also enables you to understand the way you actually go about networking. It helps you recognize your communication strengths and weaknesses and empowers you to adopt networking methods that fit your personality style.

May I Help You?

An important component of knowing who you are is knowing what you have to offer. At the start of Ana's job search, for example, she found that she had to do some careful assessment of her skills and strengths in order to convince people to interview her. It wasn't enough for her to say that she had an interest in finance; she also had to take a look at the skills she had developed as a lawyer and see which ones would be of use to the financial world. Selling people on your skills is not just limited to networking for job hunting, either. If you want people to invest their time in helping you reach your career or business goals, they have to know you're worth the trouble. You have to let them know that you have valuable experience, skills, or personal qualities that could be an asset to them, or to their profession or industry as a whole, or to the clients or customers you might be seeking.

How do you achieve this self-awareness? Some of it comes from experience. The more experience you have in your career, and life in general, the easier it is to say what you like and don't like, what you do well, and in which kinds of environments you thrive.

Although lots of experience helps, you can acquire self-awareness at any age or career level, however, by doing some careful self-assessment. Self-assessment methods range from the informal, like simply thinking about who you are, to the formal, such as testing offered by career counselors and other qualified professionals.

Many people do just fine with the more informal methods. You can sometimes gain a lot of self-awareness just by sitting on a hillside contemplating a blade of grass and thinking about who you are. Keeping a journal of your thoughts and observations on your experiences can also be useful.

Other people, though, find that they need some kind of structure to guide their thoughts so they can determine more effectively their interests, strengths, values, and priorities. Many of the books listed in the career planning and job search sections of Appendix D include exercises that help you identify your personal qualities and get them down on paper in a methodical way.

If you want to be even more thorough in your self-assessment, you might want to consider formal assessment—that is, testing administered by a qualified professional. Interest inventories, skills assessments, values clarification questionnaires, and personality style measures can give you an objective read on who you are. While the term "test" is commonly used among those of us who do this type of assessment, most of these are not actually tests per se because there are no right or wrong answers. They are instead inventories of your self-expressed preferences. Many of the more common ones have personalized reports or supplementary materials that list career fields, specific types of jobs, or work environments that match your results. While they can't provide all the answers and only rarely reveal any hidden talents that you were hoping to uncover, they can be powerful ways to find out what makes you uniquely you.

Popular Career and Personality Tests

Strong Interest Inventory & Skills Confidence Inventory

Campbell Interest and Skill Survey

Holland's Self-Directed Search

Myers-Briggs Type Indicator

Sixteen Personality Factor Questionnaire (16PF)

Career Anchors

These tests are available only through qualified professionals including career counselors as well as some psychologists, social workers, college career centers, and human resource departments. (The Myers-Briggs Type Indicator is described in Appendix D under "Resources for Understanding Your Networking Personality.")

Know What You Want

Equal in importance to knowing who you are is knowing what you want. As you learned in chapter 2, having clear goals, and thus being able to define objectives to reach those goals, is essential for effective networking. Knowing what you want also strengthens your self-marketing efforts. Let's look at an example of what can happen if you aren't clear on what you want.

Peter is a college senior trying to figure out what he wants to do with his life, so he meets with an alumnus of his school who works in advertising (since that's one field Peter is considering). The purpose of the meeting is to get information about that field to help him determine if it's the right career for him. Here's how the conversation goes:

Alum.:   "What are you looking for in a career?"

Peter: **"I don't really know. That's why I'm here."**

Alum.:   "Well, I can tell you about the different types of jobs in advertising, and maybe that will help you."

> (He then proceeds to talk for a while about the nature of the work, satisfactions and frustrations, typical salaries, and skills needed for the many different specialties in advertising.)

Peter: "So do you have any idea of which area would be right for me?"

Alum.:   "I can help you make that decision if you can tell me things like what your main strengths are, what kinds of people you want to work with, and what kinds of work responsibilities motivate you. What's most important to you in a job?"

Peter doesn't really have an answer. He has some vague thoughts on these issues but hasn't done enough self-assessment to be able to determine if he's more suited for being in account management, media planning, production, or any of the many other areas within the diverse field of advertising. In this case, he's not expected to know exactly what career he wants because that's why he is in the meeting in the first place. So, he doesn't need to have his career goal perfectly formed, but he does need to be able to put some parameters on what he is looking for.

He would have been a more effective networker if he had said, "I don't know what area of advertising is best for me, but I do know that I want to combine some creative work with a lot of client contact. I also want to use skills like persuading, negotiating, and just generally schmoozing with people. Making money is also important to me, so I want to get on a career track in which I can advance and grow." In that case, the alumnus might have pointed Peter in the direction of an entry-level position in account management. Peter would have provided enough concrete information about himself and what he wants for the two of them to get him closer to a career focus.

Peter also would have impressed the advertising executive with his self-awareness and clear convictions about what he wants. In other words, he would have been a more convincing self-marketer. In fact, he might have impressed the advertising executive enough to have that person go from being a strategist to a target—someone who would not only give him advice but possibly hire him as well. So, whether your networking encounters are for the purpose of choosing a career, finding a job, managing your career, or developing a business, it is important that you come across as knowing who you are and what you want.

Marketing Yourself with a Personal Pitch

Once you've assessed who you are and what you're looking for, you should be able to construct a personal pitch—the cornerstone of your self-marketing efforts and of almost all communication with your network. A personal pitch is a brief statement that typically takes about thirty to sixty seconds to say, or if in writing, is a brief paragraph of a few or several sentences.

The pitch introduces you and your situation and explains why you're worth the listener's or reader's attention. Depending on the situation, your pitch might also include how you were referred to the person with whom you are communicating, as well as what you want out of the contact. Your pitch will vary slightly as you use it in different situations, but the core elements of it should be fairly consistent.

Why You Need a Personal Pitch

A pitch helps you convey information about yourself in a concise and effective manner. Instead of rambling, you can get your point across quickly. Efficiency is needed when dealing with busy people who have only limited time to talk on the phone or read a letter. Concise communication is becoming increasingly important as more and more interaction takes place in ways that don't readily accommodate extraneous verbiage, such as e-mail correspondence, online chat sessions and message boards, and voice mail messages.

Constructing a personal pitch also makes it easier for people to speak on your behalf. There are many occasions in networking when you need people to pass the word along to others that you are looking for a job, seeking a promotion, or offering a particular product or service. What often happens, unfortunately, is that your "message" loses something in the translation.

For example, your message might be that pet owners should use you as their dog trainer because you had twenty years of experience working in kennels and volunteering for the ASPCA before freelancing. If you convey that message in a long-winded fashion, such as listing every job you have held over twenty years and giving too much detail, the person who passes on your message to potential customers is not likely to pass your message along in an accurate and effective way. For example, she might just say to someone, "I think he'd make a great dog trainer for you because he has a lot of experience." That's not a very convincing sales pitch.

An additional reason for developing a personal pitch is that it's a great time-saver. Every time you have to make a cold call, respond to the popular interview opener "So, tell me about yourself," or compose a letter, you can use your personal pitch as an opener. Using your pitch as the cornerstone of all types of communication keeps you from having to reinvent the wheel every time you face a new networking situation.

Constructing Your Personal Pitch

There are so many things you can say to introduce yourself to someone and to present yourself in a positive light, that it can be difficult to know what to include and what to leave out. The way to choose the best information for your pitch is to think of what is relevant to the person you're communicating with, your goals, and the situation at hand. The points you include can come from the three main categories of self-identification information described in the following sections.

Putting Yourself on the Map

Putting yourself on the map means establishing who you are in terms of your work or educational status, situation, and roles. What that might mean is any of the following:

➤ **Your Work Role.** This includes (job title, career area, functional area, or overview of your experience). Examples: "I have 15 years of sales experience, most recently for AT&T…," "I'm a physical therapist at Hope Hospital…," or "I interned last summer at MTV.…"

➡ **Your Education.** This includes (graduation year, class, and your major). Examples: "I'll be graduating from Smith College next spring…," "I received my B.S. in business from Bentley College in 1996…," "I have an M.B.A. from U.C. Berkeley…," or "I'm currently completing my associate's degree in administrative studies…."

Pitching Your Strengths

Here's where you mention the positive points that will help you reach your goals. These points might cover the following categories:

➡ **Skills.** Examples: "I am fluent in Spanish and Russian, both written and spoken…," "I am proficient in most major word-processing and database applications for IBM and Mac…," or "I have strong research and writing skills…."

➡ **Areas of Expertise.** Examples: "I have a broad knowledge of human resource functions including recruiting, training, and benefits administration…," or "My interdisciplinary major exposed me to many current issues in education, politics, and sociology…."

➡ **Personal Qualities.** Examples: "I'm the kind of person who gives 110 percent when I care about something, and I care about the problems of the homeless…." "My bosses have always commented on my reliability and willingness to take the initiative…," or "I'm a good problem-solver…."

➡ **Accomplishments.** Examples: "I coauthored two books on arts and crafts…," "I received a Telly Award for my video on job interviewing…," "I received the customer service award of distinction at my company three years in a row…," or "I maintained a B+ average all four years of college while working twenty hours a week the whole time and serving as editor of the yearbook my senior year…."

What You're Looking For

A final component of your pitch is to clarify what you want or need. What you say here should reflect the goals and objectives you established in chapter 2.

Examples: "I'm hoping to expand my business into the southwestern region of the U.S....," "I need to make a decision about the kind of work I want to do after graduation...," or "I'm looking for a position as a sales manager in a company with a strong entrepreneurial focus...."

A Common Mistake to Avoid

When marketing themselves and communicating who they are, people too often include information that drags down their pitch. Extraneous detail or information that can be seen as negative should always be left out. If you're a recent grad applying for jobs that are not related to your major, for example, don't mention your major, at least not right off the bat. If you're making a transition to a field you've never worked in but you have transferable skills, talk about those skills before getting into details of your work history. In other words, be strategic about how you present yourself in conversation and in writing. Information that is not directly relevant to your goals should not be offered until after you've stated the more positive, relevant aspects of your qualifications and experience. Then, when the less relevant points are raised, you should de-emphasize them as much as possible. It is a matter of putting your best foot forward.

Some Examples of Personal Pitches

The following samples of personal pitches give you an idea of how pitches can sound. Remember that the most important thing about a pitch is that you include only positive information that is relevant to your objectives. The samples labeled "Spoken Pitches" are written as if someone were speaking them instead of being intended for written presentation. They would be adapted slightly if they were for letters, e.g., shorter sentences and a bit more formal. You'll see that the samples labeled "Written Pitches" are slightly different in tone from the spoken ones.

Remember, too, that a spoken pitch is just part of an overall conversation. The information you see here would go along with formalities like saying hello, stating your name, how you were referred to the person, and so on. Also keep in mind that pitches can be shorter than the samples here, particularly when being said at the start of a phone call. The samples provided here are a little long to illustrate better what can go into a pitch.

Spoken Pitches

A pitch from a salesperson to a potential strategist for help in making a career transition and planning a job search:

⟹ I have 15 years of sales experience, most recently at AT&T, and am now looking to bring my expertise to a smaller, start-up company where I can initiate new business practices. Throughout my career, I've always been commended for my ability to identify and establish new markets, not just service existing ones. I'm now trying to target firms where I can use my strategic planning, business development, and management skills and be less directly involved in sales. Since you have such a good handle on the telecommunications industry, I was hoping I could take you to lunch and hear your ideas on which companies would be best for me to approach.

A pitch from a college senior to a potential strategist for help in defining a career focus:

⟹ I'm calling to see if it would be possible to meet with you to discuss careers in the not-for-profit sector. In a few months, I'll be graduating from Smith College where I've done extensive community service and majored in cultural anthropology. I want to pursue a career in nonprofit but am not sure if I'm best suited for fund-raising, programming, or direct service. I've done a lot of research on the field and now would like to speak with you for help in making my decision. I'm the kind of person who gives 110 percent when I care about something, and I care deeply about issues like homelessness (appropriate if this pitch is to someone in an organization related to the homeless). I'm just not sure in which area I can make the most difference.

A pitch from our case study Sam to one of his role models (a mentor) asking for advice on how to get a promotion:

⟹ Martha Jameson suggested I call to see if you might have the time to advise me on a career move I'm trying to make. I'm currently an art director at MM&G and am hoping to move into a creative director position either at my agency or elsewhere. I know I've got the qualifications—one of my print ads was nominated for an ADDY award this year, and I've been taking on more management responsibilities to complement my creative work. I'm just not sure what else I should be doing to best position myself.

Written Pitches

Remember that a pitch is simply one element of a letter or e-mail, so the sample written pitches that follow are not complete written communications. They are just the core element that would be surrounded by some introductory and closing remarks. Examples of complete written communication are provided in chapter 6.

A pitch for an e-mail from Monica to a target (a prospective client for her consulting business):

➠ Ben Weinberg suggested I contact you because he thought you might be interested in hearing about my Web site consulting services. I have put together some very successful sites for real estate businesses like yours and also handled the Lanford Realty account when I worked for WebWorks. I'd like to learn more about your business and see how I might help you grow through a presence on the Web.

A pitch for a letter from John to a possible strategist who can help with his career decision:

➠ My interest in a health care career stems from my solid background in science, experience as a laboratory technician, and strong interpersonal skills. As a high school science teacher for the past several years, I have developed a commitment to educating others and have had to stay apprised of current developments in the sciences. I would now like to make a transition into a health care profession and was hoping to speak with you about genetic counseling as an option.

Assembling Self-Marketing Materials

Once you've laid the foundation for self-marketing by doing some self-assessment and constructing a personal pitch, you're ready to put together your self-marketing materials. Networking invariably requires that you have written materials that describe who you are and what you can offer. How you present yourself on paper is an important element in your networking success because these materials are essentially an extension of your overall professional image.

Depending on your situation, the materials you'll need might include resumes, bios, reference lists, letters of recommendation, portfolios, and business promotional literature. Preparing these documents can be very time-consuming, so it is important to spend time on them before you start networking heavily.

There are, of course, lots of things to say about self-marketing materials. Bookstore shelves are filled to capacity with guides to writing resumes, as well as job search guides that include good advice on gathering references, putting together portfolios, and other such topics. Appendix D lists many of the better of these books that provide all the details of how to put these materials together effectively. So, in the remainder of this chapter, I do not attempt to provide comprehensive guidelines for writing resumes, assembling portfolios, and so on. Instead, I focus on tips related to these documents as a part of networking—not just as a part of a job search or business marketing plan.

Resumes

Too often, resumes are seen simply as chronicles of your work history and lists of your credentials, rather than as a marketing tool. When you buy a product at the grocery store, are you first attracted to the fine print on the back listing the ingredients or to the snazzy packaging on the front? Even if you're an avid label-reader, chances are that you wouldn't even notice the product if something about the packaging didn't attract your attention.

It's the same with resumes. Some people do want to know all the details, but they also want quick answers to two basic questions: what do you have to offer me or my organization, and what are you looking for? These questions are not only asked when you're applying for jobs, but they're also salient when you're networking. They can be very helpful when you are trying to make a career choice or to plan the strategy for a career transition. Besides all the obvious advice about having no typos and other critical issues addressed in resume guidebooks, there are some special considerations when your resume will be used primarily for networking purposes.

Generally speaking, your resume will need to be more versatile than it would be for a job search. What I mean by that is that you are likely to interact with many people outside your own career field or industry while networking, so your resume needs to be relevant to all of them. John, for example, found that he needed to downplay terminology relevant only to teaching and highlight his more transferable skills of interpersonal communication, research, and science aptitude. This made his resume more meaningful to the health care professionals who would be reading it. The following are some specific ways to make your networking resume versatile:

➡ Consider having a profile or summary statement at the top of the resume. This usually consists of a brief paragraph or a bulleted list of points that gives a concise overview of your background and qualifications. This kind of section helps the reader quickly identify who you are and what you have to offer. You usually don't mention specific jobs in an overview statement, just transferable skills and areas of expertise.

➡ Make sure that any job descriptions in your resume are generic enough for readers not well versed in your field to understand. Minimize the use of job-specific or industry-specific jargon (unless it would be relevant for the reader). Also avoid describing every job duty in painstaking detail. Just give people a big picture view of your main areas of responsibility on a job, rather than every task.

➡ Instead of having any job descriptions at all, you might want to design your resume in a functional format. A functional resume consists of three or four experience sections, each with a heading like "Management," "Research," "Project Coordination," or any other functional areas relevant to your experience. You then describe your experience and accomplishments in a brief paragraph or list of state-ments after each heading. If you want people to know your work history as well, you can include a brief employment history section at the bottom of the resume—usually a single-spaced list of job titles, employer names, and dates of employment. (More details on functional resumes and samples can be found in JIST's *The Quick Resume & Cover Letter Book, America's Top Resumes for America's Top Jobs,* and the *Gallery of Best Resumes*, as well as in other books listed in Appendix D.)

➠ Emphasize your accomplishments and successes, not just your responsibilities. Even though you're using the resume just for infor-mation and leads, not for an actual job search, you still need to do some self-promotion.

Bios

A bio is a one-page overview of your experience written in the third person. It usually isn't divided into any categories like a resume, but instead is written more like a story, giving the highlights of your work experience, educational background, accomplishments, areas of expertise, and occasionally personal information. (My bio at the end of this book is an example of one way to put together this document.)

Bios are rarely used in a job hunt but are often helpful for professional networking situations. They can be a handy way to introduce yourself to someone when you send a letter requesting an informational meeting (sending a resume could look like you're asking for a job, when in fact all you want is information). Bios might also be requested when you are to give a talk somewhere or are featured in an article or other publication.

Here are a few tips about bios:

➠ Make sure that your bio conveys your unique expertise, experience, and qualities. The bio should paint a picture of you. It should not be simply an account of your experience and credentials, which can sound generic. Your bio should convey who you really are and should highlight the features of your background or current professional activities that you think best reflect you.

➡ Consider having multiple versions of your bio on hand that empha-size different aspects of your background to use with different groups.

➡ Always have both a complete bio (usually one full page) including most information about you, as well as a very brief bio that can be used in situations where the long one is too much. A typical situation where a brief one is called for is the moment when you're being introduced as a speaker. If you leave it up to the person who intro-duces you to edit the complete bio down to a 30-second introduc-tion, you might be disappointed with what the individual chooses to leave in or take out.

If you're not sure how to put together your own bio, ask your co-workers and other professional colleagues if you can see theirs. You can also hire a public relations consultant or publicist to help you write one. Some career counselors and executive coaches also assist with bios. (See the Allied Forces section of chapter 3, as well as Appendix C, for more ideas of experts who could help you put together a bio.)

References

Having a list of bosses, professors, and clients who will recommend you for opportunities is usually required only when job hunting and applying to educational programs. Only rarely in a networking situation will you be asked for a reference list or letters of recommendation, but it doesn't hurt to have them on hand. While this is a fairly straightforward process, consider the following guidelines:

➡ **Ask for a letter immediately.** Try to request a letter of recommenda-tion as soon as possible after a class, project, or job ends. You will get a better letter if you're still fresh in the instructor's, supervisor's, or client's mind.

➡ **Give guidelines to the writer.** Don't assume that you're going to get a great letter just because the person likes you. Give the people whom you would like to recommend you a list of points you'd like them to include and remind them of ways you distinguished yourself from your classmates or coworkers (or competitors if in your own business).

➠ **Make your objectives clear.** Always let the person recommending you know what the letter is going to be used for and which personal qualities and skills you'd like the individual to emphasize so that the letter will reflect the goals you are striving to achieve.

➠ **Don't ask for recommendation letters at the last minute.** No one, even your biggest fan, can write a good letter under time pressure. Plus, it's just not considerate to give someone a tight deadline. Sometimes it's unavoidable, but whenever possible, ask for a recommendation long before you actually need it.

➠ **Keep a "kudos" file.** Don't just think of letters of recommendation as being from former bosses or teachers. If you receive letters, notes, memos, or e-mails for doing a job well, then you should save them. A boss, for example, might take the time to write a note thanking you for a project well done. A colleague might send an e-mail congratulating you on that same project. Or, a client might write to thank you for a great service or product you provided. Keep all of these in a file and select the best or most relevant ones for your portfolio. (Portfolios are discussed in the next section of this chapter.)

➠ **Compile a reference list.** In addition to having letters on hand, you should have a list of three to five people who can be contacted (by phone or in writing) to speak on your behalf. Type up the list as you would your resume with your name and contact information at the top; then under the heading "References," list the names, titles, addresses, and phone numbers of each reference. If your connection to the reference is not obvious from your resume (for example, a former boss is now at a different company), add a line or two briefly stating in what capacity the person knows you or worked with you. Depending on your situation and age, the list can include a combination of employers and professors or teachers, or just employers. If you're self-employed or in a job that is based on working with clients outside your organization, then all or part of your list might be made up of clients.

Portfolios

Once the sole domain of artists, designers, writers, and others who need to show tangible proof of their work, portfolios are becoming increasingly popular among people in all career fields. A portfolio is a collection of documents that serve as samples of your work and are testaments to your success. The materials can be put together in a three-ring binder with plastic sleeve pages that hold documents. You can also place your material in plastic sleeves but loose, inside a pocket folder with a flap that closes. Office supply stores typically have a selection of items you can use to construct a portfolio. What you include in your portfolio can be any or all of the following:

➤ Your resume

➤ Letters of recommendation and/or reference list

➤ Writing samples (articles, business correspondence, etc.)

➤ "Kudos" letters (see references section above)

➤ Notifications or certificates of awards or honors you've received

➤ Academic transcripts (usually not necessary if you've been working for a while)

➤ Samples from projects you've worked on

Business Promotional Literature

If you are self-employed as a small business owner, consultant, freelancer, or professional in private practice, the literature you use to describe what you do is one of the most important elements in your success—or lack thereof. Promotional literature speaks for you when you're not around, gets people to take you seriously, and helps distinguish you from the competition. Having a brochure, information packet, flyer, client list, or other document is critical for attracting business and referrals for more business. As with bios, one of the best ways to put these materials together is to look at what other people in your line of work are using. You can also find some useful tips in some of the books listed in the entrepreneurs' section of Appendix D. To get you started, here are a few pointers to keep in mind when developing or revising your promotional literature:

➠ Focus on the benefits of your services or products, not the features. Tell people what you can do for them, not every detail of how you do it.

➠ Take the time and invest the money to put together a polished presentation because your promotional materials reflect on you and the quality of your offerings. Make sure that the paper and print quality are top-notch and that the content has been carefully proofread.

➠ Don't invest a lot of time or money in promotional literature until you are certain of your business objectives, services, and target clients or projects. If you're just getting started in a solo endeavor, take some time to iron out the kinks before putting together materials that you'll have to live with for a while.

➠ It's usually not a good idea to list prices or fees in a brochure or flyer, particularly if you print many at one time. Doing so limits your ability to change fees or prices and can also scare off customers before you get to talk to them directly. In some cases, though, you might feel that listing them is beneficial or expected, so use your best judgment and do so if warranted.

Putting Your Self-Marketing Tools to Good Use

In this chapter, you've learned how important it is to reflect on who you are and what you need and to communicate all that through a personal pitch and various written materials. Congratulations! This was the final step in your preparation for being an effective networker.

In this first section of the book, you've learned what networking is all about, planned a networking strategy, taken stock of who you know, gotten organized (or at least learned how you could be organized!), and learned how to promote yourself. You're now ready to take action with the help of tips provided in chapters 6 through 10.

Quick Summary

All networking encounters involve an element of self-marketing or self-promotion. This chapter offered guidelines for effective self-marketing.

Self-marketing is a process of presenting yourself in a favorable light and projecting an appropriate professional image through the things you say about yourself and through written materials.

Self-marketing is necessary so that people will see you as deserving of the opportunities that you seek and so that they will be more inclined to share their time and expertise with you.

The preparatory steps for effective self-marketing are these:

➮ Know who you are: your interests, strengths, values, personality style.

➮ Know what you want: the goals and objectives you are trying to achieve through networking.

A first tool in self-marketing is the personal pitch:

➮ A personal pitch is a brief spoken or written statement that identifies who you are and what you need.

➮ Your personal pitch is the cornerstone of all your networking communication. It can be used when speaking to people in person or by phone and in written materials such as letters and e-mail messages.

Your other self-marketing tools are these items:

➮ Resumes

➮ Bios

➮ References

➮ Portfolios

➮ Business promotional materials

This chapter offered tips for putting these written documents together when they are to be used primarily for networking purposes rather than for a job search.

Communication
DOs and DON'Ts

Just know your lines and don't bump into the furniture.

—SPENCER TRACY

Have you ever had a conversation with someone in which you felt as if you were from two different planets? You were speaking the same language but didn't really understand anything the other was saying? Or, perhaps there was no problem with *what* was being said—the problem was with *how* it was being said. You just weren't connecting. The way you communicate with people can make or break your networking efforts.

Monica, for example, found that when she first started speaking with prospective clients for her Web site business, she was talking about herself and her services more than about the needs of the client. As a result, she wasn't closing deals. Ana also ran into some communication problems in her attempts to network. She found out that her telephone voice was not conveying energy and enthusiasm, so the people she was contacting had less incentive to want to meet with her or help her. Sam's communication problems arose when he first met with someone he hoped would become a mentor. The two of them just didn't seem to click, yet Sam was determined to become this person's protégé, so he kept trying to develop a relationship that just wasn't happening.

The problems that Monica, Ana, and Sam faced are representative of the three essential elements of communication: content, delivery, and rapport. Content was a problem for Monica, whose conversations focused more on herself than on the other person. Ana's communication problems lay not so much in what she said but in how she was saying it. Her problem was with delivery. And Sam found that he was having difficulty establishing rapport.

This chapter offers DOs and DON'Ts for effective communication in content, delivery, and rapport and also provides tips for communicating by telephone, through public speaking, and in writing. This chapter serves as a "communications primer" before you venture into the networking situations described in chapters 7 through 10.

Content—How to Say the Right Thing

The personal pitch that you developed in chapter 5 is a good starting point for the content of many of the conversations you'll have with your network contacts. Remember that the pitch enables you to convey who you are and what you need in a concise but convincing manner. It is a particularly important component of your communication when you are networking for career choice or career management. In those situations, you have to convince people, subtly but powerfully, that you are worth helping.

Remember too, though, that networking is a two-way street. To develop solid relationships, you can't just talk about yourself and what you need; you have to demonstrate a genuine interest in the other person. As you saw in Monica's case, doing so is particularly important when you are networking as a way to generate customers or clients for your business. To clinch the deal, you can't talk just about yourself. You have to find out what the other person needs and then tailor a discussion of your products or services to those needs. This same idea is important in networking for a job as well. If you are communicating with people as part of a job search, it helps to assess the needs of the prospective employer rather than focus just on what you need.

When you consider the content of a conversation or written communication, keep the following in mind:

⟹ DO present yourself in the best possible light, but never embellish so much that you're telling lies (or even half-truths).

⟹ DO avoid controversial topics like politics or religion (unless that's the focus of the conversation).

⟹ DO avoid using industry- or job-specific jargon and acronyms unless you're speaking to someone in your own field who will understand what you're saying.

⟹ DON'T say anything negative about a current or former boss, colleague, teacher, classmate, or just about anyone or anything else. People like, and will respond better to, a positive person.

⟹ DO have an agenda for the conversation in mind so that you cover everything you want to.

⟹ DO speak with strong action verbs, saying, for example, "I communicate well with customers" instead of "I am good with customers."

Special Tips for Your Conduct at Networking Appointments

Always be on time. Being late is inconsiderate and reflects poorly on your commitment level and organizational abilities.

Don't be too early. Showing up more than ten or fifteen minutes before a scheduled appointment time is often an inconvenience for the person you're meeting and a waste of your time.

If you're the one who requested the meeting, come with an agenda so that you don't seem disorganized and waste the other person's time.

If the length of time for the appointment was not settled in advance, clarify it early on so you know how much time you have. Be considerate of other people's time.

Make an effort to establish rapport. Ease into your agenda after some small talk; then don't just talk about yourself—be sure to learn about the other person. In addition to appearing more personable, you are likely to get some great information.

Keep your agenda flexible so that your interaction is natural and conversational, not mechanical.

If you're in the meeting for information, gently but assertively press for specific, concrete information, not just vague ideas.

Be courteous and show appreciation.

Leave when time is up. Don't hold the other person up from other appointments or responsibilities.

Send a thank-you note or e-mail (if you initiated the meeting) within 48 hours. If the appointment was a mutual idea, thanking is not so crucial; but you do want to maintain the relationship, so follow up promptly with a note saying you enjoyed the meeting.

Delivery—How You Say What You Say

Delivery of your message is as important—in some ways more important—than the content of your message. As Ana found when calling people as part of her job search, she had to make a conscious effort to keep her tone of voice positive and upbeat. She found this difficult at times because there were days when she was so tired of job hunting that making yet another phone call was about the last thing she wanted to do. If you're looking for a job, though, you have to remember that each person you speak with by phone or in person needs to be treated as if they're the first person you've contacted in your search. Your voice, as well as your overall physical presentation, needs to be fresh and enthusiastic.

This advice isn't just for job seekers either. No matter which goal you are working toward in your networking, the style in which you deliver your "message" is critical. The tone and pace of your speech are just a couple of aspects of that delivery. You also need to keep in mind how you are presenting yourself from head to toe, particularly when the communication is face-to-face. To ensure a top-notch delivery, keep the following ideas in mind:

➡ DO be concise. Don't ramble. If what you have to say is complicated or convoluted, edit it in advance so you can convey it smoothly and efficiently.

➡ DO speak clearly. Don't garble your words or mumble.

➡ DO convey energy and enthusiasm. Avoid speaking in a monotone or tired manner.

➡ DON'T speak too fast or too slowly.

➡ DO pay attention to the volume of your speech. Make sure you're not shouting or whispering without realizing it. Project but don't scream.

➡ DON'T get rattled. Try to remain composed and relaxed. Pause and take a deep breath if you feel yourself getting nervous or talking too fast. Asking questions can give you a breather and help you relax a bit.

⟹ DON'T crowd others' physical space when communicating in person. Keep a comfortable distance between you and the other person.

⟹ DO convey a confident air, but don't be aggressive.

⟹ DO pay attention to your overall image and self-presentation. Are you well groomed? Are you dressed appropriately for the occasion?

⟹ DO minimize distracting body language.

> ➤ Are you blinking a lot—or hardly at all?

> ➤ Do you have any nervous twitches?

> ➤ Are your arms and hands flailing wildly?

> ➤ Are you making eye contact (but not staring the other person down)?

> ➤ How's your body position? Slouching? Overly stiff?

Here's Looking at You, Kid

According to Kate Weil, a New York-based image consultant, first impressions are made in an average of just seven seconds and are based overwhelmingly on nonverbal factors. Research has shown that the impact you make depends 55 percent on your appearance and body language and 38 percent on your tone of voice. "With your actual words accounting for only 7 percent of the impact you make, paying attention to your image is essential," says Weil. "If your image conflicts with your verbal message, you're going to have an extremely difficult time getting that message across. And if you want people to believe that you are successful, confident, and capable, your image must say this even before you open your mouth to speak."

Rapport—How You Connect with People

In addition to paying attention to what you say and how you say it, it's also important to strive for connecting with the people to whom you're writing and talking. Perfecting your pitch, rehearsing conversations, developing a flawless speaking voice, and having impeccable grooming and comportment can actually have a downside; you can come across as an automaton, not a fellow human being.

As discussed throughout this book, networking is not just about making a good first impression, having a quick interaction with someone, and then going on your merry way. Networking is based on relationships, so the way you establish rapport with the people you meet is directly linked to the success or failure of your overall networking effort.

Sam learned this during an initial failed attempt to acquire a mentor for help in steering his advertising career in the right direction. He had been attending a particular monthly meeting for people in his area of the advertising industry and had met a woman there named Susan, who was very successful in her career. He had been familiar with Susan's work even before meeting her and had always viewed her as something of a remote role model. He now hoped to get to know her and have her serve as a mentor of sorts for him. So, for three consecutive months, he made a point of speaking to her at the meetings and then got up the nerve to call her and request that they get together for lunch. Even though she had been a bit cold to him at the meetings, he hoped that she would be receptive to his request. Well, she wasn't. Susan ignored his repeated attempts to contact her, and then finally had her assistant call Sam to say that she was too busy to meet with him at any time in the foreseeable future.

What went wrong? A number of factors probably led to this failed networking attempt. Sam may have pushed the relationship too quickly. He could have waited to get to know her better at the meetings before attempting to set a lunch appointment. He might also have talked too much about himself and his own career needs during their brief encounters at the meetings. The main reason, however, might simply be that they just didn't connect on some intangible level, and nothing Sam could have done would have made a difference. If you're looking to have a mentoring relationship with someone, then it's important that the chemistry be there from the start. You can't force people to like you, and you certainly can't force people to take you under their wings and help you develop your career. If the rapport is not there, no relationship exists. Sam soon realized this and turned to other people in his role models STARS category to find a mentor.

Rapport is a factor not just when you network for career management purposes. All of the networking goals—career choice, job search, business development, and career management—require that you establish solid rapport with people to enlist their help.

When you are trying to establish rapport, consider the following pointers:

- ⮞ DO smile. As you talk to someone, try to notice if your face is frozen. This can happen without realizing it. Relax your facial muscles and smile naturally. You don't have to beam incessantly as if you were on the lead float of the Rose Parade, but do try to have a generally pleasant look on your face.

- ⮞ DO be courteous. Be respectful of other people's time and sensitive to others' needs and feelings. A little tact goes a long way.

- ⮞ DO be down-to-earth. If there's one mistake that people most often make in career-related communication, it's to come across as overly formal.

- ⮞ DO be sincere. If you don't have a genuine interest in the people you're communicating with, you have no business talking to them. Insincerity is easy to spot and is one of the quickest ways to squash rapport.

- ⮞ DON'T be unfriendly. Even if you're having a bad day or are extremely busy, try to be patient and pleasant in all your dealings with people.

- ⮞ DO listen to the other person. Don't tap your foot and get an impatient look on your face while the other person is talking. Trying to monopolize the conversation won't do you any good—in fact, if you talk a lot more than half the time, you may be in trouble (even during a job interview). Listen attentively; don't act as if you're just waiting until it's your turn to talk next.

➤ DON'T interrupt. Wait until a pause in the conversation to speak. And when you do resume talking, make sure that what you say is related to the preceding points. Otherwise, you give away the fact that you weren't listening to the other person.

➤ DO get to know the other person. Ask questions and show interest—in fact, be interested. Again, insincerity is usually easy to spot.

➤ DON'T rush the process of establishing rapport. Although you can establish immediate rapport by using simple techniques like smiling and being courteous, lasting rapport develops over time. So, try to be patient and don't rush it.

➤ DO be attuned to the chemistry (or lack thereof) between the other person and you, and be prepared to back off if the other person just doesn't seem to want to connect with you.

Communicating by Phone

As long as you're not having a video conference, communication by telephone can be very convenient. It won't matter that you're having a bad hair day or wearing the ugly tie that your kids gave you for Father's Day. Barring a case of laryngitis, phone communication seems fairly easy compared to all the nonverbal and image issues that are so critical in face-to-face encounters. Beware, though, as that ease can lull you into a false sense of security or overconfidence. Phone communication has its own set of pitfalls to avoid and tactics to employ. The content of what you say over the phone still has to share the spotlight with your phone "presence."

When you communicate by phone, remember the following:

➤ DO pay special attention to your tone of voice, as well as to the pitch, speed, and volume of your speech.

➠ DON'T litter your speech with uhs and ums. These are much more noticeable when someone is only hearing you, not hearing *and* seeing you.

➠ DO sound energetic and positive. Your voice is the only clue to your enthusiasm.

➠ DO stand up while talking on the phone if you need a quick energy boost.

➠ DO make sure your background is quiet—no barking dogs, screaming kids, chattering room-mates, or loud music or TV.

➠ DON'T have an unprofessional or overly personal message on your answering machine or voice mail if you're actively networking for professional purposes.

➠ DON'T let a child or housekeeper answer the phone if you're doing business from home (unless they are able to answer the phone in a professional manner, stating the business name rather than saying "hello"). You can even gain stature and prestige if the caller thinks you have an assistant who answers the phone for you.

Tips for Leaving Messages on Answering Machines and Voice Mail

State your name slowly and clearly, and spell it if the spelling is not obvious.

Say your phone number clearly and slowly as well. People often race through their number because they're so used to saying it and know it so well. Remember it's new to the person you're calling, so slow down! It is also helpful to repeat it at the end of your message in case the listener wasn't able to write it down the first time around.

Make it easy to reach you. Give times when you'll be available.

Briefly state your reason for calling if your call isn't expected.

Don't waste time leaving the date and time of your call if you're pretty sure you're speaking in a voice mail system, because it will auto-matically record the date and time. (It's okay to do so, though, if you want to be extra clear about the time you left your message.)

⟱ DO have a notepad and pen handy, as well as any materials to which you might need to refer.

⟱ DO disable call waiting if you're going to be on an important business call.

⟱ DO make note of the time difference when calling people in other time zones.

Public Speaking

Speaking in public is often an efficient and effective way to make contact with large numbers of people at once. It lets people get to know you and makes them aware of your particular expertise. Since being visible is an important element of successful networking, public speaking can be a useful vehicle for communication.

For our purposes here, public speaking can refer to anything from formal speeches to informal small gatherings and everything in between. For a formal speech, you might find yourself standing at a podium in front of an audience of hundreds of people, while an informal setting could be a workshop you conduct for a small group of people sitting in a circle of chairs. Whichever setting you find yourself in, the following are some tips that can help you do it right:

⟱ DO carefully prepare your presentation or speech. No matter how much you know about your subject, it's not a good idea to wing it.

⟱ DO practice how you're going to deliver your talk or conduct your seminar, but don't try to memorize your talk or lecture word-for-word.

⟱ DO know your audience and make sure your presentation is relevant to them.

⟱ DO ask questions of your audience to involve them. If people aren't readily forthcoming with answers or comments, simply ask for a show of hands as a reply to your question. Even the most shy, inhibited audiences will usually raise their hands to indicate yes or no. Asking for a show of hands is also useful when your audience is large and interaction is difficult because of its size.

➤ DO use visual aids like overheads, slides, or flip charts whenever possible.

➤ DO make your notes readable. A few main points in large print on index cards to jog your memory are much easier to follow than pages of detailed notes in small type.

➤ DO keep an eye on the time. In an informal situation with a small audience (perhaps about twenty-five people or less), it is not unusual for the speaker to pause and ask how much time is left. Doing so is preferable to running out of time at the end or to going overtime. In more formal talks, however, or to larger groups, you should not interrupt the flow of your talk to inquire about the time. If there's no clock in sight, be sure to have a watch positioned nearby within your line of vision (not on your wrist).

➤ DO be as down-to-earth and informal as you can be, given the circumstances.

CEOs Say the Darnedest Things

The best example I've ever seen of a speaker being down-to-earth and relating to her audience was Anita Roddick, founder and head of the enormously successful company The Body Shop. She was the third in a series of keynote speakers to appear at the opening session of a conference for leaders from community service and volunteerism. After the audience had sat through two long speeches, Ms. Roddick came onto the stage in front of nearly a thousand people, clad in a colorful sundress, and opened her talk by saying, "I know you're all probably wondering when is it time for us all to have a pee, so bear with me. [My talk] won't be long, but it'll be intense." Needless to say, the audience was a bit taken aback at first, evidenced by the nervous murmur that swept across the room for a few seconds. But then a collective laugh broke out through the crowd—not a tense, polite laugh, but a genuinely relaxed reaction to her irreverent remark.

Yes, we *had* all been sitting in that overly air-conditioned room listening to speeches from politicians and corporate bigwigs far too long. And, yes, most of us probably could have used a restroom break at that point. She was right on target. In the popular film *Jerry Maguire*, the wife of Tom Cruise's character tells him, "You had me at 'hello.'" Well, Anita Roddick had *us* at "hello."

➡ DON'T talk about things you don't know anything about or don't believe in.

➡ DON'T open with a joke unless you can really pull it off and only after you've tried it out on some guinea pigs. If they don't laugh, scrap it. A joke at which no one laughs can kill your entire presentation.

➡ DON'T read from a script unless you're giving a very formal speech to a large group or in cases where accuracy of facts and figures is key. Whatever you do, do not read your talk unless you have been trained to do so. Nothing turns off an audience as fast as someone who is poor at reading a speech.

➡ DO keep distracting body movements to a minimum.

➡ DON'T wear busy, patterned clothes, particularly if your presentation will be taped or televised.

Written Communication

Many networking situations require written communication. Letters to request meetings, e-mail to check-in with people in your network, letters to promote your business, and thank-you notes all have one thing in common: not only must they be well written, they must be strategically written. Here's how to do so:

➡ DO review your objectives for the correspondence before writing (and keep them in mind as you write).

➡ DO state early on in a letter why you're writing.

➠ DON'T start a letter with "Hello. My name is...." Who you are should be evident from your signature and typed name at the bottom and/or your name on the letterhead.

➠ DO use your personal pitch as the cornerstone of your correspondence.

➠ DO back up any claims you make about yourself or your business with two or three concrete examples.

➠ DO use a minimum of words to have maximum impact. Don't ramble or be verbose.

➠ DO use correct grammar, punctuation, and spelling.

➠ DON'T have any typos or other errors in a letter.

➠ DO make sure that your letter is visually appealing—balanced on the page; on clean, unwrinkled paper; and with no messy white-out or erasure marks.

➠ DO use proper business format. (See the following sections for examples.)

Letter Formats

Most typed, professional correspondence related to your job, business, or career planning should be laid out on the page in a way that conforms to standard business letter format. You have three basic choices of formats (they are displayed on the following pages): indented, block, and modified block. Which one you choose is up to you. Simply pick the style that you like the best or that best reflects the content of your letter.

By the way, if you are writing your letters on stationery that already has your name, address, and phone number at the top and/or bottom of the page, you don't need to repeat that information. The formats in the following examples include the sender's information for people writing on plain paper, not personalized letterhead.

Indented Style

Sender's Address
City, State, ZIP
Phone, Fax, and/or E-mail

Date

Recipient's Name (first and last)
Job Title (if applicable)
Organization Name (if applicable)
Internal Address (for example, Suite or Floor #)
Outside Address (Street or P.O. Box)
City, State, ZIP (and country if applicable)

Dear Ms./Mr./Dr. : (Can use first name if familiar with recipient)

    Indent the first line of each paragraph one tab from the left margin. Continue the rest of the paragraph like this with lines starting at the left margin.

    Skip one space between paragraphs.

Closing,

Sender's Signature (first name only if the recipient knows you well; otherwise, sign first and last names)

Sender's Name (typed first and last)

Encl. (Can also type "Enclosure"; use this if you send anything with your letter.)

Block Style

Sender's Address
City, State, ZIP
Phone, Fax, and/or E-mail

Date
Recipient's Name
Job Title
Organization Name
Internal Address
Outside Address
City, State, ZIP

Dear Ms./Mr./Dr. :

Justify all lines of the paragraph flush with the left and right margins (also called justified).

Skip one line between paragraphs.

Closing,

Sender's Signature

Sender's Name Typed

Encl.

Modified Block Style

Same as regular block, but sender's information, date, and closing are on the right-hand side of the page.

Sender's Address
City, State, ZIP
Phone, Fax, and/or E-mail

Date

Recipient's Name
Job Title
Organization Name
Internal Address
Outside Address
City, State, ZIP

Dear Ms./Mr./Dr. :

Justify all lines of the paragraph flush with the left and right margins (justified).

Skip one space between paragraphs.

Closing,

Sender's Signature

Sender's Name Typed

Encl.

Sample Written Communication

The following letters, notes, and e-mail are provided as samples of written communication for various networking situations. (For examples of thank-you notes, see chapter 14.) Only the bodies of letters are included here as samples to illustrate effective content. In reality, these letters would have the recipients' and senders' contact information as shown in the letter style guides on the preceding pages.

Requesting an Appointment to Discuss a Career Transition—Formal Example

Dear Ms. Mansour:

Dr. Susan Tyler of the neonatology department at St. Bartholomew's Hospital suggested that I contact you to discuss the field of genetic counseling. As someone with a strong background in science, an interest in bioethics, and experience as a science teacher, I think I am well suited for work as a genetic counselor. Before I make this career transition, however, I would like to speak to people already working in this area for further insight into the profession.

I have already done extensive research into the nature of genetic counseling work, outlook for the field, and educational options, so I would be coming to you with focused questions to help me make the right decision.

Dr. Tyler spoke highly of your work, so I would welcome the chance to meet with you. I realize you are busy, so I would very much appreciate any time you can spare to speak with me for a few moments. I will call you in a few days to see if we might arrange an appointment. Thank you.

Sincerely,

Signature

John Stevenson

What makes this a good letter:

➠ It balances sounding as if he's not fully focused on a career goal with a bit of self-promotion.

➠ It flatters the reader.

➠ It is very courteous and respectful of the reader's time.

➠ It gets to the point of what he wants early in the first paragraph.

➠ It shows he's already done his homework.

➠ He takes the initiative to follow up instead of waiting for a reply.

E-Mail Requesting an Appointment to Discuss Business Strategy—Informal

Hello Dave,

Janet Beezley (who was my roommate at USC) thought I should contact you to learn more about your Web site consulting business. She said you've been very successful and might not mind sharing some insights with me—I am launching a similar venture here on the West Coast. I've been on the technical staff of WebWorld for the two years since graduation and have been designing sites for friends on the side as well. I want to build this freelance work into a serious business and have some questions about strategy. So, if you can spare a few minutes to talk about life as a full-time Webmaster, I'd be much obliged. Could you let me know a good time to call you? Thanks a lot.

Monica Chu

What makes this e-mail effective:

➡ Has casual and friendly tone—appropriate for the situation

➡ Clearly defines connection to referral source

➡ Makes it clear that she's not a competitive threat to the reader's business

➡ Gives a concise overview of her background so she'll be taken seriously

➡ Flatters the reader

Informal Note to Check In with a Network Contact

Dear Gloria,

Saw this article on the new convention center in Albuquerque and thought of you—looks like a great facility. I still have nice memories of that wonderful conference you coordinated in the old one a few years ago.

Sorry to have been out of touch. The last few months have been hectic as I'm now managing two departments: domestic and international travel. I hope you're doing well. Would love to see you and hear about your current projects. Things should settle down for me in a few weeks, so I'm making a note to call you then to set up a lunch.

Regards,

Emily

What makes this note effective:

➡ Sends a relevant article as a good excuse for getting back in touch.

➡ Has a warm and friendly tone.

➥ Has informal sentence structure—a style that implies "I'm a busy professional, but I'm taking the time to write you a quick note."

➥ Contains some self-promotion, but does it subtly.

➥ Shows interest in the reader.

➥ Flatters the reader.

Letter as Part of a Large Mailing to Update a Network

Dear Friends and Colleagues,

As the one-year anniversary of the founding of Day-Ja News approaches, we want to thank all of you for your support. Your advice, encouragement, and referrals have enabled Day-Ja News to grow from a glimmer of an idea on a cocktail napkin to a thriving enterprise. The following are the highlights of our year:

- Acquired ten major corporate clients needing monthly news-letters and special quarterly publications.

- Expanded our staff to include three top-notch graphic designers.

- Were one of three finalists for an award from the Association of Corporate Communicators.

Our plans for the coming year include expanding our electronic news-letter services and continuing to strive for being the best desktop publishing and communications consulting firm in the Chicago area. We will keep you posted on our progress. Please let us know if there's anything we can do to help you.

Best Regards,

Merrill   Jon
Merrill Day   Jon Jacobi

What makes this a good letter:

➥ It's a "brag" letter, but it balances boasting with a genuine show of appreciation for the readers' role in their accomplishments.

➠ It is well designed, having three distinct parts with successes highlighted as bulleted points.

➠ It highlights specific areas of their success, and it doesn't just make general, vague claims.

➠ It contains an offer to help the reader.

➠ The salutation ("Dear Friends and Colleagues") is appropriate for a mass mailing. Each recipient does not have to be addressed by name since the content of the letter makes it obvious that the correspondence is part of a large-scale mailing. If they wanted to personalize the letter for some recipients, they could have handwritten a brief note on each letter in which they addressed the recipient by name.

➠ It is also appropriate that the senders signed only their first names, not first and last, as doing so is in keeping with the personal, friendly image they want their business to convey.

Quick Summary

Networking is all about interpersonal interaction and developing relationships, so effective communication is a key to success in networking.

This chapter focused on three key elements of communication:

➠ Content—what you say

➠ Delivery—how you say it

➠ Rapport—how you connect with the other person

Communication DOs and DON'Ts for each of these three elements were covered.

Tips and examples were also provided for communication by phone, through public speaking, and in writing.

Fact-Finding Missions:
Networking to Make Decisions

A single conversation across the table with a wise man is worth a month's study of books.

—CHINESE PROVERB

Have you ever made what you thought was a pretty good decision, only to find out later that if you had just consulted other people, you could have made a better choice? That's what "fact finding missions" are all about: getting input from reliable sources who can help you make better decisions. Relying solely on what you read or on your own knowledge about career or business choices is simply not enough. Good choices are based on complete, accurate, and up-to-date information; even better decisions are based on all that, plus experience and wisdom. That's where your network of contacts comes in. They can provide the information and experience you need to supplement what you've read or what you already know, so that you can make a better decision.

What Are Fact-Finding Missions?

A *fact-finding mission* (FFM) can be defined as any interaction you have with one or more people in which you seek information that you need in order to make a particular decision about your career or business. An FFM can be a formal meeting where you go to someone's office for a scheduled appointment, or it can be an impromptu encounter that turns into an FFM. It might also be an exchange of information by e-mail, letters, or phone. The purpose of an FFM is to collect information about options you are considering, and to get input from "experts" on decisions you are making. By experts, I mean anyone who has knowledge and experience that you do not possess yourself.

FFMs are particularly useful in the career choice process but can also come in handy during a job search or as a career or business management tool.

Careful Consideration Is Key

Consider the case of Martin, a menswear buyer for a major department store. Martin wanted more autonomy in his career and had an entrepreneurial drive that wasn't being satisfied working for someone else. After several years in the retail industry, he had developed a strong sense of style and good customer relations skills and felt that he had a natural talent for advising other people about their appearance, all of which could be put to good use if he were to become a freelance image consultant. Since he was aware of the ups and downs of being one's own boss, he was reluctant just to dive into self-employment without careful consideration. So, he proceeded to go on fact-finding missions to get all the information he needed to make the right decision and feel comfortable with it. He met with several image consultants specializing in female clients—good choices since he planned to specialize in male clients, so the consultants he interviewed would not view him as competition and would be more forthcoming with advice and trade secrets. He also met with other professionals tangentially related to image consulting, such as photographers and stylists to get their take on the work. He also talked to a few entrepreneurs in fields completely unrelated to his to get insight into the self-employed life. After all his hard work, Martin was confident that he knew what he was getting into, and that the choice was a good one for him. He then set out to plan a strategy for his transition (strategy sessions are discussed in chapter 8) and gradually began to take action toward his new goal.

Where FFMs Fit in the Career Exploration Process

Too many people involved in the career decision-making process think that they can skip over fact-finding missions because they already know what a given field entails. Doing so can be a mistake, though. Martin, for example, could easily have transitioned right into self-employment since he already had a basic understanding of the work of an image consultant. Just knowing about a given career option is not enough, however. You have to know if it's right for *you*.

FFMs don't just tell you things you already know. They give you an opportunity to take what you know about yourself—your strengths, priorities, and life goals—and compare that self-knowledge with what a particular career field has to offer. The process of talking to people and getting outside opinions on the decision you're making is a proactive approach to matching your priorities with the best option.

FFMs also serve as important reality checks. Just because you already have an inkling of what a career option entails doesn't mean that you necessarily know enough to make a significant life decision. And, even if you've read everything there is to read on a particular option, you might still be lacking real-world information that can only come directly from people with experience in the field.

John, for example, found that he still had unanswered questions even after reading everything he could get his hands on concerning the profession of genetic counseling. One of the main reasons for conducting fact-finding missions was that he wanted to learn more about the skills and personal qualities he needed to become an effective genetic counselor. He knew from his reading that the work requires a combination of interpersonal skills and aptitude for science, but he didn't have a good sense of how that combination actually plays out in the daily work routine. He needed to talk to practicing genetic counselors to discuss his concerns about his lack of counseling experience and his fears that he would not be patient and empathetic enough with patients. These were concerns that a book or career profile on a Web site could not address. He needed to discuss these issues with people working in that field.

How FFMs Differ from Informational Interviews

You might be familiar with the term *informational interview*— a concept that has been quite popular for a number of years. The description you have read of fact-finding missions so far might be sounding a lot like informational interviews, but there is one critical difference. A primary goal of FFMs is to engage others actively in your decision-making process, and that's where FFMs differ from informational interviews. In an informational interview, you can easily lapse into a passive stance. You sit back and soak up information and then go off to make a decision about whether to rule in or rule out that career option. Sure, you do have to take something of a proactive stance to interview the person for the information you need, but it's not as active a process as engaging the person in the decision making with you. That's where an FFM is different.

You *are* taking in information about a given occupation, but you're also putting the other person in the role of surrogate career counselor, having the individual help you decide what you should do. You're on a mission to get specific information that you have identified as being key to your decision-making strategy. You are on a mission to make a decision, not just to collect random information. In an informational interview, the emphasis is on asking open-ended questions about work responsibilities and other facts, getting an answer, and then going on to the next question. In a fact-finding mission, you ask the same type of questions, but you also describe who you are so that the two of you can evaluate whether the work fits your preferred work style, strengths, and goals. An FFM is an opportunity to test assumptions and strategically obtain answers to your questions as they directly relate to your goals.

John took advantage of fact-finding missions in this strategic way. He did not simply ask questions about the nature of the work and personal qualities needed in genetic counseling; those questions had been answered in the reading and Web site browsing he had done. Instead, he discussed his own "profile" (interests, skills, experience, and personality type) and asked the people with whom he was meeting to help him determine if that profile sounded like someone with potential to be a successful genetic counselor. Doing so enabled him to learn where his strengths and weaknesses were in relation to that profession, thus enabling him to make a well-informed decision.

Where to Find People for Your FFMs

You may already have people in your network who can provide the information you need to make the decisions that you're facing. Look at the people listed in your STARS categories of chapter 3 and see who might help you with your FFM. (Strategists and role models are often the best sources.)

If the people you know in those categories are not knowledgable about the career fields or business opportunities you're investigating, you'll need to turn to other sources to cultivate new contacts. For fact-finding missions, alumni networks of high schools, colleges, and graduate programs are among the best places to find people who are amenable to the idea of meeting with you. If you're not already part of an alumni club or in possession of an alumni directory, contact your alma maters (or current institution if you're still a student) to see what services are available.

Also ask coworkers (past and present), clients, customers, suppliers, and other people you know through work to connect you with people they know in the fields you're considering. Remind them that you're not asking to be put in touch with people who can hire you, but rather those who can simply provide information and have input into your decisions. Professional and trade associations are excellent sources of new contacts as well. (See Appendix B for a list of associations.)

Be as creative and persistent as possible in tracking down people with whom you can conduct FFMs. It's easy to say, "I've thought about looking into arts administration, but I don't know anybody who does it, so I have no one to talk to." In addition to meeting people by simply attending a meeting or conference of an arts administration professional association, you can also think of someone you know who might know someone in that field.

Sometimes the connections are a bit remote. Do you know anyone who's an artist who might have applied for a grant through a nonprofit arts organization? Do you know a teacher who might have once arranged a student field trip at a museum and therefore has had contact with a museum administrator? There are an infinite number of ways to get connected to anyone in any field. You just have to do some brainstorming. Appendix A does some of the work for you, listing connections between career fields and industries. That list is just a start, though, and doesn't include individual connections, like the fact that your sister's husband's brother's podiatrist knows someone in public relations.

Don't forget about career counselors as people to have FFMs with, too. Career counselors often know a lot about various career fields and definitely should know how to guide you in reconciling who you are with what your options offer. They don't always know as much about a particular field as the people who work in it daily (and that's not really a career counselor's primary role anyway), but they can help you take what you've learned from reading and from other FFMs and make a good decision.

Where and When Fact-Finding Missions Take Place

People who take an active role in managing and shaping their own careers actually hold impromptu as well as planned FFMs all the time, not just when they're facing a major decision. In today's world of work, we can all benefit from being like reporters constantly researching the next story. People who are naturally curious collect a lot of interesting, useful information as they go through life. Then, when a career turning-point or crisis arises, this information can come in quite handy.

The settings and circumstances of fact-finding missions are less important than the actual exchange of information. An FFM can be an official, scheduled meeting at someone's workplace or on the phone, or it might be a brief conversation that takes place in an elevator, in an office hallway, on a train or plane, or just about anywhere else. You can also conduct FFMs in writing if distance prevents you from meeting with someone or if you don't want to incur expensive long-distance phone bills. Ideally, though, FFMs should take place in person, preferably at the workplace of the person you're meeting with. Because that's the most common method, that's what the tips in the following section focus on.

How to Prepare for a Fact-Finding Mission

There are several bases that you must cover before you can conduct an FFM. First, you need to determine which "facts" you need to find. Then you should make an effort to gather those facts through books, magazines, journals, and Web sites. At that point, you can contact people for fact-finding missions, knowing that you have done adequate preparation. The following sections provide more detail on ways to prepare.

Know What You Are Looking For

The most important thing that you can do to prepare for an FFM is to determine what you need to know. This only makes sense, right?

What this really means is that you have to know what data is preventing you from making a good decision. For example, you might be a recent college graduate considering entering the book publishing field as an editorial assistant. Everything you've read about the field makes it seem right for you; you like to read, write, edit, proofread, and follow developments in contemporary literature. You're also aware that publishing is a business and not just a bunch of literary people sitting around in tweed jackets reading manuscripts and going out to lunch with authors. While you *think* the field is right for you, you're not certain. That's where an FFM comes in. You don't need to talk to someone just to learn the basic duties and responsibilities of an editor—you need to sit down with somebody to ask pointed questions that will help you understand what publishing is *really* all about. FFMs are not just for entry-level people either. The same fact finding is necessary for mid-career and senior-level people who need to uncover the subtle nuances between career options in order to make good choices.

Questions Monica Asked in Her Fact-Finding Missions

After reading books on entrepreneurship and consulting, Monica still had questions about the best way to proceed in developing her Web site business. Her questions included:

➡ What is the best way to advertise my business?

➡ If I am not an outgoing, aggressive person, will I have difficulty promoting my business?

➡ Should I refer to myself as a Web site consultant or as the president of a Web site company?

➡ Is it worthwhile to join the entrepreneurial professional associations I have read about?

➡ Do you think I have enough Web site development and maintenance experience to start my own business?

Research

To make the most of an FFM and to be sure you don't waste anyone's time—yours or the person's you're meeting with, be sure that you've done your homework. That means reading as much as possible about the career or business options you'll be discussing in the FFM. It's helpful to think of your research as having four main layers:

⇒ **World of Work Overviews.** Books that provide an overview of the whole world of work (or most of it) are a good place to start to get brief descriptions of the fields that you are considering and to get a sense of how those options relate to other fields. The Department of Labor publishes two handbooks for this purpose: the *Occupational Outlook Handbook* (known as the *OOH*) and the *Dictionary of Occupational Titles* (often called the *DOT*). These are accurate, objective reference books found in most public libraries and school libraries. These books are good places to start your research, but they probably won't be very satisfying for those who already have an advanced knowledge of the work world.

Additional books with good overviews are found in bookstores and libraries with career resource collections. These books, which often give more detailed descriptions of career fields than are found in the *OOH* or *DOT,* include such titles as *Job Smarts: Careers with a Future* by Martin Yate (Ballantine, 1997); *The Complete Guide for Occupational Exploration* (JIST, 1993); and *America's Top 300 Jobs,* 5th Edition (JIST, 1996). (Complete references for these and other books are found in the bibliography of Appendix D.)

⇒ **Information on Specific Careers.** The books mentioned in the preceding bulleted item provide just a brief description of a given career field or occupation. To get more complete information, you should next turn to books that focus on just one career area. Books with titles like *Hot Health Care Careers* (McNally & Schneider; Master Media, 1993), *Career Opportunities in the Music Industry* (Field; Facts on File, 1995), and *Careers for Writers* (Bly; NTC Publishing Group, 1995) are just a few of the many occupational guides you'll find in bookstores' career sections, public libraries, and college or community career centers. These books describe the nature of the work, typical salaries, qualifications needed, career paths, and employment outlook for a particular career field, or set of related occupations.

Many of the Web sites listed in Appendix C are also good sources of information on specific career fields. Some sites post career field or industry overviews and may also feature various occupations in chat rooms or auditorium events.

➠ **Inside Information.**   Career fields and professions themselves are often good sources of information about your career options. Many professional associations publish free or low-cost pamphlets on career paths in their field; or, at the very least, the organization's membership packet can offer insight into what the field is all about. Also informative are the magazines, journals, or newspapers for a particular trade or profession.

➠ **Creative Sources.** In addition to the traditional places to find occupational information, be on the lookout for less obvious sources. Popular magazines and newspapers can give insight into the inner workings of various fields. Articles that are not written for the purpose of educating readers about an occupation can nevertheless do so inadvertently. Business magazines and newspapers are obvious examples. For example, reading about a merger between two corporations gives you insight into the work of investment bankers and lawyers. Articles about a new advertising campaign for a familiar product can shed light on how advertising executives and other media professionals do their job. Try to get in the habit of reading with two objectives in mind: reading for news and reading for useful *career* news.

John, for example, found helpful articles related to his career choices in the science and health sections of his local city newspaper. Monica gained insight into entrepreneurial endeavors by reading *Inc.* and *Success* magazines. They provided "real world" news that was a nice complement to the books she read on small business and consulting.

When you've gone through a thorough research process in libraries, bookstores, and online, you're ready to test what you've read, by talking to people for more real-life accounts of life on the job in the field you're considering. FFMs can supplement what you've read with up-to-the-minute, experiential information needed to make your decisions. FFMs can also answer questions that books can't answer—for example, how does this or that option fit with who I am and what I want?

Protocol and Strategy for Fact-Finding Missions

Once you are prepared for FFMs, you can go ahead and begin to set them up. The following sections describe how to do so.

Requesting the Meeting

An effective FFM strategy begins with how you request the meeting. You may do so either in writing (by regular mail or e-mail) or over the phone. The pros and cons of each method are about equal, so there is no one best way. Choose the method that fits with your best communication style, the time frame you're working under, and how well you know the person you want to meet with. Sending a letter or e-mail is preferable if you don't know the person and if you're not under tight time pressure. It's also the better method for those who dread making "cold calls" and get a little tongue-tied talking to strangers or distant acquaintances. If you're comfortable on the phone, however, and need to schedule an FFM as soon as possible, or if you know the person fairly well, using the phone is the better approach. Whichever way you ask, make sure that your request includes the following points:

⇒ Who you are (your name and any other relevant identifying information)

⇒ How you got the contact's name

⇒ Why you're calling (that is, to obtain advice, information, and help with a decision)

⇒ Your broader objectives (that is, to make a decision about a specific career direction)

⇒ How much time you need—usually at least 30 minutes to get anything accomplished, with 45 to 60 minutes being preferable (Some job search experts suggest asking for only 15 to 20 minutes for this type of meeting, but that's hardly enough time to get the pleasantries out of the way.)

What to Wear

The most important guideline for your attire at an FFM is that you should dress to fit the environment. If you are going to a conservative business setting, wear an appropriate suit; to an informal business environment, dress down a notch but still look professional and well-groomed. Since an FFM is not a job interview, you don't have to be as formal as you might for an actual interview, but you should still show respect for the person and the organization you're visiting. Like all face-to-face encounters, a fact-finding mission is a chance to make a good first impression; so even though you're not there to apply for a job, it never hurts to look the part of a serious job candidate. If you're not sure what to wear, ask someone familiar with the career field, industry, or specific organization you'll be visiting.

By the way, you might think that you don't have to worry about what you wear when you conduct an FFM over the phone (unless it's a video conference), but think again. Do you feel professional and confident lounging in your pajamas and fuzzy slippers or sweatpants with holes in them? Some people actually find that they come across better if they make phone calls wearing business attire—or real clothes of some sort!

Protocol During the Meeting

Whether the FFM is conducted by phone or in person, be respectful of the other person's time, sticking to the agreed upon schedule. If no time limit was set in advance, ask how much time has been set aside for your meeting so you can be sure not to wear out your welcome.

It's OK to take notes in front of someone since an FFM is not a job interview. It's also acceptable to read from your own notes to remember questions you want to ask. Just make sure the interaction isn't too mechanical; be sure to make it conversational rather than just reading from a list. If the person you're speaking with is freely forthcoming with information and talkative, try not to interrupt the flow by relying too heavily on your list of questions. Sit back and take it all in; then turn to your notes to make sure all your questions were addressed.

Avoid asking personal questions unless the person starts volunteering such information. If you're tempted to ask about salaries, just ask in general terms, such as "I've read that typical starting salaries in this field are in the mid-twenties nationwide. Would you say that's accurate for jobs in this city?" That question is preferable to saying "How much do you make?"

Phases of Fact-Finding Missions

Generally, FFMs consist of several stages that include the following:

➡ **Greetings**. State your first and last name clearly and listen closely to the other person's name if you were uncertain about pronunciation. Convey energy, enthusiasm, and confidence. If face-to-face, give a firm handshake.

➡ **Chitchat**. It's natural for the conversation to begin with a moment or two of small talk. Stick with positive comments and neutral topics like the weather, some nice feature of the office, or something about the person you know in common (if that's how your FFM came about).

➡ **Gratitude**. Open the meeting by expressing your appreciation for the person's agreeing to meet with you, taking time out of his or her busy schedule, and so on.

➡ **Objectives Statement**. Reiterate why you asked for this appointment—what specific information you need, what kind of decision you're trying to make, and where you are in the fact-finding process (for example, how much you know already from your prior research or other meetings).

➡ **Fact Finding**. Here's where you get what you really came for—the information, advice, and counseling that you need to be better informed about your career options.

➡ **Problem Solving**. This is the part that distinguishes an FFM from a traditional informational interview. Using the facts you've gathered in the preceding steps, you now engage the other person in your decision-making process. In the "Facts to Gather During a Fact-Finding Mission" section at the end of this chapter, you'll find a list of topics to cover during the fact-finding and problem-solving stages of an FFM.

➠ **Resources and Referrals**. As you begin to wrap up the meeting, be sure to ask for the names of other people to talk to, as well as any other resources you might not already be familiar with, such as Web sites, professional groups, publications, or conferences for fields you're investigating. If you have discussed such names during the meeting, you do not need to ask for them as a separate step near the end.

➠ **Closing and Plans for Follow-Up**. In addition to expressing your thanks for the meeting and saying good-bye, the closing is a time to establish how future contact and activities, if any, will proceed. This is where you confirm anything the other person has agreed to do for you, like place a call to a colleague on your behalf or circulate your resume. Now is also the time to ask permission to contact the person in the future if you have any additional questions.

After your meeting, be sure to follow up immediately with a thank-you letter or, at minimum, with a thank-you call or e-mail. Tips on thanking (and gift-giving where appropriate) are provided in chapter 14, along with sample thank-you notes.

Tips for Conducting FFMs in Writing

As mentioned earlier, there are times when it's not convenient or possible to meet with someone face-to-face or even to speak over the phone. In those cases, you might find yourself writing letters or sending e-mails to request assistance with your career decisions and hoping for a response by mail or online. The most important strategy for this situation is to keep your requests concise and to the point. Don't make blanket requests for information or advice. You have to keep the readers' time in mind and not overwhelm them. You're not likely to get a response if you ask for the world. In other words, be as specific as possible.

I sometimes get letters or e-mails from people considering becoming career counselors who essentially say, "Hello, I'm looking into becoming a career counselor and was wondering if you could offer any advice or assistance." Of course, the correspondence is somewhat more detailed than that, but that's the way it comes across to me. Sometimes people are closer to being on the right track in that they do ask specific questions for me to answer. Still, though, the letters are off-putting because they ask too many questions or ask for basic information, revealing that they've done no initial research on the field. If you're going to use letters or e-mail for your fact-finding missions, do your homework first, limit your requests to one or two specific questions, and be very appreciative in advance, acknowledging that the reader's time is valuable.

Facts to Gather During a Fact-Finding Mission

The following topics are just a sampling of information you might need to gather for help in making your career decisions. You should choose from this list and add to it according to your individual needs. Also note that issues related to both traditional career choices and decisions about entering self-employment have been included.

Nature of the Work—Daily

Questions about day-to-day activities on the job should ask the following information:

➡ Typical responsibilities and the percentage of time spent with each duty

➡ Amount of travel involved, if any

➡ Work environments (in office or outside, cultures, norms, level of formality, and so on)

➡ Satisfactions and frustrations of this field

➠ Typical methods of being evaluated

➠ Opportunities to advance

➠ On-the-job training opportunities

➠ Typical starting salaries and projected future earnings

Nature of the Work—Long-Term

Longer-term considerations should include the following:

➠ Typical career paths in this field

➠ Future outlook for the field in terms of job growth and industry developments

Qualifications Required

You should also ask whether a particular job or field has requirements, such as the following:

➠ Educational credentials

➠ Specific skills and expertise

➠ Specialized training for entry

➠ Licenses, certificates, or other registration requirements

Resources for More Information—People and Print

Some of the most important information you can gather is additional contact information:

➠ Other people with whom to hold FFMs

➡ Professional associations and other networking groups for this field

➡ Journals, newsletters, and other publications for the field

➡ Meetings and conferences to attend

➡ Web sites and Internet newsgroups related to the field

➡ Best places for education or training to prepare for the field

Problem Solving for Your Decision

To get the to the "bottom line," ask the following questions:

➡ Based on what I've told you about my strengths, interests, and priorities, do you think this career choice would be a good fit for me?

➡ In what specific ways would this be a good choice for me?

➡ Given what you know about me, do you anticipate any trouble spots—reasons why I would not be satisfied or successful in this field?

Quick Summary

A fact-finding mission (FFM) is any interaction in which you seek and receive information that assists you in making a decision and in which you actively engage others in your decision-making process.

FFMs are particularly useful when you make career choices. They give you a reality check on a given option and help you decide if it's the right career or business venture for you.

FFMs can take place almost anywhere—either as a formal appointment in someone's office or over the phone, or as an impromptu conversation with someone you've just met.

Preparation for a fact-finding mission involves knowing what questions you need to get answered and researching a field through print and online resources. This enables you to ask more informed questions and prevents you from wasting your contacts' time asking things you should already know.

You should follow proper protocol for requesting FFMs and for conducting them as well. Guidelines were provided in this chapter.

The agenda for a typical FFM includes greetings, chitchat, thanks, objectives statement, fact finding, problem solving, request for more resources and referrals, and the closing and plans for follow-up.

Always send a thank-you note or call promptly after a fact-finding mission.

Strategy Sessions:
Networking to Reach Your Goals

The winds and waves are always on the side of the ablest navigators.

—EDWARD GIBBON

As you learned in chapter 2, it takes a carefully planned strategy to reach your goals, whether those goals are related to career choice, job search, career management, or business development. Your strategy is the driving force behind every step you take toward your goals. It is the guiding vision that determines what you should do day-to-day, week-to-week, or month-to-month to get to where you want to be in your career or business. Having a well-thought-out strategy keeps your efforts from being haphazard and prevents you from taking wrong turns. A good strategy is like a trusted navigational device: it tells you where you are and how you can get to where you're going.

So how do you develop an effective strategy with clear objectives and a feasible plan like the samples you saw in chapter 2? A strategy session is one of the best ways to do so. Remember that one key to successful networking is to interact with people who have expertise, experience, and knowledge related to your needs—the idea expressed in that tongue twister from chapter 1, "who knows what you need to know." Well, in strategy sessions, you meet with the people who know what you need to know—that is, those who can help you devise a strategy for making a career choice, finding a job, managing your career, or developing a business.

What Strategy Sessions Are

Strategy sessions take over where fact-finding missions leave off. Fact-finding missions provide the information and expert advice that help you make informed decisions and set career or business goals. Strategy sessions then enable you to plot a course for reaching those goals. Fact-finding missions get you only so far. They enable you to decide what you're going to do, but they don't always tell you how you're going to get there.

John, for example, chose to pursue genetic counseling and research rather than other health care careers as a result of what he learned in fact-finding missions. Once he had made that decision, he then conducted strategy sessions to find out what steps he should take to transition into that field. Similarly, Ana used FFMs to decide which career area within finance made the most sense for her. Then she used strategy sessions for help in planning her job search. Sam used strategy sessions to plot a course for his long-term career growth. Monica used strategy sessions to develop a strategy for launching her business (having decided to start a business as a result of advice she got in fact-finding missions). So, the main objectives of an FFM are to make a decision and set goals, while the objectives of a strategy session are to learn how to implement that decision and reach those goals.

During a strategy session, you speak with someone who knows what it takes to succeed at the endeavor you're about to tackle—perhaps that's searching for a job, negotiating with your boss for a raise, or launching a consulting practice. The strategy session gives you an opportunity to plan a strategy that is based on reality, not just on your assumptions of how you should go about reaching your goals. It is also a chance to get valuable feedback on the "tools" of your search or business. Showing your resume, cover letters, thank-you letters, portfolio, or business promotional materials to someone who knows what works—and what doesn't—is an excellent way to polish your approach. You can also practice your interview technique, negotiation or workplace communication style, or business sales pitch in a strategy session.

The sample questions in the sections that follow will give you a more specific idea of what can be discussed in a strategy session.

Questions to Ask During Strategy Sessions—Job Search

Following are questions that you might need to ask if you are holding a strategy session during a job search:

➡ Here's how I plan to conduct my job search. Where am I on target, and where am I off base?

➡ How effective is networking as a way to get jobs in this field (as opposed to other job search methods, such as answering classified ads or sending out unsolicited resumes)?

➡ Would employment agencies (or executive search firms) be good sources for my target job? If so, which ones do you recommend?

➡ Which other job search methods are typically effective in this career field or industry?

➠ On which method(s) should I concentrate most of my time and effort?

➠ How did you get your job when you were at my level?

➠ Are there newsletters or other publications that list jobs and contacts for this field?

➠ Which Web sites do you recommend for my job hunt?

➠ Do you know of any meetings, conferences, or other networking opportunities coming up soon that I could attend?

➠ What are the strengths and weaknesses of my resume? How can I improve it?

➠ If you were a prospective employer receiving this cover letter (or follow-up letter), would you be impressed by it? How could I make it more effective?

➠ Can you help me refine my interviewing technique?

➠ How do I come across in general (communication style, voice, energy level, image)? What could I do to improve?

➠ If this were an actual job interview, would I be dressed appropriately?

➠ Am I coming to this job search with any serious deficits in skills or experience? How might I bridge the gap?

➠ Do you know of any positions available?

➠ Do you know of anyone I could speak to who might know of job openings?

➠ Do you know of anyone else I could speak to just for further strategy advice?

➠ Do you know of any organizations that often or occasionally have openings in my target area (whether or not you know of any current openings there)?

⟶ How long should I expect my job search to take?

⟶ May I stay in touch with you for help with my strategy along the way?

Questions to Ask During Strategy Sessions—Career Management

The following are some typical questions people ask in strategy sessions when they are trying to manage their careers more successfully. These are offered only as basic suggestions, however. Career management strategies tend to vary significantly from one person to the next, so you may find that you have needs not addressed here. If so, just use this list as a starting point and tailor it to fit your own situation. The questions in this list are grouped into four main categories that reflect the typical areas addressed in career management strategy sessions.

➤ How can I be more effective on my job?

Specifically, how can I…

➤ manage my time more efficiently?

➤ be more productive?

➤ be more creative or innovative?

➤ solve problems more quickly or effectively?

➤ How can I improve my communication style and interpersonal relationships in the workplace?

Specifically, how can I…

➤ be a better team player?

➤ be a more effective leader?

➤ manage other people more skillfully?

➤ have more harmonious relationships with co-workers, bosses, or subordinates?

➤ deal with office politics more successfully?

➤ How can I enhance my professional image?

Specifically, how can I...

➤ be a more confident or polished public speaker/presenter?

➤ be more skilled at writing for business purposes?

➤ avoid making business etiquette or protocol errors?

➤ improve my attire or personal grooming?

➤ become more visible?

➤ How can I advance and grow in my career?

Specifically, how can I...

➤ negotiate a raise?

➤ position myself for a promotion?

➤ gain more responsibility?

➤ move laterally to a new position for fresh challenges or a new routine?

➤ negotiate a different schedule or flexible working arrangement?

➤ plan my long-range career track?

➤ develop new skills?

Questions to Ask During Strategy Sessions—Self-Employment

When conducting strategy sessions for self-employment purposes, you might have questions related to starting, promoting, expanding, or maintaining a business. Following are some questions you might need to ask depending on your specific circumstances:

Questions about starting a business, consulting practice, or freelance endeavor:

➡ Is my business idea a viable, marketable one?

➡ Is it unique enough? How can I identify a unique angle?

➡ Do I have the background and credentials to succeed in this type of business?

➡ Which of my qualities are my best selling points?

➡ What's the most important part of a business plan for this type of endeavor?

➡ Could you critique the business plan I've prepared?

➡ What are some potential funding sources for my business?

Questions about promotional materials and marketing strategies:

➡ Are the plans I have for marketing and promotion likely to be effective?

➡ Are direct mail campaigns effective ways to advertise my services and products?

➡ Which promotional methods do you think are most effective?

➡ Is my brochure, information packet, flyer, ad, or direct mail piece effective?

➡ How can they be improved?

➡ May I practice my pitch to prospective clients and customers with you?

Questions about expanding or maintaining an established business:

➡ Is there a secret to your success?

➡ Could you help me troubleshoot weak areas of my business?

➠ Here is my plan for expanding my business. Does it sound appropriate?

➠ Do you know of any organizations or other resources I should be using to grow?

➠ Has your business ever had slow periods? How did you handle them?

➠ Are my business growth objectives realistic?

➠ May I keep in touch with you for occasional input into my business decisions?

When to Conduct Strategy Sessions

Strategy sessions should be conducted before taking action toward any career goal. John, for example, could have just jumped right into the process of becoming a geneticist after fact-finding missions helped him decide on that career direction. He could have applied to any graduate programs he came across, and randomly sent out resumes for entry-level jobs or volunteer positions related to that work. Instead, though, he went back to some of the genetic counselors and research scientists who had been helpful at the FFM stage and asked for further advice. He let them know that he had looked into the field in-depth based on their suggestions and had decided that genetics was definitely the field he wanted to pursue. He then asked if they would be willing to give him a little more of their time to discuss in more detail how he could get into the field. They agreed, and he set up both phone and face-to-face meetings with them for strategy sessions.

In those sessions, they gave him input on which schools to apply to and where he could do volunteer work to get some experience. They also gave him names of more genetic counselors and researchers who could provide further strategy help. He then had strategy sessions with those people during which he had his graduate school essays critiqued. He also identified gaps in his experience and skills and learned ways to make up for those in order to be a better candidate for graduate school and jobs.

Conferring with people knowledgeable about the jobs, career path, or business you're striving for is essential for avoiding wrong turns along the way to your goals. So, like John, you should conduct strategy sessions as soon as possible after setting your goals, instead of striking out for those goals without the input of some knowledgeable strategists.

How to Find Strategists

Anyone familiar with your career field, target job, or proposed business is an appropriate choice for a strategy session. Also appropriate are the allied forces in your network, particularly career counselors, job search coaches, and career management or executive coaches. While these people may not necessarily be experts on your field or industry, they do have expertise in the techniques that lead to success in your career or business. In other words, it is their job to help you plan a strategy for most any kind of career or business endeavor. (See Appendix C for ways to find these professionals and chapter 3 for a description of the Allied Forces.)

Coaching You to Success

When plotting a strategy for managing your career, you may find an executive coach (known also as a career management coach) to be a valuable ally. Executive coaches are experts who can help with the day-to-day management of your career, as well as help you plot a course for your future. Found in outplacement firms and consulting firms as well as in private practice, executive coaches have backgrounds in business, psychology, or social work—or ideally some combination of the three. If you work for a savvy corporation, your employer might send you to an executive coach, but you can also seek out one on your own. (The Job Search Coaching, Career Counseling, and Executive Coaching sections of Appendix C list resources to help you locate and select a qualified executive coach.) According to Sheryl Spanier, a consultant with the Strickland Group and an executive coach in private practice in New York City, "It's not necessary to wait for your company to do this for you. Smart executives increasingly are taking charge of their careers by getting a 'career physical and booster shot.' Working with an executive coach, especially one who has experience in your industry or knowledge of your own company's corporate culture, can give you information, insights, reality checks, and if nothing else, an anonymous, confidential sounding board. As people manage their own careers, it's really important for them to be aware of not only how they are perceived by others in their company, but how they fit into the corporate culture as a whole. What may have worked yesterday may not work today and probably will not work tomorrow."

The people you select as your fellow strategists might be some of the same people with whom you had fact-finding missions. In fact, some FFMs turn into strategy sessions in the same meeting. While asking the questions listed in chapter 7, you might also go ahead and start asking about strategy. If you didn't already get into strategy with your FFM people, you can still contact them to say that you have made a decision and would now like advice on strategy. Most people will be receptive to this request, particularly if you closed and followed up on the FFMs properly as suggested in chapter 7—that is, asking their permission for continued communication and following through with a nice thank-you.

In choosing strategists, be sure to select at least one or two people who are far enough along in their careers or businesses to be able to advise you from a position of authority based on substantial experience. It is also helpful to network with at least one or two people who may be close to your career level and who perhaps have just recently gone through a job search, gotten a promotion, or started a business. Their fresh perspective on the process and up-to-date contacts and resources can be invaluable as you plan your strategy. Meeting with both experienced strategists and those who have recently achieved the goals you are striving toward will give you a balanced perspective.

Where to Hold Strategy Sessions

Like fact-finding missions, the setting for a strategy session is less important than the exchange of information that takes place. Since a strategy session is basically a guided conversation, it can take place in person or over the phone, as well as in writing, through letters, or by e-mail.

One difference between strategy sessions and FFMs, however, is that strategy sessions are often quick meetings by phone or an exchange of e-mails rather than scheduled, face-to-face meetings. The reason for this is that when you are in the thick of a career transition—job searching, trying to advance in your career, or starting or expanding a business— questions undoubtedly arise as you go along. It's not always realistic to hold your questions for an appointment scheduled at a later date; you may need answers right away.

Ana, for example, found that during her job search there were a couple of people—strategists—to whom she could turn for ongoing advice. These people came in especially handy when she had questions about how much she should follow up with prospective employers. There was one time in particular when a "mini" strategy session (a ten-minute phone call to one of her strategists) proved extremely valuable. She called the strategist for advice on how to handle a situation in which she had left several messages for someone to whom she had faxed her resume the week before. She wanted to make sure he had received it and discuss the possibility of her coming in for an interview, but he hadn't returned her calls.

She was perplexed by his lack of response because he had actually requested that Ana fax him her resume after a phone conversation they had had the week before. Now that he had her resume, was there something in it that he didn't like? Did he no longer have any positions available? Was he still interested in her but was just too busy to call back? She didn't know the answer to these questions. As a result, she wasn't sure if she should keep calling, send her resume again, or just give up and hope that he would eventually call her back. To determine what her strategy should be, she called one of her strategists for advice.

The strategist recommended that she leave another message for the target, but that this time she say something like, "I'd really like to speak to you as soon as possible because I am in the final rounds of interviewing with another company but wouldn't want to accept an offer there without first seeing about the possibilities at your company." She also recommended that Ana remind the prospective employer of her strengths and qualifications by briefly stating her personal pitch. Doing so might remind him of the interest he had expressed in their initial phone conversation. Saying all that was more likely to elicit a response than the weaker message she had been leaving which was, "Just calling to see if you got my resume." The strategy session paid off. Ana left the new message and got a call back the same day.

While such "mini" strategy sessions can come in handy along the way to your goals, it is important initially to have a few strategy sessions of substantial length (thirty minutes to an hour or more) to map out a plan for reaching your goals. Then, as career crises or pressing needs emerge along the way, you can check in with your fellow strategists for input.

How to Prepare for Strategy Sessions

The first step in preparing for a strategy session is to make sure that you're ready for one. Have you carefully researched your options; made a career or business decision that you're comfortable with; and set realistic, clearly defined goals? If so, you are ready to start plotting your course. If not, you may need to go back to the research stage, including conducting fact-finding missions. In order to make the most of the strategy session, you need to be able to state your job search, career management, or business objectives clearly and without hesitation.

The second step is to put some thought into your strategy yourself before asking for input from others. Your fellow strategists are more likely to be able to help if you come to them with a rough plan in mind that they can critique. Monica, for example, crafted a rough draft of a business plan before her strategy sessions so that her strategists would have something to work with. Before having his strategy sessions, Sam thought of ways he could advance his career—for example, attending certain professional meetings, making more of an effort to bring in new accounts to his agency, and developing new graphics skills through classes. His strategists were then able to evaluate the strengths and weaknesses of that plan and to suggest additional activities.

If you need help strategizing on your own to prepare for your strategy sessions, consult some of the excellent job search, career management, or business strategy books that are readily found in bookstores and libraries, as well as advice dispensed through Web sites. Many of these books are listed in Appendix D, and Web sites are found in Appendix C. By using these resources, you can develop on your own a rough strategy that can then be critiqued and refined in strategy sessions.

These resources can also help you prepare the "tools" that you need to reach your goals. These include resumes, cover letters, and a portfolio for job search or career management purposes, or promotional materials and a business plan for a self-employment endeavor. Having at least a rough draft of the tools that are relevant to your situation is crucial for making the most of strategy sessions. If you're going to send letters and resumes for jobs, for example, why not have those materials critiqued by someone comparable to your target employers? You'll get important feedback that will help you make your search as effective as possible.

Doing so worked well for Ana, who needed to convert the old resume she had used in the past for jobs in law into a resume suitable for jobs in finance. She needed to come to her strategists with at least a rough draft since she couldn't expect them to help her write it from scratch. She wasn't sure how to write a resume for a career change, though, so she consulted a couple of good books on resume writing. Following the guidelines in those books, she was able to put together a solid working draft that her strategists were then able to help her adjust and finalize, based on their knowledge of qualifications needed for jobs in finance.

The final step in preparing for strategy sessions is to set an agenda and objectives for the strategy session itself. You don't want to waste your time or your fellow strategist's, so it's important to think through in advance what questions you have and what topics need to be addressed. The questions provided earlier in this chapter gave you some idea of what might be covered in a typical strategy session.

Strategy Session Protocol

Keep in mind that, like all networking encounters, a strategy session is not a meeting for which you just show up, sit back, and passively soak up advice. You need to do your homework first to make the most of the meeting, and you also need to do your share of the work during the meeting. You don't want to say, for example, "How should I write a cover letter for this kind of job?" You should say instead, "Here's a rough draft of a cover letter I've written for one of my target employers. Is this a good letter for the kind of job I'm seeking? How could I improve it?" Additional tactics for a strategy session are discussed in the following sections.

Requesting the Meeting

As with fact-finding missions, you may request a strategy session by phone or mail. Since strategy sessions are often held with someone you already know (but not always), you're likely to request most of them by phone. When you ask for a meeting, consider the following:

⟶ If you need a strategy session as part of a job search, emphasize that you're not asking for a job interview, but that you are simply planning a strategy before actively searching.

⟶ Ask for permission to bring your resume, letters, business promotional materials, business plan, or whatever is relevant to your situation so that you can have them critiqued.

⟶ Let your prospective strategist know what you've already done to plan your strategy, so that it's clear you don't have to be spoon-fed.

⟶ Give a minor, subtle "sales pitch" for yourself so that your strategist knows you are committed to your goals and that they are realistic for you—that is, that you're worth your prospective strategist's time and effort.

What to Wear

The guidelines for strategy session attire are essentially the same as those for a fact-finding mission (see chapter 7). Strategy sessions, however, are one step closer to an actual job interview (for those of you networking for job search purposes), so you might want to take extra care with your appearance, making sure that you look professional in a way that is appropriate for that environment. Even if you're not job seeking (networking for career management or business development purposes, for example), you're still one step closer to your goals when you are at the strategy session stage, so you should start to look the part. If, for example, you're strategizing about starting a business as a management consultant, you should dress for a strategy session as you would for a client. If you're meeting with someone to plan how you can get a promotion at work, you should dress like someone who deserves a promotion.

Protocol During the Session

As with FFMs, be mindful of the other person's time and show appreciation at both the beginning and the end of the meeting. It is also acceptable to take notes and refer to your own notes as with an FFM since you're there for information gathering, not to be interviewed for a job.

As with FFMs, you can expect strategy sessions to unfold in certain phases. These include the following:

➤ **Greetings**. If this is someone you haven't met before, state your first and last name clearly and listen closely to the other person's name if you were uncertain about how to pronounce it. Be sure to convey energy, enthusiasm, and confidence in order to make a strong first impression.

➤ **Chitchat**. As with all networking meetings, strategy sessions should start out naturally with a few minutes of conversation on noncontroversial, positive topics.

➤ **Thanks**. Early in the meeting, thank the other person for agreeing to meet with you, being generous with their time, and offering to share their expertise.

➤ **Objectives Statement**. Restate the purpose of the meeting. If you're there to discuss a job search strategy, make it particularly clear that you are not there as an official job candidate. (Don't worry, if you come across well in the strategy session, you will certainly be considered for any jobs that might happen to be open.)

⟩ **Strategizing**. This is the main part of the session during which you map out a plan that will enable you to reach your goals. The questions in the following section of this chapter can help you conduct this part of the meeting.

⟩ **Critiquing of Tools**. Here's where you ask for feedback on your resume, letters, portfolio, business plan, or any other materials you've brought with you, unless these items were already discussed during the strategizing.

⟩ **Resources and Leads**. Before closing the meeting, be sure to ask for recommendations of any materials (such as newsletters listing jobs, books on small business marketing, etc.) that could help you attain your goals. This is also the time to ask for any leads to jobs, client referrals, and so on, if they haven't already been offered.

⟩ **Closing and Plans for Follow-Up**. As the appointment wraps up, express your thanks for the meeting and the advice; but before saying good-bye, also be sure to establish the boundaries for future follow-up. Ask if it is OK if you contact the person if you have further questions. At this point, you should get a sense of how available the strategist wants to be to you in the future.

As always, follow up with a thank-you note. (Sample thank-you notes are provided in chapter 14.) Since strategy sessions are likely to take place in bits and pieces over time instead of being just one formal meeting, you won't need to write a note after every phone call or e-mail. In those cases, you should keep track of how often you've expressed your appreciation and write thank-you notes periodically. If someone works with you long term, either in a professional capacity or informally as a mentor, it is common courtesy to acknowledge that individual's role in your success when you get a job, solve your workplace problems, or launch your business. A well-thought out thank-you letter or small gift is appropriate at that point and helps reinforce that person as an ongoing member of your network.

Quick Summary

Strategy sessions take over where fact-finding missions leave off. FFMs provide the information that helps you make informed decisions and set career goals. Strategy sessions help you plot a course to reach those goals.

To avoid making mistakes, you should conduct strategy sessions before you act toward any career or business goal.

Strategy sessions can be scheduled meetings in person or by phone, but may also be brief conversations when you need advice along the way to your goals.

To prepare for a strategy session, make sure that you're ready for it—that is, that you've set clearly defined goals. Also do some work first so that your fellow strategist doesn't have to start from scratch. Be sure to set objectives for the meeting.

The phases of a typical strategy session include greetings, chitchat, thanks, objectives statement, strategizing, critiquing of materials, requesting resources and leads, and the closing with plans for follow-up.

As always, send a thank-you note promptly after a strategy session. If you're receiving ongoing advice from someone, an occasional phone call or note will suffice. You don't need to send a formal thank-you letter after every brief encounter.

Referral Meetings: Networking to Develop Business

Everyone lives by selling something.

—ROBERT LOUIS STEVENSON

A referral meeting is essentially any interaction in which you let others know what kind of people or information they can refer to you to support your career or business. Like strategy sessions, referral meetings can be formal appointments or might simply be quick phone conversations. Referral meetings are an important tool for anyone who wants to be more productive in a job or to develop a business.

Successful entrepreneurs, salespeople, consultants, and others whose livelihood depends on acquiring customers, clients, or projects have always known that they can't just sit back and wait for business to roll in. To generate business, you have to generate activity, which means that you have to expend energy. Holding meetings with people who can generate some of that activity for you is a good way to expend your energy strategically. Look at it this way: You can put a lot of effort into bringing in one prospective client, which might yield one client. Or, you can put effort into cultivating one referral source—someone with access to the kinds of clients you're seeking—and that effort can yield an endless stream of clients. It's obvious which approach helps you conserve time, energy, and resources.

The same rationale explains why referral meetings are important for career management purposes as well. Referral meetings are not the sole domain of entrepreneurs and people in sales. If you're employed in an organization—whether corporate, not-for-profit, or government—you, too, can benefit from referral meetings. With job security being non-existent in today's world of work, everyone has to take an active role in his or her own career stability and success. It's not enough just to do your job; you have to do it well and make sure the powers that be *know* you're doing it well.

Strategy sessions with key advisors and guidance from role models is one way to do that. Another way is through referral meetings in which you gain access to people and information resources that can help you do your job more effectively. I know of one human resources manager, for example, who regularly has meetings (by phone and in person) with people who can refer top-notch candidates for positions at the large corporation for which she recruits. Then there's our friend Sam who keeps in touch with people who can refer talented freelancers that his ad agency can use—copywriters, designers, photographers, stylists, and others who can make his campaigns the best in the business. Think about what kind of resources you rely on to do your job well and con-sider holding periodic referral meetings with people who can lead you to those resources.

Referral Meetings in Action

Consider the following examples of the role that referral meetings can play in various career management or entrepreneurial situations.

Madeline, a real estate agent specializing in residential sales and rentals, took Joan, a corporate human resources executive, out to lunch. Joan's company actively recruits new employees from around the country, most of whom need a good realtor to help them find a new home to go with their new job. Joan's company also brings in its own employees from branch offices worldwide for short stints in the headquarters office. Madeline could arrange short-term residences for these people. This lunch meeting was a first step for Madeline to cultivate a relationship with Joan so that she would become the realtor of choice when the company Joan works for has relocation needs.

Stuart was a clinical psychologist at a large mental health clinic with a small private practice in the evenings and weekends. After several years, his client flow was steady enough to let him cut back his hours at the clinic to part-time and expand his private practice to a few days a week. Before making the transition, however, he set up a series of referral meetings over a three-month period. He made office visits to fellow psychologists and therapists, college counselors, physicians, career counselors, and others who were in a position to refer clients to him. The meetings ensured that he had a strong referral base to support the expansion of his practice.

As a sales rep for a small environmental products company, Alvaro had been selling items such as water filters and air purifying systems, mainly to individuals for household use. He began to realize that many of his company's products would be suitable for businesses as well, and that commercial contracts would be more lucrative, so he set a goal of breaking into new markets. He started with a strategy session with his friend Suzanne in the purchasing department of a large corporation. She helped him develop a plan for promoting himself and his products in a way that would appeal to corporate clients. He then set up referral meetings with five people whom Suzanne had put him in touch with. In some respects, these were traditional sales calls in that he hoped some of the five would buy his products, but they were also referral meetings in that they opened doors to other companies. The five people had been chosen for their high visibility and involvement in their industries as a whole, not just in the companies for which they worked. They could therefore be good sources of referrals to other companies, thus substantially expanding Alvaro's network.

How to Prepare for Referral Meetings

Referral meetings are usually less structured than fact-finding missions and strategy sessions since referral meetings are more like conversations between two colleagues than the quasi-interview format of the former meetings. It is all the more important, therefore, that you prepare carefully so that the interaction isn't just a social conversation with no real purpose. The following sections describe what you need to do to prepare for a referral meeting.

Know What You Have to Offer

Since you're there to promote your business or professional service, it's essential that you articulate clearly and concisely what you have to offer. Your personal pitch becomes key here. When delivering that pitch in a referral meeting, it is particularly important to take a tip from tried and true advertising and marketing principles: sell the benefits, not the features. What that means is that you might say, "As a time management consultant, I help people get their act together so they can be more productive and efficient," instead of saying, "As a time management consultant, I assess people's organizational deficits in the areas of paperwork and clutter, setting objectives, and scheduling their time." The first statement cuts right to the chase, telling people how you make a difference. The second description is just a litany of the things you do to make that difference. There's always time to get into the details of specifically what you do and how you do it if the other person is interested. Until then, concentrate on emphasizing the result of your work, not the means to the end.

Similarly, if Monica is trying to market her Web site design and maintenance service, she might say, "I help my clients expand their businesses exponentially by developing a presence on the Internet and maintaining it so that they are free to do their work, instead of getting bogged down in the administrative details of managing a Web site." From this statement, we know the features of this business—setting up and maintaining Web sites, but those rather ordinary services are couched in more exciting benefits. This approach is much more powerful than simply saying, "I design and maintain Web sites."

Knowing what you have to offer is not just a task for entrepreneurs, either. Take the example again of that human resources manager who seeks referrals of qualified job candidates. In order to persuade people to make referrals to her, she has to "sell" the strengths of the company she recruits for. She has to show people that her company is a great place to work, so that they will feel comfortable referring job candidates to her.

Support Your Claims with Relevant Examples

It's not enough to make claims about your business or your employer; you have to prove those claims with hard evidence. If your business involves making a product that you can bring to a meeting, that's great, but in most cases, it's not possible to trot out examples of your work. This is especially true in this age of information. Businesses based on intangible products and services can back up their claims with stories that provide powerful examples of their benefits. Before going to a referral meeting, think of a few examples of clients or customers you've helped or projects you've completed with much success. Recounting tales of your accomplishments brings an objective twist to your self-promotion; you're essentially saying to the other person, "Don't just take my word for it, here's evidence."

I find this technique to be quite effective when I am speaking to prospective clients for my private practice or to people who could refer clients to me. For example, I recently received a call from a man who was considering sending his thirty-three year old son to me for career counseling. The son had started college several years back but had never finished and had since drifted from job to job with no career focus. The son's self-esteem had sunk so low, and he had developed such an apathetic view toward life, that the father was concerned that his son would never "get his act together." As the father described his son's situation to me, I could sense that the father doubted that I—or any career counselor for that matter—could make a difference in what seemed to him to be a highly unusual and impossible situation.

I did want to work with this man's son, and I knew that his situation was actually not that uncommon, especially in my practice. Basic career counseling methods along with a little extra attention were all it called for. So to reassure the man that having his son meet with me would be worth while, I decided to give an anonymous example of a similar client I had worked with. Doing so was more effective than simply saying, "Yes, I can help your son. I've handled similar situations." Instead I said something like, "Yes, I can help your son. I have something of a specialty in difficult situations like his. For example, I'm currently working with a young man who hasn't held a job in several years because of some family problems that caused him extreme emotional distress. Here's what I'm doing with him that seems to be working well…." By providing even sketchy details of another situation, the father felt less alone in his dilemma and also developed confidence in my ability to help.

Know to Whom You'll Be Talking

Just assessing your own strengths and preparing examples of them is not enough. If you don't consider the perspective of the person you'll be meeting with, then your sales pitch might fall on deaf ears. Consider the work that the other person does and choose relevant examples of your business accomplishments. Also consider potential needs of the other person and think about ways you might meet those needs with services or products from your own business. You might also be able to help with resources to which you can refer that person.

This point proved important for Monica, who made a few wrong turns when she first began to promote her Web site business. She found that she was making a false assumption in assuming that all the prospective clients she approached wanted their businesses to grow through a presence on the Internet. She learned that she needed to do as much research as possible before referral meetings and ask many questions at the start of referral meetings before making such assumptions. She then had to alter her pitch to appeal to the interests, concerns, and business goals of the person with whom she was speaking.

Prepare Your Promotional Materials

Be sure that any written materials related to your business are in good shape and that you have an ample supply of them. If all you use is a business card, then take several so that the potential referral source you're meeting will have a few extras to hand out to people interested in your services. If you have brochures, information packets, flyers, or other print materials, take at least one, or more if you think they're warranted. Don't overload the other person with bulky materials, however. Take a reasonable amount and then mail more after the meeting if the person is interested in having a supply to pass on to others.

Protocol and Agendas for Referral Meetings

Many of the strategies recommended in chapters 7 and 8 for fact-finding missions and strategy sessions apply to referral meetings, as do the networking tips offered throughout this entire book. Meeting for the purpose of generating referrals does require some special tactics, however.

Requesting a Meeting

The key to requesting a referral meeting is subtlety. There's a real danger that your request will come across as "Let's get together so you can refer some business to me." Even if you don't think that's what coming out of your mouth, that's how it can sound to the other person. The way to avoid this is to stress two points: 1) that you'd like to offer yourself as a resource and 2) that you'd be getting together out of interests common to both of you. You want the meeting to sound like a collaborative, cooperative effort, not a one-sided sales pitch. As mentioned at the beginning of this chapter, a referral meeting really isn't a sales call. It's a two-way street—an effort to see how two (or more) people can be resources for each other.

During the Meeting

Subtlety is still important once the meeting is in progress. Keep in mind that referral meetings should be a two-way street, and don't bowl the other person over with an aggressive sales pitch. Take the time to establish rapport—get to know the other person's business and particular needs and interests. At the same time, though, be sure you meet your objectives for the meeting. Subtlety doesn't mean passivity. You should be assertive in getting your points across—that is, the benefits and evidence of what you have to offer. That means maintaining a careful balance between talking about yourself and listening to the other person. That also means not being shy about handing over your promotional materials.

Developing Your Business on a Shoestring through Bartering

Exchanging products or services with fellow entrepreneurs and small businesses—instead of paying fees—is a great way to keep your start-up or operating costs down and to gain visibility. In doing so, you'll be in good company, as all the advanced civilizations of the ancient world were based on bartering. In ancient Egypt, for example, onions and beans were the main currency until about 500 B.C. when coins came into use. Think of who might want your "onions and beans" and who has something you need, and approach them about a possible bartering arrangement.

Typical Agenda for a Referral Meeting

The flow of a referral meeting is likely to be much looser than that of a fact-finding mission or strategy session. The interaction is more of a two-way conversation between peers or colleagues, so you don't necessarily need to go in with a strict agenda in mind. It is helpful, though, to have a general sense of how you want the meeting to proceed. Keeping a mental list of topics to cover and social courtesies to address can help keep you on track and ensure that your objectives are met. You can expect the following phases during a typical referral meeting:

➠ **Start with greetings and thanks.** As always. convey warmth and enthusiasm when you first meet. This is particularly true since you are a reflection of your business. If you initiated the meeting, be sure to express your thanks for the other person's time and effort.

➠ **Get to know each other or reestablish rapport with an old acquaintance.** If the two of you are meeting for the first time, take some time to get to know each other. Ask questions about the other person's business, or offer a compliment on something positive you've heard about him or her. If you already know the other person well, still take some time to get reacquainted and caught up on things. In referral meetings, you always want to show genuine interest in how others are doing and in any new developments in their businesses or personal lives (if appropriate).

➠ **Weave your benefits and evidence into the conversation.** Try to have your subtle self-promotion flow naturally into the conversation, rather than abruptly shift gears from a two-way conversation to a one-sided sales pitch. You might say, for example, "Oh, it's interesting you should mention that problem. I've found some new ways to help my clients get around that issue. For example, I worked with someone last month who...." By linking your business' benefits directly to a concern or an interest the other person has voiced, you're sending a much more powerful and meaningful message.

➠ **Look for follow-through "gems."** As the conversation progresses, be on the lookout for bits of information or resources that the other person seems to need. Sometimes these needs will be stated openly— for example, "Do you know of a good book on...?" Other times, you'll have to read between the lines to detect what might be useful. These become your "follow-through gems," those clues to how you can have an excuse to stay in touch after the meeting is over and how you can be of use to the other person. You can then send a relevant article, phone number, or other bit of information to keep the relationship going after the meeting and to put yourself in the role of "informational clearinghouse" for that member of your network.

➠ **Provide your promotional materials or business cards**. If you haven't done so already, offer your materials as the meeting winds down.

➠ **Remember to follow-through**. If you initiated the referral meeting, or if it worked primarily in your favor, then the focus of your follow-through will be to thank the other person, often in the form of a letter rather than a call or an e-mail.

If the meeting was initiated somewhat jointly for your mutual benefit, your follow-up will include thanks for the other person's time, but that should not be the main focus. You should focus instead on strengthening the relationship by stating how you enjoyed the meeting and mentioning any ways that the meeting was informative or enlightening. With someone you know well, you might send an e-mail or fax, or you might mail just a brief note. Regardless of the nature of the relationship or who initiated the meeting, the follow-up communication is the time to make use of those follow-through gems. If you have an article, a reference to a book, a referral to another person, or any other relevant information, now is the time to provide it. Sending something useful to the other person (or leaving a phone message about it) is more effective than simply sending a thank-you note.

Quick Summary

Referral meetings are important networking interactions for anyone trying to start or grow a business, consulting practice, or freelance endeavor. They are also useful for people who are not self-employed, but who can benefit from referrals of people or information they can use to do their jobs better.

Referral meetings are essentially conversations between two or more peers or colleagues from the same or different industries or functional areas. In these conversations, the parties involved get to know each other's business needs and determine how they can help each other.

A referral meeting is not a sales call in which you're just trying to sell your products or services to that one person with whom you are meeting. It is instead a time to cultivate a relationship with someone who can refer business to you and who may, or may not, partake of your products or services directly.

Touting the benefits of your business should be based on a careful assessment of your strengths and successes and should be backed up with actual examples of your business accomplishments.

The conversation in a referral meeting should be balanced and not just a one-sided sales pitch on your part. The promotion of your business should be subtle and weaved into the conversation.

During a referral meeting, it is appropriate to give out your promotional materials; at the very least, you should provide several of your business cards.

After a referral meeting, you should follow up not only with a thank-you note or call, but also with any information that could be useful to the other person, such as a relevant article, book, or name of someone else to speak to.

Places to Network: Conferences, Job Fairs and Other Gatherings

In the dime stores and bus stations, people talk of situations, read books, repeat quotations, draw conclusions on the wall.

—BOB DYLAN

Networking can happen just about anywhere, from casual conversations in elevators to major conventions that include scheduled networking sessions. Whether you are interacting with people at a formal networking event or simply in an impromptu situation, it is important to keep certain guidelines in mind to make the most of each encounter. This chapter provides those guidelines, covering *dos* and *don'ts* for networking at structured events like conferences and conventions, career or job fairs, and other professional gatherings. You'll also find tips for connecting with people in settings where networking is not the main focus but has the potential to take place. Such settings include eateries, social gatherings, classes or seminars, and the Internet, as well as impromptu, serendipitous situations.

Structured Networking Events

Some of the best places to meet people, or to reconnect with existing contacts, are professional events where networking activities are either a direct or an indirect part of the agenda. These include conferences and conventions, networking clubs, professional and trade association meetings, and career and job fairs. (If you need a reminder of what these events are or how to find them, refer to chapter 3.)

These settings offer chances for you to meet people, cultivate relationships, and gain valuable information. They also offer opportunities for full-scale or modified fact-finding missions, strategy sessions, and referral meetings. Of course, they are also opportunities for plain old conversations that can be informative as well as enjoyable.

Monica found conferences to be a particularly useful networking setting as she was getting her business started. During the first several months of self-employment, she attended the national Women in Business conference, an annual event sponsored by the American Women's Economic Development Corporation (AWED). AWED is a professional association made up of women business owners and consultants from a wide variety of career fields and industries (see Appendix B for AWED contact information). At the first AWED conference she attended, Monica spoke with many entrepreneurs who had all sorts of successful businesses. Each conversation she had became a kind of mini strategy session, in that it gave her the opportunity to get advice on how she could develop her own business. She also met one experienced entrepreneur who turned out to serve as a role model for her. Over the months that followed the conference, this person gave Monica extremely valuable advice about her business. She also suggested that Monica apply to be a speaker at the AWED conference the following year. She helped Monica put together a proposal for a workshop on how to promote a small business on the Internet. The proposal was accepted, so Monica attended the conference the next year, not just as a participant, but as a knowledgeable expert listed in the conference program. The visibility paid off with several solid referrals of new clients.

DOs and DON'Ts for Structured Networking Events

Whether you are attending a national professional conference, major trade show, or just a ten-person breakfast meeting of a small networking club, the following strategies are effective in just about any group setting:

➡ Shake hands with everyone you meet. Use a firm, but not bone-crushing grip.

➡ Introduce yourself as you shake hands, clearly stating your first and last name. Don't wait to be introduced by someone else or to have to be asked for your name.

➡ If you're standing with one or more people when a new person approaches, take the lead in introducing everyone to each other.

➡ To remember the name of someone you've just met, focus carefully on the name when you're first introduced (we usually have a million other thoughts running through our minds and don't even listen to the name). You should also try to use the name in the first few minutes of conversation to reinforce it in your mind.

➡ When wearing a name tag, wear it on your right side. This is a more natural place for people to cast their eyes as they shake your right hand with their right hand.

➡ Take plenty of business cards and keep them within easy reach. (It's always a good idea to wear clothes with pockets.) If you are self-employed, take your promotional materials to hand out; and if you are job hunting, always have your resume handy, but remember not to force your material on someone who doesn't seem interested.

➡ When people give you their business cards, store them in a pocket different from where you carry your own so you won't have to fish through a jumble of cards when handing out your own card.

➡ As soon after each networking encounter as possible, make notes on the back of each business card you receive, so that you don't get confused about who each person was and what was discussed.

➡ Don't spend too much time with any one person. You don't want to come across as clingy, and you should try to meet a range of people. Even if you are attending an event primarily to connect with just one person, it's not a good idea to monopolize that person's time. Also, you never know how you might benefit from interacting with some of the other people in attendance.

➡ If possible, identify in advance the people whom you want to meet or get reacquainted with, so that you'll be sure to connect with them. This tip is especially important when you are attending very large events. It is easy to get a little overwhelmed when you're faced with a large crowd of people and to forget which ones you came to meet.

➡ Set objectives concerning the type or number of people you want to meet, the information you want to collect, points about yourself that you need to convey, or resources you need to find.

➡ Keep one running list of things you need to do after the meeting to follow up—that is, letters or e-mails to write, calls to make, Web sites or books to look up, projects to take on, and so on. This is especially important at a meeting that lasts more than one day, because you can easily lose track of follow-up notes and reminders scattered here and there in the materials that you collect over the course of the event. You can keep your list in your appointment book or planner or on the notepad that is often provided in conference materials.

Staying Organized at Conferences

When attending a conference, particularly one out-of-town that lasts for more than a day, take along several file folders or accordion files to keep track of the mountains of information that you are likely to collect over the course of the event. Label the files according to functions, such as "to file," "to call," "to write," and "to do." That way, when you get home or back to your office, you can pull out the "to write" file, for example, and get all your correspondence taken care of easily since the names, addresses, and other relevant information are all in one place. You'll also need a few files in which you place miscellaneous information that might not fit into the functional categories. When you return to your hotel room at the end of each day, take some time to sort through the session handouts, promotional materials, and business cards you collected that day. Throw out what you don't need to lug home, and file the rest.

(I want to share the credit for this tip with Linda Rothschild, President of the New York-based professional organizing firm ~~CROSS IT OFF YOUR LIST~~, who advocates a similar method. Organized minds think alike!)

The DOs and DON'Ts listed previously apply to most any group event, but there are also a few strategies to keep in mind for each specific type of gathering you might attend. Tips for various settings are provided in the following sections.

Conferences and Conventions

When attending a conference or convention, consider the following tips:

⯈ Take some time at the start of the conference to study the agenda and mark the sessions and events that you want to attend. This will help you maximize your time at the event because you will be sure to hit the most promising sessions. With sessions you're interested in, but have to miss because a more important one is being held simultaneously, mark those in another color. (It is helpful to carry with you highlighter pens or markers in a couple of different colors.) Since even parallel sessions often don't end exactly at the same time, you can go by the rooms where those conflicting sessions were held to see if anyone is still there. (They usually are.) This gives you a chance to pick up any leftover handouts and perhaps to meet the session leaders and some attendees.

➡ Also take time at the start of the meeting to go through the list of participants (both attendees and exhibitors) and mark the people you want to meet or "re-meet." Transfer the names to a separate sheet of paper or index card to have a handy list you can consult throughout the conference. Check off the names of people you meet, so you can track your progress.

➡ Some conference exhibit halls have a "freebie table" where anyone can leave promotional or educational handouts without paying the often exorbitant exhibitors' fees. These are great for entrepreneurs on a tight budget, so be sure to take a stack of your brochures or other literature to leave on such a table if there happens to be one.

➡ Try not to skip the scheduled social events at conferences as they often provide a more relaxed setting in which to meet people. While an occasional evening alone in your hotel room with room service can be rejuvenating and pleasant, it doesn't offer much in the way of networking. Sometimes to network effectively, you have to do what doesn't come naturally. (You can always "veg" in the room after the gathering, and then you won't have to feel guilty about it!)

➡ At conference meals, try to sit with people you don't know and with a different group at each meal.

➡ Also take part in any side trips to local sites that are sometimes arranged for conference attendees. These often take place outside the formal conference agenda (sometimes before the official start of the conference or after it ends), so they may require some advance plan-ning regarding your travel arrangements, but they are often worth the extra effort.

Networking Clubs

As discussed in chapter 3, there are groups all around the country that are formed solely for the purpose of professional networking. These are particularly popular among salespeople and entrepreneurs who share leads for potential business. They also exist for other career areas as well as for people who join together along gender or racial lines.

The events that these groups hold range from small meetings in which a handful of people get together to give each other tips and advice, to large "networking socials" where a hundred people or more might mingle over cheap white wine and hors d'oeuvres. Whichever type of event you attend, certain rules of etiquette and strategies prevail:

Bonding in Unexpected Places

Some of the best networking at a conference takes place on "field trips." I once attended a conference of a few hundred educators, many of whom were excellent potential referral sources for my career counseling practice. Of the thirty or so people I got to know at the conference, which ones turned out to be my best referral sources? Not the ones I met at the sessions or conference meals, but rather several people I met briefly on a crowded van ride from a museum back to the hotel during an outing at the end of the conference. There's something about a shared experience outside the professional arena, even one as mundane as a ride in a van, that bonds people together in a powerful way.

➡ **Don't be selfish.** Make sure you're being true to the give-and-take nature of networking by sharing advice and leads as well as receiving them.

▫▸ **Follow through.** Since fellow members of the group often go out on a limb to provide you with contacts, be sure to follow through on the leads they give you, or graciously explain why you don't plan to do so.

▫▸ **Promote yourself.** If you meet regularly with a group of people, you might start to take for granted that they know you're great at what you do. Don't assume anything! Familiarity can breed forgetfulness, so keep the group apprised of your successes, accomplishments, and strengths so that they have an incentive to help you.

▫▸ **Be positive.** These groups can take on a "gripe session" quality over time, so be sure the supportive environment doesn't lure you into sounding negative or pessimistic. Remember you always want to convey an air of enthusiasm and confidence to maximize your effectiveness while networking.

▫▸ **Focus on quality over quantity.** Networking is something of a numbers game, and large gatherings are great places to expand your network exponentially. Don't, however, get caught up in the free-for-all atmosphere of a large networking event and race around the room trying to meet as many people as possible. Keep an eye toward quality, making sure you have at least a few substantive conversations, and really make an effort to get to know people.

Professional and Trade Association Meetings

Associations often hold events in which networking is not the main objective, but is simply a by-product of the gathering. These types of events include: lectures, seminars, discussion groups, and other professional development activities. Since networking is not the main aim, it is particularly important to have a strategy for creating networking opportunities while participating in the event. Things to remember include the following:

▫▸ **Be subtle.** Remember that the visibility you gain just by attending a professional meeting can be powerful. You don't need to bowl people over with your presence and thus be seen as disinterested in the main purpose of the event, especially if that purpose is educational or charitable.

⟶ **Share war stories and successes.** These gatherings are excellent opportunities to interact with like-minded colleagues. If the aim of the event is to help members develop their professional skills, knowledge, and expertise, such as with a continuing education seminar or a lecture, then the atmosphere is often one of collaboration and commiseration. Take advantage of this chance to bond with your colleagues.

⟶ **Look for ways to distinguish yourself.** In professional and trade associations, you are networking with a fairly homogeneous group in terms of career interests and pursuits. Make sure that you let people know exactly what you do and find out about others' jobs or businesses so that you know how to help them in the future.

⟶ **Take on a leadership role.** Just attending professional and trade association events is not enough. To gain true visibility, you need to volunteer for some kind of official role or even run for elected office.

Career and Job Fairs

Career fairs and job fairs (the terms are used somewhat interchangeably) are usually viewed as places to get jobs rather than as networking events. That thinking can be misleading, though, since rarely do you actually *get* a job just by showing up at a fair. Jobs result from fairs because you networked effectively with the *people* at the event.

Job fairs can also be good places to conduct fact-finding missions. Early in his career exploration process, John attended a job fair for health care professionals sponsored by several hospitals. He was not looking for a job because he did not yet have the training or credentials needed to get one, and he had not yet decided which health care career to pursue. (He attended this fair before he had narrowed his choices to genetic counseling and research.) At the job fair, he was able to get a good sense of the employment outlook and typical salaries for various health care occupations. This information helped him to make an informed decision eventually. He also made valuable contacts at the fair; these came in handy down the road when he did need a job.

All the rules of communication described in chapter 6, along with general networking strategies given throughout this book, apply to your conduct at job fairs. In addition, there are a few strategies to keep in mind specifically for these events:

➧ **Research.** If it's possible to find out in advance which organizations will be represented at the fair (and it usually is), try to do some research on the ones that most interest you. Since many corporations, not-for-profit organizations, and government agencies have Web sites, you can learn the basics about a large number of organizations in a fairly short time. Doing so will enable you to have more substantive conversations with those organizations' representatives at the fair.

➧ **Perfect your personal pitch.** Since job fairs are often crowded, hectic environments with all too brief and superficial interactions, you have to make an impact on prospective employers in less than ideal circumstances. A strong, concise personal pitch is one way to do that. It enables you to convey who you are, what you have to offer, and what you're looking for to a recruiter who only has very limited time to spend with you.

➧ **The early bird gets the worm.** Try to arrive right at the start of the fair when it's likely to be a little less crowded and when the recruiters are fresh and don't yet have that glazed-over look. If you must attend after the event is well under way, be sure to allow yourself ample time there so that you can meet everyone you want to meet. Be prepared for possibly long lines at some of the employers' booths and don't expect to be able to "pop in and pop out."

➧ **Distinguish yourself.** Making yourself stand out is important in any group setting, but it is particularly important at job fairs. Recruiters can meet hundreds of job seekers at fairs, so it's important to distinguish yourself from the pack. Besides just introducing yourself and providing your resume, add some bit of information that's likely to stick in the recruiter's mind. You might mention some fact about the organization that attracts you to it (here's where that research comes in handy), or give a brief example of one of your accomplishments.

➡ **Follow up immediately**. Follow-up is particularly important after job fairs. When recruiters get back to their offices, the faces that go with the resumes on their desks are mostly one big blur. Sending a carefully crafted letter mentioning something specific that you talked about can put a face with your resume. By the way, don't take this advice too literally and send a photo! That's a no-no for all job seeking except modeling and the performing arts.

Unstructured Networking Settings

Unstructured networking settings offer some of the best opportunities to connect with others, simply because networking is not the main focus. In a class or seminar, for example, you have the opportunity to connect with people out of a common interest or to bond with each other while working on a group project. Solid relationships are cultivated this way, and they are often more lasting than the superficial connections made at actual networking events.

How to Find Career Fairs

The National Association of Colleges and Employers (NACE) has a career fair clearinghouse on its Web site, listing more than 1,000 fairs. These are searchable by keyword, date, and location. There is also a college career fairs database with more than 2,000 career events. You can find these databases at: www.jobweb.com

Social events such as parties, weddings, and other gatherings also offer opportunities to get to know people in a nonpressured atmosphere when people are usually relaxed and having fun. Restaurants, bars, and cafes are included in the unstructured category as well because many people make plans to get together over lunch (or coffee, drinks, or a snack) only to find that they don't really know how to handle the meeting. Networking over meals or drinks falls into that murky area in which social and professional pursuits overlap, making it difficult to know how to balance social courtesies with your own career or business objectives. All of these situations require that you be extra clear about your goals and networking objectives so that you can subtly, but assertively, work them into the conversation, all the while making sure not to turn a casual social occasion into a hard-driving business meeting.

Eateries

When you are mixing networking with food and drink, keep the following in mind so that you don't cause yourself or others indigestion:

➠ **Choose a convenient location**. When you are deciding where to go, the rule of thumb is to choose a place convenient to the other person if you're initiating the get-together. After all, it's the courteous thing to do. If the other person has initiated the invitation, or if the get-together is a mutual idea, then just be sure to be flexible in any discussion of where to meet. Try to find a mutually convenient place, or better yet, make the generous gesture of offering to meet near where the other person lives or works.

➠ **Keep the cost appropriate**. Take into account the income bracket of the other person and be sure that no one suggests a place that will be too much of a financial burden on any-one. If you need to choose an inexpensive restaurant and are embarrassed to reveal that you're on a tight budget, suggest a place that you know is reasonable, but cite its convenience, quiet atmosphere, great soup, or whatever feature gives you an excuse for proposing it.

➠ **Understand who should pay**. Here, the rule of thumb is that whoever does the initiating should offer to pay the bill—and should be prepared to do so. If, however, you're just getting started in the working world and ask to go out with someone older or more experienced than you, then that person might offer to pick up the bill, and it's OK to let them do so (though you should at least protest a bit).

If you were invited by the other person, you should still be prepared to pay in case they don't offer, so make sure you have adequate cash or a credit card with you. Be aware that many people who network frequently get in the habit of going dutch, which is a good policy so that neither of you feels obligated to the other.

➠ **Make the food a secondary focus.** When someone wants to get together over a meal, try to opt for just a coffee break instead. The focus should be on talking with each other, not on consuming lots of food and drink, which can distract from the conversation. This is often unavoidable, however, as some people have time to meet with you only during a lunch break or for breakfast. So, if you must network over a meal, it is better to eat light so that you can focus on the conversation; you can always grab something later to satisfy your hunger.

➠ **Order food that's easy to eat.** Since the focus of the meeting should be on conversation, not the food (unless you're both in the food or hospitality business!), order something that won't be awkward to eat. Spaghetti dangling over your chin or cheese from French onion soup stretched across the room doesn't do wonders for your professional image. Also avoid food that will cause a spectacle. Anything that the waiters have to light on fire or that requires you to wear a bib is a bad idea, as are orders that inspire the restaurant staff to ring bells and sing to you.

➠ **Hold your liquor.** In many professional circles, drinking is not a smart move since there's no telling what you could end up saying or doing that you might regret. If you do go to a bar with someone or have a drink with a meal, keep an eye on how much you imbibe and stay well below the limit at which you are usually affected. A networking meeting with someone you've never met is not the time to discover what the fuss over martinis is all about.

➠ **Watch out for no-business policies at clubs.** If someone invites you to a country club or other private social club that you're not familiar with, don't assume you'll be openly doing business. Some exclusive clubs have a policy of no business in their dining rooms and will seriously frown on the fact that you've spread papers and other business paraphernalia across the table.

Social Gatherings

Social events, such as weddings, parties, charity functions, and small gatherings, need to be handled delicately. Here's how to do so:

➡ **Strike the right social and business balance.** It's extremely important that you don't push people into talking business when they would rather be socializing. Read situations and people very carefully, and be sure not to cross the line between low-pressure networking and being overbearing. Also, it's particularly rude to rope an event's host into a business discussion. The mother of the bride, for example, probably has other priorities that take precedence over discussing your career.

➡ **Initiate a business contact and make plans to follow up.** Related to the first point is the idea that you should simply broach the subject of your career or business with someone at the social gathering, and then turn back to discussing nonbusiness topics. Just make sure that you get people's office phone numbers or cards so you can continue the conversation at a more appropriate time and place.

➡ **Don't try to do business if you've had one too many.** As mentioned earlier, drinking too much can really foul up professional interactions. While you might enjoy the fact that a drink or two rids you of your inhibitions and makes networking a little less intimidating, don't get yourself in an embarrassing situation by having too much at a party where potential professional contacts are around.

➡ **Keep your follow-through expectations realistic.** In the relaxed atmosphere of social gatherings, lots of promises are made that aren't always kept after the party's over. Keep your expectations realistic and realize that just because on Saturday night your date's Uncle Louie said he'd get you a job, it doesn't mean he'll even remember who you are when you call his office on Monday.

Classes, Lectures, and Seminars

Educational settings are great places to network. When you have a chance to connect in such environments, be sure to do the following:

➠ **Get to know the instructor**. The people who teach classes and lead workshops are often a great source of contacts and resources. Be sure you are known to them as more than a name on a class roster. Make an effort to talk with the instructor during office hours or some setting other than class.

➠ **Get to know your classmates**. As with instructors, your fellow students and workshop participants can often lead you to people, places, and information that can get you closer to your goals. Try to get together with people after class.

➠ **Use class materials as sources of contacts**. The textbooks, articles, and handouts used in most classes are a largely untapped source of networking opportunities. Pay attention to who wrote the things you're reading or to people mentioned in what you read. Some of them might be more approachable than you think.

➠ **Be on the lookout for organizations cited in your class materials**. For example, if a research study is listed as being funded by a particular foundation and you're exploring careers in foundation work, you've just found a place to approach for information or to apply for a job.

The Internet

The World Wide Web and other areas of the Internet are revolutionizing the way that networking takes place. If you're a cyberspace neophyte, you probably hate hearing statements like that. It can be overwhelming if you don't know where to begin or how to make the most of this vast network. You might think to yourself, "So what if I can communicate with billions of people and find ten million citations that match my interest areas? I just want one good contact who can help me make a career decision and lead me to a job." Well, those of you who are skilled net surfers know that the process of tracking down people and information on the Internet *can* be frustrating, but you know also that it can be amazingly convenient and thorough as well.

Several good books are on the market, including *Using the Internet and the World Wide Web in Your Job Search* (see Appendix D), which can help you make the most of this miraculous tool. You may not be looking for a job, though, but networking instead for career choice, career management, or developing your own business. The Internet and the Web have plenty to offer in that regard also. Many of the Web sites listed in Appendix C are good sources of information on career and business topics beyond job listings.

While Web sites are one very important networking avenue in cyberspace, be sure to make full use of electronic networking through these additional tools:

➡ **Use e-mail**. Of all the possible networking methods, e-mail may be the most convenient one ever to come down the pike. With the click of a button, you can contact anyone anywhere (anyone with an on-line address, that is) at any time. You can send e-mail at any time you choose, while the recipients can read them any time they choose).

With e-mail, there's no excuse for not checking in frequently with people in your existing network or for not contacting people you don't know, but would like to add to your network. It's becoming more and more common to see e-mail addresses publicized. Authors of books and articles are starting to list their addresses in their creations; letters-to-the-editor sections in magazines and newspapers often include e-mail addresses so that you can enter into a dialogue with people who write on topics that interest you; editors and reporters of magazines and newspapers can also be reached; and Web sites of corporations and other organizations often connect you with people who a few years ago would have been much harder to contact. Tips and protocol for e-mailing are offered throughout this book to help you take advantage of this powerful communication method.

Be Thankful You're Networking at the Brink of the 21st Century

As the Internet becomes commonplace, most of us are already taking for granted the ease with which we connect to people around the globe. A thousand years ago, networking was slow sailing—literally. In A.D. 1100, the

Arabs invented the lateen, a triangular sail which allowed ships to sail against the wind and sped things up a bit, but that travel was nothing like the speed and ease with which words and ideas fly through cyberspace these days. You wouldn't have fared much better globe-trotting in the 1930s either, when the British concocted a grand plan for regular passenger service by blimp to faraway lands in their world empire. On the maiden voyage, the first blimp made it only as far as France when an accident felled not only that trip but also the whole plan. Virtual travel has both these methods beaten by a mile.

Source for historical facts: *World Access: The Handbook for Citizens of the Earth* by Kathryn and Ross Petras. Fireside/Simon & Schuster, 1996.

➡ **Explore Web sites.** Web sites are the most popular Internet destinations. While they tend to be better sources of information than actual connections to people, they are, nevertheless, important parts of your networking efforts. (And some do provide e-mail access to people who are affiliated with the site, some of whom may be valuable experts for the allied forces portion of your network.) Exploring the sites of businesses, individuals, and other organizations is an important way to stay in touch with resources that can help you reach your professional goals. And, they do offer opportunities to interact with people through chat rooms and events held in virtual auditoriums—sometimes even in real time.

Caution—This Is a Very Public Forum

If you're using the Web for job hunting, be careful when you post your resume online. While doing so can be a great job search method—in that it lets your resume work for you 24 hours a day with little or no effort on your part—keep in mind the downside of this visibility. Is there a boss, competitor, or client whom you'd rather not make aware that you're looking to make a move? They can easily see your resume online, and the consequences might not be pretty.

Appendix C lists some of the more useful sites for information and guidance in career planning, career management, job search, and small business management. When you find sites you like, be sure to bookmark them for easy access.

➤ **Join newsgroups**. There are more than 10,000 newsgroups available to you on the Usenet portion of the Internet (a separate area from the World Wide Web). Newsgroups are kind of like virtual community centers—places you can go to talk with people who share an interest of yours and to read information on a given topic. People post questions, announcements, and other information on message boards that you can review and respond to if you'd like. You can also be a silent member (also known as a lurker), just reading other people's dialogues or the posted articles and notes without actively participating.

You can also branch out from a newsgroup to carry on a private correspondence by e-mail with someone you meet through the newsgroup. Some of the best sources for lists of newsgroups are www.dejanews.com, www.careermosaic.com/cm/usenet.html, and www.careermag.hub.

When first getting involved with a newsgroup, be sure to read the FAQs (Frequently Asked Questions) for new members so you won't break any cyberspace etiquette rules.

➤ **Use the Web's people and business directories**. There are many Web sites that let you track down an address, phone number, and e-mail address for just about any person or business. These include AOL NetFind (for America OnLine subscribers), at www.aol.com/search/htm12/person.html and www.aol.com/search/htm12/business.html; Big Yellow, at http://sll.bigyellow.com/; Four11, at www.Four11.com; Galaxy, at www.einet.net/galaxy/Reference.html; Switchboard, at www.switchboard.com/; WhoWhere?, at www.whowhere.com/; and 555-1212.com, at www.555-1212.com

Sometimes Networking Just Happens— The Serendipity Factor

As mentioned in chapter 2, the "serendipity factor" is just as important an element in networking as are the scheduled events. You never know where the next great contact, lead, or tidbit of information is going to come from, so it's important to be open to all possible opportunities, not just to those that are part of your premeditated networking plan.

Think of all the places in which you interact with people who might become valuable members of your network. These include the office waiting rooms of doctors, dentists, accountants, lawyers, and other professionals; your barbershop or beauty salon; realtors' offices; buses, trains, and planes; and the gym or health club. The list is endless— wherever you are, that is where you can network with people.

DOs and DON'Ts When Networking Just Happens

To handle these serendipitous situations with aplomb, keep the following DOs and DON'Ts in mind:

⟶ DO start a conversation with a simple hello or neutral comment or question, instead of trying to be overly witty (unless you truly are witty!) or instead of opening with a comment that could be controversial.

⟶ DO stretch past your comfort zone and make contacts even if you don't feel like doing so.

⟶ DO exchange business cards with anyone who seems to be a worthy candidate for your network.

⟶ DO maintain a professional tone, vocabulary, and posture so that your overtures can't be misconstrued as romantic or inappropriate in any other way.

➠ DON'T be a pest. Don't bother anyone who seems busy, depressed, or distracted or doesn't continue a dialogue that you initiate.

➠ DON'T put your foot in your mouth by saying something that might be controversial or offensive; wait until you know more about the person before you move into potentially sensitive areas, so that you move into those kinds of areas only if you really have some need to do so.

➠ DON'T open a conversation with anyone who looks menacing or dangerous, and exercise caution even with seemingly friendly people. And, don't ever go anywhere alone with someone you've just met.

Quick Summary

Networking can take place just about anywhere, from casual conversations to major conferences with scheduled networking events.

This chapter discussed two main types of networking settings:

➠ Structured networking events including conferences and conventions, networking clubs, professional and trade association meetings, and career and job fairs.

➠ Unstructured settings in which networking is not the main focus but can be if you make an effort. These include restaurants and bars, social occasions, classes and other educational settings, and the Internet.

This chapter also covered DOs and DON'Ts for your conduct in all these typical networking settings, as well as for making the most of the "serendipity factor."

Dealing with Difficult People and Surviving Sticky Situations

He looked at me as if I was a side dish he hadn't ordered.

—RING LARDNER, JR.

While networking is often a pleasant and rewarding pursuit, you inevitably will face occasional challenges and frustrations. Since networking is all about human nature in action, it is bound to be difficult, awkward, or downright annoying at times. For example, you might go to lots of trouble to track down just the person you need to talk to, only to have him not return your calls after repeated tries. Or, what if you do get through to someone, but she's not able (or willing) to meet with you? Connecting with others—or trying to—can tax the limits of even the most patient souls. And the rejection it often brings can crumble even the toughest cookies.

Not only are difficult people hard to avoid, but so are the sticky situations you're likely to face. These are those disastrous (or, at the very least, moderately unsuccessful) networking encounters that make you wish you could turn back the clock and try again. When you interact with large numbers of people in your professional life, the basic law of averages dictates that you are occasionally going to say the wrong thing or lose your composure. Following the communication techniques discussed in chapter 6, as well as other tips offered throughout this book, can minimize the chances of that happening. It is important, though, to be prepared to deal with sticky situations nonetheless. In this chapter, I describe typical types of difficult people and situations and offer strategies for dealing with them. The scenarios I chose to include here are those that my clients frequently report experiencing, as well as ones that I have had to deal with myself.

Difficult People

There are some people who are just plain hard to connect with—either literally in that you can't get in touch with them, or figuratively in that they're not pleasant to deal with. As you network, you are bound to encounter people who are overtly or covertly difficult. In this section, I give you some pointers for dealing with the most common types of difficult people. We'll take a look at the "elusive ones," the "false promisers," the "rejectors," and the "pains in your neck."

The Elusive Ones

As you try to network, you will run into your fair share of people whom you just can't seem to get a hold of. These are the people who don't return your calls and thus leave you in that awkward position of not knowing when and how often it is appropriate to call back. They may also be the ones you can't even leave a message for because they have the world's most impenetrable screeners standing in your way—diligent assistants or receptionists whose sole focus in life seems to be to stand between you and their boss. The elusive ones aren't just problematic in networking by phone, either. They are also skilled at ignoring your faxes, e-mails, and letters and could probably even manage to look the other way if you sent a singing telegram to their door. When it comes to some people you'd like to have in your network, you might feel you'd have an easier time calling up the dead in a seance. Trying to reach the elusive ones is one of the most frustrating, time-consuming, and perplexing aspects of networking.

Why Some People May Elude You

There are many reasons why certain people might be unresponsive to your attempts to reach them. Often, the reasons have more to do with circumstances than with personal character. They may simply be too busy to take your calls, respond to your phone messages, or reply to your e-mails or other correspondence. Aside from circumstances, however, a common reason why people are elusive is that they assume—usually wrongly—that they can't be of any help to you. Even if you're just approaching them for advice or information, they might assume that you want them to find you a job, or, if self-employed, that you want to sell them something. If they don't have a job for you or aren't in the market for your product or service, they simply don't respond. Then there are those who do realize that you just need advice or information but are afraid that you'll take up too much of their time. And, finally, there are some people you might contact who are simply a bit shy or introverted and make it a habit of not responding to people they don't know. Whatever the reasons, the strategies suggested in this chapter for dealing with elusive types can help you overcome some of these hurdles.

When dealing with the elusive types, remember the tips in the following sections.

Keep Trying

The rule of thumb for tracking down elusive types is to be more persistent than you probably think you need to be (unless you're usually very aggressive by nature). Career management experts repeatedly find that people they coach through networking and job hunting tend to give up too early. It's easy to assume you should give up if someone hasn't returned your call after you've left two or three messages. In many cases, though, it's perfectly OK to keep trying.

Remember that you're most likely not a top priority for the people from whom you're seeking advice or information, particularly in the case of networking for career choice or job search purposes. Depending on the occupation and lifestyle of the people you're trying to reach, they are likely to be too busy to have even a few minutes to spare for getting back to you. Since they're likely to have other priorities besides you, whatever extra time they do have is probably not going to be spent calling or writing to you. It's not fair, but that's the reality. The good news, though, is that this doesn't necessarily mean they don't want to speak to you. I've worked with countless clients who are amazed to find that when they finally get through to someone who has been elusive, that person is friendly and happy to talk to them. So keep trying! As in most things, persistence pays off.

Persistence Pays Off

That was the case with Ana, who once made almost thirty calls over a period of a couple of weeks to someone during her job search. He was a financial trader (one of the most hectic occupations in this country), did not have a secretary or voice mail, and did not have a direct phone line. Every time Ana called, another trader at a desk adjacent to her target's would answer the phone and suggest that she call back later. She did keep calling back, trying different times of the day and different days of the week, knowing that she would eventually catch him. Half the time she called, she left a message with whoever answered the phone, asking the trader to call her back, but the other half of the time, she did not leave a message. By not leaving a message some of the time, the ball remained in her court, making her more free to call back without feeling intrusive. By the time she had made about her twentieth try, she started to feel a little uncomfortable and considered giving up. She called the strategist who had given her the trader's name in the first place and asked what she should do. That person acknowledged that the trader was almost impossible to reach and suggested that Ana keep trying. She did, and he eventually came to the phone. Ana just about fell off her chair when she found herself actually talking to this elusive target! She was relieved to find that her persistence had not been at all inappropriate and actually paid off. The trader apologized profusely for being so hard to reach and thanked Ana for her persistence. He then agreed to pass her resume on to some people in his company who he knew were looking to hire analysts.

Make Your Objectives Clear and Simple

In addition to lack of time or priority, some people don't respond to your attempts because it's not clear why you're contacting them. Think about it. If you're busy and get a phone message just saying to call someone you'd never heard of before, would you have much incentive to call back? Probably not.

Phone messages and e-mails that make vague requests aren't likely to get results, particularly if the person doesn't recognize your name. Avoid saying things such as "I'd like to speak to you for some advice about my career" or "I'm trying to develop my business and thought you might be able to help." These wide open requests for assistance can scare people off. They sound like dealing with you will be too much trouble and too time-consuming. Try instead to be more specific in your request, using some of the examples in chapter 6. By putting some parameters (limits) on your request, you make it less overwhelming, and thus you are more likely to get a response.

The preceding broad statements, for example, could be made less intimidating as follows: "I'd like to speak to you for about fifteen minutes to discuss a few specific questions I have about making a career transition from advertising to marketing." Or, "I'm launching a new Web site development business and was hoping to get your opinion about two specific aspects of my business plan." These statements make it clear that you are coming to them well-prepared and won't waste their time.

Dangle a Carrot

Some people need more incentive to respond to you than just the basic desire to help others. These kinds of people need to believe that they might somehow benefit from talking to you before they'll bother. This is an unfortunate set of circumstances that does present itself occasionally, so it's helpful to be on the lookout for it.

Name-dropping is one useful incentive to use in this situation. If you can mention the name of someone who is already part of your network and who will impress the person you're trying to reach, by all means do so. You might say something like, "I've been talking to a number of people in your industry, including Jane Harrell at XYZ, Inc., and John Simpson over at The BCD Group. They encouraged my efforts to get into this field and suggested I talk to more people like you." Notice that Jane Harrell and John Simpson did not necessarily refer you to the person you're now calling, but you are able to use their names because you have spoken to them. These, of course, would need to be names of prominent figures in a given industry or top companies, or at least in some way would need to be recognizable to the person you're calling. This name-dropping establishes you as something of an "insider" and can also imply to the person you're calling that you have valuable connections you could share with him or her.

Also think of anything you might be able to offer the other person as a sort of reward for helping you. This doesn't mean showering the individual with lavish gifts (see chapter 14 for appropriate ways to show appreciation), but instead simply offering something like information, resources, or support. In the course of researching fields or industries (or potential markets in the case of self-employment), you're likely to come across a lot of interesting data that could be of use to the people you're trying to reach. Try to work such tidbits of information into the conversation when you are making a request. You might say, for example, "I'd like to discuss with you the pros and cons of my making a transition into X. I came across an interesting Web site recently that cited studies showing X as a #1 growth industry. I'd be happy to give you the address or could bring you a copy of information I printed out if we were to meet." If the information you found was relatively obscure (don't offer information or resources that would be obvious and well-known to the person), chances are that person would welcome the information. Dangling this carrot won't guarantee that the individual will respond, but it might help.

Charm the Gatekeepers

If you keep getting a "gatekeeper" such as an assistant, receptionist, or other coworker every time you call, the best thing you can do is to get that person on your side. Try to remember that that person is a fellow human being. It's easy to fall into the trap of being too impersonal with gatekeepers or venting your frustrations on them. Try instead to remember that they're just doing their jobs and don't have a personal vendetta against you. Being courteous and considerate with them will get you far. Also, when leaving a message, don't just state your name; introduce yourself. Instead of saying, "Please have Ms. Jones call me. My name is Cliff Bowers," say, "My name's Cliff Bowers. How are you doing?" After the response, Cliff could ask, "May I have your name please?"

The False Promisers

Sometimes you do get through to people, only to find that they don't follow through on promises they made to help you. A common example of this situation occurs in the job hunting process when someone offers to forward your resume or make a call to a colleague, but doesn't get around to doing it, or at least doesn't call to let you know it's been done so that you're left in the dark. The same thing can happen in the career management or self-employment networking processes as well. Someone might offer to put you in touch with people who can help you advance in your career or your business, but never get back to you with the names and numbers. Dealing with the false promisers presents challenges to networkers, particularly regarding how assertive and aggressive one should be.

In the following sections are some tips on dealing with people who promise more than they deliver.

Maintain As Much Control As Possible

The best way to solve the problem of the false promisers is some preventive medicine. By taking some simple steps to maintain control over these situations from the start, you can often prevent the problem from happening in the first place. Let's say you're having a strategy session with someone who is critiquing your resume and offering job search advice. At the end of the meeting, she says, "When you've finished revising your resume, send me a few copies, and I'll pass them around the company." That's a nice offer, but what often happens is that you send the resumes and follow up with a call about a week later, only to find that she didn't get around to passing them on. She promises to do so soon; but knowing how busy she is, you suspect that it could slip her mind again. You're left in an awkward position of not knowing how much more you can follow through without being too pushy, and you may be hesitant to ask if you can send the resumes out yourself, because that might seem to imply that you don't trust her to do it herself.

This situation might have been avoided if you had been more direct when the offer was first made. You could have said, "That's a very nice offer. Would it be possible for me to send the resumes directly to the people you suggest and mention you in the cover letter? That way, I'll save you some effort, and I won't bother you with follow-up calls to check on the status."

Most people won't object to this request because it saves them time and effort. However, if you think that there is substantial benefit to having the person send the resumes herself, or even hand-deliver them, don't send them yourself, but do ask for the names of people they'll be going to. That way, you can follow up directly with the recipients; and if they haven't gotten your resume, you can send it yourself.

This tactic works for other networking situations as well. If you're already in a situation where someone is not following through and you weren't as direct as you should have been at the beginning, it's usually not too late to regain some control midstream. Just tactfully ask to take over the task for the other person.

Reevaluate Your Own Qualifications and Networking Technique

Most of a lack of follow-through by people in your network results from time management issues, not from a lack of desire to help you. People usually have the best of intentions, but just don't get around to following through because they're very busy or lose track of what they're supposed to be doing.

There are, however, occasions when their lack of assistance results from concerns about your qualifications or credentials or because something about your networking technique is not quite working. When people offer to help, they often do so with incomplete information about you. Say, for example, that you're self-employed and someone offers to refer lots of business to you. After the first customer, though, the referrals dry up and you wonder what went wrong. While there may be many simple explanations, you can't entirely rule out the least desirable explanation— that something about your work did not meet the referral source's approval. Now, I don't mean to send anyone into a tailspin of self-doubt, but it never hurts to take a second (or third) objective look at the way you conduct business, your qualifications for a job, or your approach to networking in general.

Are you treating your clients or customers with impeccable service or products? Are you going after jobs that fit with your background and skills? Are you networking with courtesy, being considerate of others' time, and showing appreciation? If you have any doubts about these issues, you can either ask for feedback directly from the "false promiser" or turn to one of the role models in your network for insight into the problem.

How Monica Learned the Hard Way about False Promisers

When Monica first got her Web site business up and running, she was excited to tap into an excellent source of referrals. The source was a small business advisor who worked for the public library system and also saw private clients and led seminars around the community. Since he came into contact with so many people who were starting or running small businesses, he was a great source of people who might need Web site services. Soon after Monica's business officially got started, he sent her one of her first clients, saying that this would be the first of many he would send. Monica acknowledged the referral with a nice note and small gift, then had no contact with the business advisor for a couple of months. No further referrals came from him during that time, and she couldn't imagine what was wrong. He had seemed so enthusiastic about wanting to send her a lot of business, but now the referrals had dried up. She decided to call him to check in and to try to find out what the problem might be. When she did so, he was candid with her and told her that the first client he had sent had not been completely pleased. Though the client was more than happy with his Web page, he had not liked certain ways she did business. He had complained to the business advisor that Monica had not returned his calls promptly while they were working together and had been two weeks late in getting the page set up. Monica knew that these were valid complaints. She *had* been overextended when she first started the business and had not ironed out the kinks in the day-to-day operations. Never had she imagined, though, that what she saw as minor problems would offend the client so much and would turn off the referral source. After all, the actual product she provided was top-notch. The business advisor told her that just providing an excellent product is not enough. Customers expect good service as well. Monica promised to make amends and eventually restored her reputation in the referral source's eyes, but did so only after learning a hard lesson.

The Rejectors

Every networking effort brings an occasional bout of rejection. Like the common cold, rejection in networking is inevitable, annoying, and temporarily incapacitating, but usually not life-threatening. It can seem at times, however, to take on catastrophic proportions. You invariably will be putting a good deal of effort into networking, so it can be a real setback to have someone turn down a request or be unresponsive to you. Nobody likes rejection, but it is especially difficult if you're a sensitive person who tends to take rejection personally. It can also be particularly hard to deal with if you are networking after a blow to the ego such as being fired or quitting a job that didn't work out. Or perhaps your ego is a little fragile because you've just gone into business for yourself and haven't built up your entrepreneurial confidence yet.

If you get rejected, it is no time to quit and go home. There are ways to handle even these difficult situations.

Keep a Balanced Perspective

Realize that having someone turn down your request for assistance or your offer to go out to lunch is not the end of the world. Rarely is one member or prospective member of your network so critical that you absolutely must have that person's assistance. The old advice about other fish in the sea definitely applies to networking. If you have trouble downplaying feelings of rejection, try these tricks on yourself:

➠ Recall past positive networking experiences to remind yourself that they *do* work sometimes.

➠ Make a list of all the reasons why you deserve the attention and assistance of others. Cite your positive personal qualities, skills, and accomplishments. In addition, consider how the person who helps you can benefit from helping you.

➠ Think of all the things in life that are worse than rejection. It's not a terminal illness, a death in the family, or a plane crash. These may seem like morbid thoughts, but what better way to put a little rejection in proper perspective!

➠ Treat yourself to something pleasant. When you're feeling a little down, it often helps to give yourself a treat of some sort. That might mean buying something you've been wanting, taking the afternoon off to have fun, or just relaxing. Find whatever works for you to alleviate the rejection blues.

Don't Internalize the Rejection

Once you've put the rejection in perspective, the next step is to make sure that you don't internalize it. Doing so can prevent you from forging ahead with your networking efforts. Internalizing rejection means that you take it to heart—you make it a part of you. In other words, you take it too personally. Instead, you need to view rejection as situational. It is simply something that happens sometimes. It happens when someone else, for whatever reason, does not respond to you in the way that you had hoped. This need not have anything to do with you. Rejection is not a character flaw. In fact, it can't be because it is a situation, not a part of you. So, when you are faced with rejection, try to look at it simply as a fact of life that you will come across now and then—not as a problem within you that you carry with you.

Adopting a Sales Pose to Deal with Rejection

Ellis Chase, a New York City-based career management consultant, executive coach, and member of the International Association of Career Management Professionals (see Appendix C for information on IACMP), suggests adopting a sales pose to deal with rejection. He recommends that you "understand that people will occasionally treat you like dirt. Someone will stand you up, not return your call, or keep you waiting without an apology. You have to realize that it's not your problem, it's theirs. Adopt a sales pose and move onto the next step. Networking is partly a quantity issue." Even though you might not see yourself as a salesperson (unless that happens to be your occupation), you *are* a salesperson of sorts whenever you network. If you are looking for a job, trying to advance in your career, or promoting your own business, you are selling a product, and that product is you. So, just as real salespeople can't take it personally and give up every time someone doesn't want to buy their product, you too should adopt this sales pose and keep plugging away. A sales pose is a frame of mind that keeps you somewhat immune to rejection. It helps you realize that rejection is a natural part of life and is not something that should be internalized.

The Pains in Your Neck

I've said it before, and I'll say it again: networking is human nature in action. Since there are always a few rotten eggs in the basket, there are invariably going to be people who are just plain difficult to deal with. They might be rude, inconsiderate, curt, overly critical, inattentive, or downright nasty. Whatever their particular "affliction," they can make networking quite unpleasant. Fortunately, you're not likely to come across true pains in the neck all that often, but it helps to be prepared when you do.

Don't Deal with Them

Nothing says you have to welcome everyone you come across into the hallowed halls of your network. There are times when you have to say to yourself that someone isn't worth dealing with. Successful networking does not require that you subject yourself to abuse and punishment. Carefully consider whether this pain in the neck is absolutely essential to your network. Rarely is someone so critical to your network that you must put up with that person.

Flattery Will Get You Everywhere

Some people whom you come across are difficult because they're on some sort of power trip or because their brusque facade masks insecurity or low self-esteem. One of the best ways to deal with narcissistic or self-doubting types is to feed their fragile egos with flattery and to play into their need for power by placing them on a pedestal. Though this tactic can work, I must acknowledge that it can be a difficult one to stomach. You might find it demeaning or against your principles to cater to someone you don't respect, so I recommend doing so only if you are sure that this person absolutely stands between you and your goals and therefore you don't have much choice.

Difficult Situations

In addition to dealing with difficult people, there are times when difficult situations arise. These can be a result of something you said or did or just may be due to unfortunate circumstances. While sticky situations are uncomfortable, there are ways to deal effectively with them. This section addresses what to do when you say the wrong thing, just don't click with someone, forget the name of someone you know, or become exceptionally nervous.

When You Put Your Foot in Your Mouth

Networking involves a lot of communicating, so the odds are that you're occasionally going to say the wrong thing. The consequences of doing so can range from mildly embarrassing to quite devastating. This problem is becoming more common as technology makes it easier to goof. Think about how close you've come at times to forwarding an e-mail to the wrong person with a quick click of a button. Or perhaps you put a memo into the fax machine, only to find that it's on its way to someone who doesn't need to be reading it and there's no getting it back. While you can't turn back the clock and erase something you have said or written, you can repair some of the damage by the way you handle yourself after the deed is done.

Monica found it necessary to do some damage control during a conversation she had with a prospective client. In talking about what people do wrong when they develop Web sites, she cited a particular company's site as an example of what not to do. She went on and on about how ineffective the site was, only to remember midway through her remarks that the person she was speaking with had until recently been employed in that company's marketing department. She knew this from some research she had done on this prospective client but had forgotten it for a few minutes. She managed to recover from the faux pas, using some of the strategies suggested in the following sections, but she just about lost the account.

Maintain Your Composure

A lot can be said for remaining as unflustered as possible after putting your foot in your mouth. Showing excessive embarrassment and nervousness tends only to exacerbate the problem. Try instead to stay calm and composed.

Get a Second Opinion

Before jumping to the conclusion that what you've said or written is so catastrophic that your mouth should be sewn shut and your computer privileges revoked, make sure it *really* was a big mistake. Turn to the strategists, supporters, or role models in your network (anyone you don't mind being embarrassed in front of) and get their opinion about how big a gaffe it really was.

Apologize, Correct, and Move On

If you've said or written something that will probably offend someone, offer a polite apology, but don't go overboard. If your faux pas was more an erroneous statement than an offensive remark, correct yourself as clearly and concisely as possible. There's no harm in offering some sort of an excuse, such as "You'll have to forgive me, but I'm just not myself today. I received some upsetting personal news just before coming here. I wouldn't have mentioned it, but clearly it's affecting my concentration." Only give excuses, however, when you've really blown it—and when the excuse is the truth.

Monica, for example, could have said, "I'm sorry, I just realized you used to work for that company whose Web site I'm criticizing. Please understand that I don't usually make a habit of saying such negative things about other Web sites, but I'm afraid that that site just contradicts what I believe makes a site effective. I'm sure that you weren't the primary architect of that site, so please don't take my comments personally." Her apology did smooth things over. Even though the person actually had been directly involved in developing that site, he respected Monica's opinion and appreciated her candor.

Consider the Blunder an Entree to Improved Communication

Occasionally, saying or writing the wrong thing can open the doors to a candid discussion with someone you haven't had a good relationship with previously. This is particularly true if you've cc'd or forwarded an e-mail, fax, or memo to a group of people and included someone by mistake—someone who might be discussed negatively in the correspondence. There's often no way to pretend that you didn't really mean what you said, so sometimes the best thing to do is to get everything out in the open and say what's been on your mind.

The preceding example of Monica's apology is also an example of this strategy. She did apologize, but she did not take back what she had said about that Web site. As a result, she demonstrated her professional integrity and commitment to quality work. Doing so impressed the person she was speaking with, making him soon forget the mild offense he took at her initial statements.

When You Just Don't Click

Sometimes you'll talk or meet with people and simply not hit it off. This is to be expected and is not a great cause for alarm. It can, though, be awkward and uncomfortable and can be frustrating if you believe that the person is a critical member of your network who can likely help you reach your goals. In phone calls or meetings, the signs of not clicking are usually fairly obvious—the other person seems distracted, bored, disagreeable, or not able to understand you. This situation can result from an age, gender, or cultural difference; conflicting values; different personality styles; or just from some basic lack of chemistry. There are things you can do to get through these situations as well.

Be Objective About How Bad the Situation Really Is

Before assuming that connecting with such a person is hopeless, make sure you're not misreading the situation. Ask yourself these questions: "Are my expectations too high? Did I expect us to become fast friends when in fact that's not necessary for an effective networking relationship? Am I being overly sensitive and presuming that this person doesn't like me? Could I just be subconsciously looking for an excuse in case the meeting doesn't turn out well for other reasons?" Also think about whether you're the kind of person who can usually hit if off with most anyone. If so, and you find a particular encounter is not going well, there really may be some problem.

Pump Up the Volume

Think of steps you can take to jazz things up a bit. Is your energy level low? Are you not conveying enthusiasm and commitment? You don't have to start singing and dancing to grab someone's attention, but you might need to put in a bit more effort. Remember, networking encounters are a two-way street. You have to do your part to make an interaction engaging and stimulating for the other person.

When You Forget a Name

Almost everyone knows that sinking feeling. Someone approaches you with outstretched hand calling you by name, and you can't think of the person's name. You then go through that awkward dance of conveying warmth and familiarity without using the person's name. And, you pray that no one else will join you who needs to be introduced to this now nameless person.

Assess How Bad It Is That You've Forgotten

You can't be expected to remember everyone's name, so in some cases it's OK not to. If the person is a remote acquaintance or someone you haven't seen in a long time, there's nothing wrong with politely saying, "I'm so sorry, but your name is on the tip of my tongue...." Most people will graciously offer their names at that point and not take offense. Remember that everyone has forgotten a name now and again, so most people will relate to your doing so.

Prompt Others into Saying Their Names

A popular technique to use in this awkward situation is to offer your name first if the other person or persons are individuals you haven't seen in a while and hope that they will say theirs. Another ploy is to encourage them to offer their names by enlisting the help of a third party. If you are at some gathering, immediately scan the area around you for someone you know. We'll call that person Janet Smith. Call Janet over to join you and the "nameless" persons and say to them, "Do you know Janet Smith?" Doing so should prompt each nameless person to introduce himself or herself to Janet.

When You are Exceptionally Nervous

Sweaty palms, cotton mouth, and other unpleasant bodily functions are telltale signs that you're not exactly relaxed. Being visibly nervous is a frequent problem in job interviews, but it can happen in any networking encounter. Following the strategies suggested throughout this book, particularly the communication DOs and DON'Ts of Chapter 6, can give you the confidence that's needed to minimize the nervous factor. Following are some additional tips for dealing with a case of nerves.

Acknowledge the Truth

If you're talking with somebody and fear that you're really about to blow the whole meeting because of your obvious nerves, the best thing to do is openly acknowledge that you are nervous. Trying to hide it will only make you more anxious. Say something like, "I don't know why I'm nervous. I usually stay relaxed in most situations." Only do this, though, if you really think that your nervousness is so obvious that it's having a seriously adverse effect on the interaction.

Try Physical Relaxation Techniques

Make sure you're breathing! Most people actually hold their breath, or take very short breaths, when they're nervous. Pay attention to how you're taking in air and try to take a couple of slow, deep breaths before continuing to talk. If you're not face-to-face with someone (and not in the view of others who may be present), you can even force a yawn to bring about relaxation. Also take note of what you're doing with your body. Are your muscles constricted? Are your hands clinched in fists? Try to loosen your grip and relax your muscles from head to toe. The physical change should bring about a mental one.

Prevent Nervousness from Happening in the First Place

To keep your nerves from taking over at the next networking encounter, make sure you are prepared and feel confident. Having a solid handle on your strengths, goals, and objectives is an important first step. Also be sure to do whatever research is necessary to feel knowledgeable.

Quick Summary

Since networking is all about human nature in action, it is inevitably difficult, awkward, or annoying at times.

The following "difficult" people were discussed:

➡ The Elusive Ones

➡ The False Promisers

➡ The Rejectors

➡ The Pains in Your Neck

Strategies were offered for dealing with each type.

Difficult situations described included these:

➡ When You Put Your Foot in Your Mouth

➡ When You Just Don't Click

➡ When You Forget a Name

➡ When You Are Exceptionally Nervous

Strategies were offered for getting through these sticky situations when they occur.

12

Networking for Introverts: 25 Painless Tips

One can acquire everything in solitude but character.

—STENDHAL

When I set out to write a book on networking, I knew that I wanted to devote an entire chapter to the networking concerns of shy people and other introverted types. Through my counseling sessions with clients and in networking workshops I conduct, I constantly come across people who admit to feeling uneasy about networking because of their tendency to be a bit reserved, introspective, or downright shy. Thus, I am frequently reminded that there is a definite need for networking advice tailored specifically to introverts. I also wanted to include this chapter out of a personal connection to the topic. You know from the preface of this book that I make no secret of the fact that I'm not a natural born networker. (If you skipped the preface—as most people do!—you might want to go back and read it now because it is not only a prelude for the whole book, but is particularly relevant to this chapter.)

What's an Introvert Doing Writing a Book on Networking?!

I asked myself the same question before taking on this task! After years of struggling to incorporate networking comfortably into my professional life, I have learned that networking is a skill that can be learned. It's a skill I have developed, and I enjoy showing others how they can too. That's why I wanted to write this book. I wanted to show introverts that they *can* be successful networkers. It just takes a little determination, a willingness to move past the boundaries of your comfort zone, and an understanding of effective networking strategies. I also wanted to write this book for extroverts who may find networking to be such a second nature to them that they never step back and assess their networking technique. Because I have had to acquire networking skills rather than possess them innately, I have had to examine the networking process closely to see what works and what doesn't. This book gives me an opportunity to pass that information along to both introverts and extroverts.

In the story that I recounted in the preface, I shared that I can fairly easily masquerade as an outgoing person, but that my preference is for being a bit of a loner. If you're reading this chapter because you are something of a loner too, or reserved when in groups, then you probably know what I'm talking about. It's the anxiety that creeps in when you have to make a phone call to someone you don't know, or the discomfort you feel when walking into a room full of strangers. It's those sweaty palms that you get when having to speak in public or the awkwardness of trying to make small talk with someone you don't know very well.

There may also be some of you who don't necessarily get nervous when interacting with other people, but who simply prefer to keep to yourself.

You may feel fairly confident in social interactions, but your preference is for more independent, solitary activities. Being "in the thick of things" with other people is simply not a priority for you. That's what true introversion is all about; being introverted does not necessarily mean you are shy.

In the 1920s and 1930s, the Swiss psychologist Carl Jung wrote extensively about personality differences among people and developed a system for psychological types, which is the basis for much modern day personality testing, career counseling, and psychotherapy. (See Appendix D for a description of the Myers-Briggs Type Indicator, a popular personality test based on Jungian concepts.) Among the psychological types are the introverts, who according to Jung, have a basic preference for focusing their attention inwardly on their thoughts and impressions. Introverts prefer to be reflective and are usually happiest when they are occupied with projects that let them be alone much of the time. Extroverts, on the other hand, prefer to focus their attention outwardly on the people and activities around them. Introverts are not necessarily shy by definition but simply have a different orientation to the world than do the extroverts. They are therefore much less likely to be inclined toward networking. If someone not only has this introverted orientation to the world but also happens to be shy, timid, or reserved, networking is going to be that much harder.

How Introverts and Extroverts Differ

Clinical psychologists David Keirsey and Marilyn Bates, specialists in psychological types, describe the difference between introverts and extroverts in their book *Please Understand Me* (Prometheus Nemesis Book Company: Del Mar, CA, 1984, p. 15): "While the extravert [*sic*] is sociable, the introvert is territorial. That is, he desires space: private places in the mind and private environmental places. Introverts seem to draw their energies from a different source than do extraverts. Pursuing solitary activities, working quietly alone, reading, meditating, participating in activities which involve few or no other people—these seem to charge the batteries of the introvert. Thus, if an extreme introvert goes to a party, after a 'reasonable' period of time—say, half an hour—he is ready to go home. For him the party is over. He is no party pooper; rather he was pooped by the party. This is not to say that introverts do not like to be around people. Introverts enjoy interacting with others, but it drains their energy in a way not experienced by extraverts. Introverts need to find quiet places and solitary activities to recharge, while these activities exhaust the extravert. If the latter goes to a library to do research, for example, he may have to exercise strong will power to prevent himself, after fifteen minutes or so, from taking a 'short brain break' and striking up a conversation with the librarian. It is quite the opposite with an introvert, who can remain only so long in interaction with people before he depletes his reserves."

Unfortunately for introverts, it's getting more and more difficult to succeed professionally without developing a broad range of connections to other people. There simply is no such thing as a job or career field in which you can be rewarded entirely for what you know and how well you do your work.

You not only have to do your job well, but also must make sure that others know you're doing your job well. This is especially true if you are self-employed. Word-of-mouth publicity is widely regarded as one of the keys to running just about any type of small business or consulting practice. Remember, it's not just what you know that counts, it's who knows that you know what you know. Visibility is key. This can be a real pain in the neck for introverts who would rather focus on their work than on their relationships at work. And, it can be downright painful for shy types who cringe at the thought of self-promotion. I have good news and bad news for introverted or shy readers. The bad news is that networking as a means of career survival is here to stay. The good news is that networking is most definitely a skill that can be learned.

How to Have the WRONG Attitude Toward Networking

"I'm Nobody! Who are you?
Are you—Nobody—Too?
Then there's a pair of us?
Don't tell! they'd advertise—
   you know!
How dreary—to be—
   Somebody!
How public—like a Frog—
To tell one's name—the
   livelong June—
To an admiring Bog!"

—EMILY DICKINSON, CA. 1861

25 Networking Tips for Introverts

Using the techniques advocated throughout this book is one way to learn the art of networking. Sometimes, though, all the best strategies in the world are not enough if seeking connections with others and promoting yourself just seem to go against your grain. That's why I've singled out twenty-five tips especially for introverts here in this chapter. By applying these tips, you will be able to network in ways that are comfortable for you and that fit your preferred way of communicating with the world, instead of having to transform yourself magically into an extrovert.

As discussed in the introduction of this book, networking works best when it's conducted in a way that fits your personality. This approach is particularly relevant for introverts or shy types. So many people don't even attempt networking because it seems like an alien way of being and thus a task impossible to fit into their daily lives. That's unfortunate because the process can be quite rewarding and occasionally even fun, once you get the hang of it.

On the following pages, I provide tips to make networking a little less painful. You will recognize some of these as being the same techniques I've recommended elsewhere in the book. I don't claim that each of these tips is unique to introverts. What I do in this tip list, however, is show how you, as an introvert, can put a unique twist on the same techniques that extroverts might use. You can think of these tips as "coping mechanisms" of sorts. They are ways to employ tried-and-true networking principles in a manner that fits your own personality style.

1. **Take baby steps.** Don't try to become a master networker overnight. A common mistake introverts make is to wake up one day and announce to themselves, "Today I'm going to become an active networker!" That proclamation is, unfortunately, about as likely to succeed as announcing that you're going to lose weight or quit smoking once and for all. If networking has not been a regular part of your life, and if it is not a comfortable process for you, then you need to take it slowly. If you try to tackle too much at once, you're likely to get discouraged or to burn out and give up. Try instead to take "baby steps" and let your confidence build slowly with each positive experience. You're more likely to succeed that way.

The Danger of Taking On Too Many Networking Activities

I frequently work with introverted or shy clients who try to take on too many networking activities and end up getting overwhelmed by the process. One such client was Roger—an administrative assistant for a large insurance company who was completing his bachelor's degree in computer science at night. Roger had just two more semesters of classes to complete for his degree and then hoped to get a job as a computer programmer, either with his current employer or elsewhere. He came to me to plan a strategy for making the career transition. In our first appointment, I encouraged him to start networking long before he needed a job. We discussed all the ways that networking could facilitate his career transition and position him for a good job. He left that appointment with a list of networking activities I recommended for him. These included having strategy sessions with classmates, professors, and alumni; joining associations for computer professionals and attending their meetings and conferences and reading their publications; and getting to know people in the information technology department of his company. I warned Roger, however, that he did not need to do all of these things at once or in a short period of time, especially considering he had told me that networking was hard for him and that he had never really done much of it. Even though I stressed that he should just try a few of the recommendations on the list rather than try to tackle them all, he said he was eager to get going and wanted to do as much as possible as quickly as possible.

Roger was scheduled to return to my office three weeks later to discuss his progress and plan the next steps. When he came in, he was almost embarrassed to admit that he had accomplished very little since his last meeting with me. Even though I had suggested that he see networking as a slow process and that he take just a few steps to get started, he had nevertheless felt overwhelmed because he had tried to do too much. After a week of making phone calls to try to set up meetings, he began to feel burned out and simply gave up. I discussed with Roger that his reaction was normal and reminded him that change—that is, becoming a skilled networker—is a process that takes time. We then agreed to work out a detailed plan that included a manageable number of networking activities per week. He soon became more motivated and came back to subsequent appointments with great progress to report.

2. **Don't assume you're being a pest.** Introverts tend to assume that they'll be bothering others if they contact them. Before making phone calls or approaching people in group settings, introverts often worry that they'll be seen as pests. While this perception is almost always wrong, it is understandable that introverts might feel this way.

   When assuming that they're bothering people, introverts might be projecting their own feelings onto others. Since introverts often prefer to be left alone—to do their work without interruptions or not to have their "own little world" invaded—they can erroneously assume that other people feel the same way. I know I fall into this trap frequently. If I'm sitting at my desk engrossed in a solitary project that involves thought and concentration, I don't particularly welcome a ringing telephone or other such interruption. As a result, I tend to project those same feelings onto others. So, before making a phone call, I often hesitate and wrongly assume that the person I've thought of calling won't want to hear from me. When I actually do make the call, though, I find that my concerns could not have been further from the truth.

   So, before you assume you're going to be a pest if you try to make contact with someone, think twice. Most people will be glad to hear from you. According to research that has been conducted on personality types, approximately 75 percent of the American population is estimated to be extroverted, so chances are high that most people you reach out to will welcome the contact.

3. **Rely on your supporters.** Of all the STARS in your network, the supporters are especially important for keeping you motivated and positive as you attempt to network. If you find that networking is something of a struggle for you because it is not second nature, you might be particularly susceptible to feelings of rejection or discouragement. As discussed in chapter 11, the networking process invariably brings challenges that can elicit less than positive feelings. This may be even more true for introverts or shy types. If you already feel as if you're coming into the networking game with something of a handicap (because you are not naturally outgoing or people-oriented), it may be particularly difficult to ride out the rough times. In

those cases, you need to have supporters you can turn to for encouragement and empathy along the way.

4. **Get the competitive juices flowing.** Try to remember that lots of people, who aren't half as capable, qualified, talented, and nice as you, are getting ahead simply because they connect with others and make themselves visible. This is the case for many clients I work with who lament the fact that they have been passed over for promotions or raises or haven't been able to get a business off the ground. They usually are aware that the people who are getting ahead of them aren't necessarily any better qualified but simply are more visible or more well-connected. What they aren't usually aware of, however, is that they can turn this negative fact into a positive result. What I mean by this is that they need to stop complaining about the injustice in that situation and start using it to get their competitive juices flowing.

Even people who don't consider themselves to be all that competitive by nature can usually muster up some competitive drive when they see how unfair it is that less-qualified colleagues are getting ahead.

5. **Rest on your laurels.** Always have in the forefront of your mind a repertoire of situations in which you excelled at an activity that wasn't a solitary one. Remember the times you've been successful in group endeavors or one-on-one interactions with others and keep these in mind to propel you confidently into the future.

I have to use this trick all the time to boost my confidence before I go into certain situations. Even though I have spoken in public thousands of times, for example, I still have to remind myself each time that I will do OK. I have led workshops for groups as small as ten people, taught classes to twenty or thirty students, and given formal talks in front of audiences of hundreds, but each time I approach a new group situation, I still have some of the same fears I had the first time I ever did any of that. Sure, some of the concerns go away with time. I no longer worry that I'll make a fool of myself—forgetting what I'm supposed to say, or tripping on my way to the podium. Instead, the fears that linger are those that most any introvert has: How will I connect with the people in this group? What will they think of me? I also still have some of these same concerns when I anticipate one-on-one interactions as well.

So how do I counter these fears? I remind myself how I have felt in the past after rewarding individual or group encounters. I try to remember that "high" I feel after a really successful class I've taught or after a great conversation with someone at a professional conference. I try to remember times when I have connected successfully with people and felt how rewarding it is to do so. These recollections then give me the courage—and encouragement—to face the next networking situation.

6. **Be a leader.** Introverts don't always seek leadership roles because these positions inevitably require such dreaded tasks as committee meetings and team projects. While that may be true, it *is* possible to find more behind-the-scenes leadership roles such as being a newsletter editor or the secretary for a professional association. These positions can play to your strengths—organizational or writing abilities perhaps—while not forcing you to be too outgoing or political.

   Another advantage of any type of leadership position is that it gives you a built-in excuse for connecting with people. It's one thing to be just a member of a professional organization and call up someone you don't know on the membership roster; it's another thing to be able to call that person and say, "Hi, I'm the new Program Committee Chairperson for the XYZ Association." Having to contact people because of your official responsibilities enables you to establish relationships with people you might otherwise have never met.

   If your schedule or workload precludes your taking a leadership role, consider other ways to be involved on an official level but with less of a long-term commitment. You might join a committee to plan one particular event, or serve as a host at an event. You could volunteer, for example, to be the person handing out name tags at the front table of a networking meeting. It's often easier to meet and greet than to meet and mingle!

7. **Don't go it alone.** If you have to attend some group meeting or large conference, try to take a friend or colleague with you. Strength in numbers can make the experience less intimidating. Be sure, though, that you don't spend all your time talking to your companion and not making new contacts. It's ideal if your companion is a good mixture of introvert and extrovert—too much introversion, and neither of you will meet anyone; too much extroversion, and you'll be left in the dust while your friend is off schmoozing.

   A little networking trick I suggest for these situations is to make a pact with your friend that you will separate from each other for a certain period of time—maybe half an hour or an hour, depending on the total length of the event—and agree to get back together at a specified time. You can make this something of a contest by seeing who can meet the most new people during that time. (Yes, I know I've said throughout this book that networking is not entirely a numbers game, but when you're getting your feet wet in the networking process, this sort of contest can be a valuable exercise. Having to introduce yourself to a lot of people can be a good way to force yourself headlong into the networking process.) If you would prefer to take a more in-depth approach to your networking encounters at that particular event, the objective of the contest could be to see who can make a meaningful connection during the specified period of time.

   While these exercises can be valuable ways to get a feel for networking, remember that they are just exercises. At some point, you will need to venture into group settings without a companion as your security blanket. Or, when with a companion, you will eventually need to network naturally—not because you're in the midst of a competition.

8. **Enlist a spokesperson.** As an introvert or shy person, you might have names of potentially valuable contacts languishing in your contact management system or on slips of paper tacked to your bulletin board. Even though you know it would be in your best interest to call them, something keeps you from doing so. Perhaps it's the "I'll just be seen as a pest" factor described in Tip #2. Or, maybe you just don't know what to say to them. Whatever the reason, you need to

find a way to make contact with people rather than miss out on valuable opportunities.

If you're hesitant to contact someone you don't know, consider having another person act as a go-between for you. If someone in your network has given you the name of a colleague, ask your contact to call the person first for you to "warn them" that you'll be calling. Most people are willing to do this.

9. **Don't underestimate the power of listening.** Networking can seem at times as if it's all about talking. As an introvert, you might worry that you'll never be a successful networker because you don't have the gift of the gab. Don't despair. Listening is just as important as talking when it comes to establishing relationships with others. Introverts often make good listeners, and there's nothing extroverts like better than having someone listen to them talk. So, don't feel you have to keep up the conversation as much as the other person. Listening well is a valuable and appreciated talent.

10. **Don't sweat the small stuff (small talk in this case).** Small talk is just what it sounds like: small. Most people don't expect you to come up with incredibly witty or profound comments when you first meet them. A sense of humor or some profound insight is nice, but there's nothing wrong with a mundane comment to break the ice like, "Large turnout, isn't it? or "This is great dip." Asking a question is often a great way to initiate a conversation. You might ask someone a question about the speaker you're about to hear; or after a lecture or meeting, you can ask what someone thought of the event. Opening with a question is a great way to draw out the other person and get a conversation going.

11. **Like birds of a feather, flock together.** If you really find group interactions difficult, survey the group for other people who look as if they are also uncomfortable and approach them. It's a lot easier to get into the networking game when you start by mingling with other introverts rather than with the intimidating woman in red who's surrounded by a phalanx of fans in the center of the room. Just don't get stuck with the introverts all night, though. At some point you do have to leave the nest and talk to the woman in red.

12. **Make the most of what you know.** Remember that what you know is just as important as who you know when it comes to successful networking. This fact comes in particularly handy for introverts. Unlike extroverts, we're likely to be the ones who did take the time to read that industry newsletter cover-to-cover. We're the ones who consider a quiet afternoon in the library or surfing the Internet to be anything but boring. In short, introverts like to know stuff. (Extroverts like to know things too, of course, but they're often more likely to keep up with people than with information.)

    Rather than fight your introverted tendencies, look at them as trump cards in the game of networking. Let people get to know you as the person they can call for the latest information on whatever is relevant to your field. Also, take the initiative to pick up the phone and share your findings with others. Calling with a valuable tidbit of information may be more comfortable for you than calling someone just to chitchat. So, if you worry that you're not going to dazzle people with your outgoing personality, then at least you can dazzle them with your knowledge.

13. **Rehearse, rehearse, rehearse.** If your phone calls are littered with uhs and ums, or if you tend to be tongue-tied when meeting someone new, try planning and practicing what you're going to say. It's likely that you find yourself having the same sort of conversations over and over with members of your network or with new people you are approaching. You might be trying to convey information about your business or are requesting fact-finding missions or strategy sessions. Whatever the nature of your conversations tends to be, it is helpful to streamline what you say. Your personal pitch (see chapter 5) is one way to do that. You may also, though, need to plan more extensive conversations.

    By suggesting that you rehearse conversations—or your side of a conversation at least—I don't mean to imply that conversations are perfectly predictable. You never know what the other person is going to say to you. You can, however, think through in advance what you plan to say, and then be prepared to make adjustments when you get into the real situation.

You also don't need to memorize scripts of what you will say word-for-word, because that's just likely to make you even more nervous. You also don't want to come across as sounding too rehearsed or robotic. It is helpful, nonetheless, to practice your side of typical conversations—perhaps with the help of a friend to simulate a two-way interaction. Doing so will help you be less tongue-tied when the real occasion arises.

14. **Get your nose out of that book!** It's easy to get stuck in the library or at the computer and never make it out into the world to meet someone. Even though you learned in Tip #12 that your knowledge can be an asset in networking, try to resist the temptation to isolate yourself completely. You're just delaying the inevitable. You have to get out there eventually.

15. **Leave a brief message at the tone.** There's nothing like having to leave a voice-mail or answering-machine message to bring out the insecurities in an introvert. If you find that you freeze up or babble incoherently when leaving messages, then get in the habit of taking some time before you pick up the phone to plan what you'll say if the person doesn't answer. Don't write out a script because your message will come across unnaturally. Do, though, list the main points you need to cover in the message. I also sometimes jot down key phrases next to certain points if I want to remember to say something in a particular way.

16. **Don't keep it to yourself.** Introverts are champions at keeping things to themselves. It's not that we mean to be secretive or selfish; we just tend to be somewhat self-sufficient when it comes to dealing with most issues of daily life. If you have some news or a problem to solve, try picking up the phone and telling someone about it, instead of mulling it over indefinitely by yourself.

Introverts tend to contact people only over the "big" things, like when they need some urgent information or advice about a major issue. Only when they see that a situation is too big or difficult to handle on their own do they reach out for help. The same is often true for announcing news as well. As an introvert, you might be more likely to pick up the phone and tell a colleague that you have a new job or that you're getting married than you are to call and tell someone about the interesting meeting you just attended or to pass on some fun and harmless gossip. Again, the psychology behind this is that introverts worry that they will bother people, so they tend to reach out to others only when they are really worried or really excited about something. Try, instead, to get in the habit of connecting with people over the small things—not just the big ones. Doing so enables you to develop better ongoing relationships and ensures that your contacts are there for you when you do need to share the big stuff.

17. **Attend events that have a purpose.** If you're likely to be uncomfortable or nervous at events that are solely networking opportunities, then instead try to attend events that have a purpose, such as educational or cultural seminars. Interactive classes and workshops are especially good bets since they often have a built-in agenda that involves structured networking. Plus, as an introvert, you naturally enjoy the world of ideas and thought, and educational settings are likely to be comfortable for you.

18. **Write often.** If you just can't get yourself to pick up the phone and make a cold call, or even a cool call, then consider writing. As discussed in chapter 6, written communication is often an effective way to connect with others. Sending a letter of introduction first can make the follow-up phone call less nerve-racking.

    While you do need to stretch past your comfort zone and get used to calling people more than you are naturally inclined to do, there's nothing wrong with making the most of written communication. As I discussed in Tip #12 ("make the most of what you know"), playing to your strengths is important. As an introvert, you might be so reluctant to call people that you never contact them at all. In that case, written communication is better than no communication at all. And, it might even be better than phone contact if you express yourself more articulately and convincingly in writing. So, if you have a preference for writing people, make the most of that tendency. Just don't let it keep you from having telephone and face-to-face contact as well. Once you've broken the ice by writing, you then have to maintain a relationship through direct contact.

19. **Get out among them.** Do you tend to hole up in your office or other workplace? This tendency is particularly problematic for home-based workers, people who sit at a desk most of the time, and anyone with a busy schedule that keeps them working long hours. No matter how much work you have to do, it helps just to get up out of the house or office occasionally and go out among people—any people. Just walk around the block, take a stroll through the park, or do anything that brings a change of scenery and a reminder that you're not alone. Although walking isn't directly networking, it does propel you out of your own little world and brings about a powerful mindset change that can lead you into networking activity.

20. **Be positive.** It's easy to become pessimistic and assume that your networking efforts will be fruitless. This is actually a defense mechanism that keeps us from being disappointed if, in fact, we do fail. Before you declare that it's not going to be worth your time to talk to Joe Shmoe or to attend a particular event, stop and think. Do you have any rational proof that the prospects are dim or are you just afraid to do so? Be honest with yourself, and if you think a networking encounter could truly be valuable, then stretch past your comfort zone and give it a shot. Almost all encounters are worthwhile, for the practice if for no other reason.

    If you *do* experience some encounters that are less than positive, try not to let the negative experience get to you. As you learned in Tip #1, networking sometimes involves taking baby steps. It is a process that evolves over time. It's easy to let one negative encounter turn you off of networking for good, but don't let it. Remember to take networking one step at a time, and try to stay positive.

21. **Consider seeking professional help.** If you think your shyness or introversion is more than just a mild nuisance, you might need to consult a psychologist, therapist, or other mental health counselor. Shyness that seriously hinders your social interactions can keep you from doing what you need to do, and you may benefit from professional treatment. Appendix C suggests ways to find someone who can help.

Online Resources for Shy Types

The Shyness Institute at www.shyness.com

A shyness newsgroup at alt.support.shyness

22. **Be comfortable in your own skin.** Sometimes reluctance to network results from insecurity about your appearance. The problem might be with your wardrobe, an accent you're embarrassed by, or something about your physical appearance. While physical attractiveness is by no means a prerequisite for being a successful networker, the "package" you present to others is important. If something about your outward image is dragging down your confidence, consider fixing what's fixable and learn to make the most of what's not. Appendix C tells you how to find image consultants and other types of professionals, including psychotherapists, who can help you be more comfortable with how you come across. Remember also that your true image comes from the inside, so being comfortable in your own skin is really about being comfortable with who you are, not how you look.

23. **Remember that networking is as much a skill as it is an innate talent.** As you get started networking, or change the way you're networking now, keep in mind that effective techniques can be learned. Introverts are often overly hard on themselves, saying things like "This should come more easily to me. It shouldn't be such a struggle." Don't expect miracles—at least not right away! Learning anything new takes time (and practice), especially when you're learning a new way of thinking and acting. Be patient and pat yourself on the back with each forward step you take.

One Introvert's Success Story

For several years, I have followed the progress of Tom, one of my favorite former clients, who happens to be extremely introverted. Tom is an accountant who had been with a large firm that folded because of financial difficulties and disagreements among the partners. Tom had always enjoyed his work as an accountant but had never liked the politics of working in a large organization and never really felt that he fitted in. He wanted more autonomy and independence in his career, so he decided to strike out on his own and start an accounting practice rather than go back to another firm. He did so with considerable trepidation, however, because he knew that running his own business would require a great deal of selling. With the exception of a few long-standing clients who would follow him from his old job into his practice, he knew that clients would not just be walking through the door. He would have to be a more active networker to spread the word about his services.

Now that Tom is established in his business, he is no longer a client of mine, but we get together from time to time to discuss each other's businesses (and to commiserate about being self-employed introverts!). The last time I met with Tom, he had been in business for about a year-and-a-half and was pleased to report that he felt he had actually mastered the skill of networking. He said that he knows it will always be a bit of a struggle and will never be his favorite professional activity, but once he realized that networking is a skill that can be developed and refined with effort and practice, he found that there was hope. He told me how he saw progress in himself from month to month. Each month he would stretch just a bit more into unfamiliar territory (the territory of extroverts), and each successful attempt gave him the impetus to stretch a bit further the next time. He was gradually having more referral meetings, making more cold calls to potential clients, and attending more meetings. He had also published an article in a professional journal and spoken at a conference. I was proud of Tom's accomplishments and inspired by them as well.

24. **Networking is like air.** A funny thing happens when introverts get involved in networking. They find that networking is as natural as the air around us. They find that it's been happening around them among people from all walks of life with all sorts of objectives. We introverts just tend not to notice until we watch for it. When you reach that point of recognition, you find that some of the mystery is gone. Networking seems like an ordinary part of daily life rather than something you have to think about constantly. That outlook may

seem a little remote if you're just getting started, but all I ask is that you have a little faith that it's true.

25. **Just do it.** Keep in mind the serendipity factor that has been discussed in other chapters. You never know where a job, a lead, or some good advice is going to turn up. Sure, networking can be difficult, anxiety-provoking, and just a plain old pain-in-the-neck, but at some point you have to abandon all the excuses, take a deep breath, and just do it.

Quick Summary

If you're an introvert, you are not alone in finding networking difficult or uncomfortable. You have a preference for being self-sufficient, independent, or nonrelationship-oriented, all of which can lead to a reluctance to network or an awkward networking style.

Not all introverts are shy. As defined by the psychologist Carl Jung, introversion is merely a preference for focusing inward rather than outward. Introverts often tend to be shy, quiet, or reserved, but they aren't always. They simply have more of a need for being alone frequently than do extroverts and more of a tendency to live in their own world instead of seeking social opportunities. Introverts aren't afraid of people or unwilling to socialize, they just need time alone or perhaps with one close friend to get their energy back after being around a lot of people.

Just like death and taxes, there's no escaping networking. Unfortunately for introverts, there is no such thing as a job or career field in which you are rewarded solely for what you know and how well you do your work. Networking is an inescapable fact of life. You will be better off if you embrace it and do it as well as you can.

Networking is a learned skill. Even if you aren't naturally endowed with the gift of gab and a tendency to reach out and connect with others, you can still become a skilled networker. The techniques suggested throughout this book can be useful for introverts, but putting them into practice might require coping mechanisms to "masquerade" as an extrovert. This chapter listed 25 tips that can serve as those coping mechanisms.

CHAPTER

13

It's Never Too Early to Start:
25 Networking Tips for Students

Education is not the filling of a pail, but the lighting of a fire.

—WILLIAM BUTLER YEATS

Networking as a student? Isn't that just for experienced people in the work world? Not at all! Consider these real-life examples that demonstrate the importance of starting to network early.

Jim was a high school senior with a history of perfect grades and stellar test scores. He was certain that after all his hard work, he would get accepted to at least one of the highly selective colleges to which he had applied. But did he? Unfortunately, he didn't get into any of his top choices. The reason? He had no extracurricular activities and had only lukewarm recommendations from faculty and advisors. Jim had spent all his time in the library and hadn't bothered to get involved in campus activities and hadn't developed relationships with key people at school. In other words, he had not networked, and it cost him.

Heather was determined to get into a top-notch MBA program, but her undergraduate grades and GMAT scores were near the minimum cutoff for most of the better schools. She did, though, have a few years of excellent work experience, wrote strong application essays, and presented herself well in the admissions interview, all of which at least put her on the waiting list. How did she distinguish herself from the other candidates and move from waiting list to acceptance? She did so by networking. Heather finally got up the nerve to call an alumnus of the business school whose name she had been given several months before by an acquaintance. He was impressed with the case she presented for why his alma mater was the right fit for her career and educational goals. She also demonstrated her ability to do the work by citing some of her past accomplishments. He then offered to put in a good word for her with the admissions office. He did, and soon she was accepted.

Patricia was a thirty-eight-year-old mother of two. She had returned to college to complete the bachelor's degree she had started many years earlier. Patricia was convinced that the degree would be her one-way, nonstop ticket to a good job. After years of being denied the jobs she wanted, she was certain that a bachelor's degree was the only barrier between her and her career goals. She was determined to finish her degree as quickly as possible, and to concentrate on getting the highest grades she could. While nothing is wrong with those goals, they turned out to be not enough when it came time to get a job. After graduating, Patricia was dismayed to find that other students her age with lower grade-point averages landed the kinds of jobs she wanted, while she could barely get any interviews. The problem? One prospective employer told her that he would rather see internships and part-time jobs on her resume than "straight A's" in English and history. In other words, she could have taken a lighter course load and taken a little longer to get her degree in order to have time to gain valuable work experience. The degree alone was not the answer to her career problems. Had she been networking effectively, she might have found this out before pinning all of her hopes on the degree and grades.

But Isn't School a Time to Learn, Not to Schmooze?

While high school and college are primarily times to develop intellectually, socially, physically, creatively, and spiritually, they are also excellent places to learn and practice valuable networking skills for a future career. The school years are an excellent time to begin cultivating a circle of contacts. Even during graduate school, which is a time to specialize in an academic discipline and develop a professional knowledge base, attention must be paid to planning for the future. While impressive, those initials after your name probably won't be enough to get you to your goals.

It's easy to say you're too young, busy, or inexperienced to network. It's tempting to assume that networking is not relevant to your life as a student. It's never too early to start, though, and it's really essential for success in your post-student life (effective networking might also help your grades!). The following sections list just some of the reasons you should network while you are in high school, college, or graduate school.

Network to Get a Job

The world of work has changed dramatically in the last several years. It's no longer enough simply to have a degree and the knowledge that comes with it. To get a good job (or at least a job that doesn't require you to wear a silly hat and operate a deep fryer), you will undoubtedly have to network. Connecting with others through fact-finding missions, strategy sessions, shadowing, internships, and other methods that are described throughout this book enables you to develop relationships with people who can help you get jobs.

When you get out in the world, grades and test scores are not always important (which should come as a relief to those of you who'd like to bury your transcripts several hundred feet below ground). What does count is your ability to convey to others that you are focused, motivated, and capable of doing the job. It's a lot easier to do that when you have a network of people helping you strategize ways to get a job and perhaps even intervening on your behalf with prospective employers.

Network to Make a Good Career Choice

Most students come out of college saying, "I guess I have some skills, but I have no idea what they are. I have so many different interests, I don't know which one to turn into a career." While there are a few exceptions, most schools do not incorporate career development classes into the curriculum. Thus, one thing that most people don't learn in college is how to choose a career.

The emphasis in college—on the part of both students and advisors—is on getting internships and postgraduate jobs. You may learn how to land interesting internships, write a killer resume, and interview like a pro, but rarely do you learn the steps involved in exploring and deciding which career field you should choose. Even if your college career center offers workshops on choosing a career, or even offers individual counseling, you may not take advantage of it. It's likely that you've said, "I don't have time for any of this soul-searching or vague self-assessment stuff. I'm about to graduate and I need a job." Or, "I'm just a sophomore; I don't have to worry about all that yet."

Every job search expert knows that one of the keys to getting a job is to know what you want. The more focused you are about who you are and the more you know about the career field in which you're interviewing, the more you'll impress prospective employers. How do you get that focus? By networking, of course! As you've seen in previous chapters, talking to people about what they do and trying out career options through experiential opportunities can help you weed out the jobs you wouldn't want to do in a million years and zero in on the ones that could make you happy as a clam.

Networking for a career choice isn't just for undergrads, either. You might have gone to graduate school because you have already identified at least a general career goal. While the graduate degree will get you closer to that goal, the graduate school process often opens up new worlds that you didn't even know existed within a given field. This can leave you confused about your career focus. It's particularly important in that case to connect with alumni of your program to evaluate the pros and cons of the various options.

Network to Learn About Yourself

Unless you're going to be a perennial student or have a career as a scholar, you'll eventually be leaving behind your life as a student. It's therefore important to start seeing yourself in ways other than as a student. Networking enables you to take a look at who you are outside the classroom, and it prepares you for the change of identity that comes as you cross the border to the real world. By getting involved in campus organizations, for example, you have the chance to test your leadership skills and see if you enjoy teamwork. By visiting people at their workplace during fact-finding missions, you experience different work environments. You also learn about the different types of people whom you are likely to encounter there. You might even learn something about your own personality, style, and values. All of these experiences help you gain the self-awareness necessary for making good career decisions and for doing the self-promotion that's necessary for getting jobs (or even into the next degree program).

Network to Learn How to Be Proactive in Shaping Your Career

School makes people passive. Think about it. High school and college have built-in networks and structures to guide you through the educational process. Advisors help you plan your course of study. Teachers and professors tell you what to study and when to study it. Classmates or roommates study with you and maybe even keep tabs on your emotional state.

In grad school, you're a bit more autonomous, but still may have networking opportunities practically handed to you on a silver platter. Professors involve you in research projects, for example, and advisors take an active role in helping you obtain internships or fieldwork experience.

All of this can lead to a disease I call SES, or Student Entitlement Syndrome. It's easy to catch, but there is a cure. There's a danger in growing accustomed to the somewhat nurturing structure of the academic environment and expecting to find the same when you set out to get a job or manage your career. You won't get far in the real world with SES, though. The belief that one can sit back and wait for the job offers and promotions to pour in is a trap even the most mature, unselfish grad can unwittingly fall into. Developing networking skills while still in school, however, can equip you with a sense of self-reliance and an ability to hold your own in that real world. When reality bites, you'll know how to bite back.

Real-World Skills You're Learning in School That Come in Handy While Networking

➡ Research

➡ Writing

➡ Oral Presentation

➡ Leadership

➡ Teamwork

➡ Global Thinking

➡ Diversity Awareness

25 Networking Tips for Students

The following list contains lots of ideas for ways you can begin to practice one of the most important skills you may ever learn: networking.

1. **Get involved.** Look for ways to explore your interests, develop your skills, and satisfy your values by joining organizations that do something you care about. It really doesn't matter if you join campus clubs or off-campus organizations; the exact focus is not so important as the fact that you are getting involved. Also look into joining the student chapters of professional associations for career fields that you are considering entering. While not all associations have student divisions, many offer membership at reduced rates for students. Be sure to see Appendix B for groups you might want to join.

How Getting Involved Pays Off

Tricia was a college junior majoring in psychology who had an interest in a future career in human resources. When she expressed this interest to a counselor in the campus career office, he told her that her college used to have a student chapter of a national human resources professional association but that the chapter had been defunct for several years. The counselor said that he would gladly help her revive the chapter and serve as its advisor if Tricia would consider being its president. She readily took on the leadership role and found that it proved extremely valuable in getting her postgraduate career launched. Through her involvement with the club during her junior and senior years, Tricia was able to meet hundreds of human resources executives who turned out to be valuable contacts when it came time to get a job after graduation. She also gained visibility in the profession while still a student by speaking at a national conference, publishing an article in the association's journal, and being featured in the newsletter. As a student interacting in professional arenas, she was something of a "novelty," making these opportunities for networking and visibility somewhat easier to come by than they would be after graduation.

2. **Attend professional conferences.** Whether you join professional associations or not, it's a good idea to attend national or regional conferences to learn more about a particular career field and to make valuable contacts. These meetings usually have reduced student rates (sometimes the regular registration fees are pretty steep). Sometimes there are special events and job fairs for student attendees. Ask your professors which conferences would be worth while for you to

attend, or contact organizations that interest you in Appendix B to find out about meetings they have scheduled.

3. **Be a leader.** Instead of just sitting on the sidelines, consider taking a leadership role of some sort in your school. Not everyone can be president of student government (nor does everyone want to be), but there are plenty of other ways to test out your leadership abilities and gain visibility.

Leadership Pays!

Students who devote time and energy to leadership positions on campus are being rewarded for their efforts. A recent survey by *U.S. News & World Report* (April 28, 1997, p. 12) reported that some colleges are now paying students salaries or giving tuition breaks for serving on student government. Annual salaries quoted ranged from $440 for the vice-president of student government at Colorado College up to a whopping $8,413 for the student body president at the University of South Florida.

4. **Make classes count.** Be on the lookout for ways to give your class projects a real-world twist. Consider, for example, designing a project or writing a paper that involves interviewing people in the business world or examining a policy that affects your community. The idea is to have an excuse to connect with the outside world in some way. These kinds of projects have been known to lead to jobs after graduation (or summer internships) based on relationships established during the project.

5. **Connect with people.** A typical high school, college, and graduate school campus is filled with a wealth of resources. Faculty members, deans, advisors, administrators, and coaches can be valuable sources of advice, guidance, and contacts. Too often, though, it's easy as a student to be hesitant about bridging the gap between you, the "lowly student," and the "almighty THEM." Or, you might be too caught up in your daily routine as a student to step back and look at how these key people can get to know you as a person and maybe even as a peer, not just as someone who shows up to class and turns in homework. Think about what you can do to change this situation.

Now is the time to start learning to cultivate professional relationships.

6. **Get to know alumni.** Just as the people on campus are valuable contacts, those who've already left the hallowed halls of your school can be important members of your network as well. They can help you make career decisions and reach your goals through FFMs and strategy sessions (see chapters 7 and 8). They can often provide leads to internships or jobs, and might even be in a position to hire you themselves. Check with your institution's career development office, guidance counselor, or alumni relations department to see how you can get in touch with alumni who do work that interests you.

Forging a Path from Campus to Career

As a high school senior, Ryan wrote a term paper for his government class on the role of "Corporate America" in politics. By interviewing numerous business executives and government officials to research his topic, and by keeping in touch with them after he finished his project, Ryan developed a large network of powerful people who came in handy later in his college career. Through these contacts, he was able to obtain a college scholarship as well as prestigious summer internships in both government and business.

When dealing with alumni, keep the following tips in mind:

> ➤ Be respectful of their time.

> ➤ Don't expect them to do everything for you.

> ➤ Be prepared with questions and clear objectives.

> ➤ Be courteous.

> ➤ Thank them promptly.

7. **Use your campus career center or guidance office.** Never again will it be so easy and convenient (and free!) to get good advice about your career as when you're a student. Your campus career center or guidance office should be an important part of your networking efforts. Think about it. The professionals in these offices come across jobs, internships, and educational opportunities and interact with large numbers of people daily. You need to get to know these counselors!

8. **Shadow.** As discussed in chapter 7, observing someone at work for a day or even part of a day is a great way to get the information you need to make career decisions and cultivate contacts. As a student, shadowing opportunities are often easy to come by as more and more high schools and colleges are establishing shadowing programs. Often held over winter or spring break, these programs match students with alumni working in careers they'd like to learn more about. If your school doesn't have an official shadowing program, ask professors or career counselors if they can help you find someone to observe.

As coordinator of the shadowing program at Barnard College in New York when I was a career counselor there, I saw how valuable the shadowing experience could be for students. I also saw some mishaps and missed opportunities, however, so I want to offer you a few pointers to help you make the most of the experience:

Always show up for your shadowing day unless you have a very good reason not to. The person you're shadowing has probably arranged her schedule around you and may have planned some special activities, so be sure to take the appointment seriously and make every effort to be there. Also, make sure that you are there on time. If you can't make it for some unavoidable reason, make sure that you get a message to the person whom you are to shadow so that she doesn't waste time waiting for you.

Tracking Down Alumni

What should you do if you attend a school that does not have an active alumni network or any official system in place for referring you to alumni? Don't despair, helpful alumni *are* out there! They just might not be listed in some handy directory or database, so you have to do a little sleuthing to find them. Ask professors in relevant departments if they've kept up with alumni doing work that interests you. Also ask your school's administrators or anyone else who is likely to keep up with alumni.

Dress appropriately for the environment you'll be visiting. Since "appropriate" can vary widely, ask someone who knows what's right. If all else fails, you can ask the person you're shadowing, because you don't have to impress the person in the same way you would if it were a job interview. The person you're observing will appreciate the fact that you want to wear something that he would approve of since he'll be introducing you around to other people at the workplace. In any case, make sure that what you wear is comfortable (particularly the shoes). If in doubt, it is always better to dress "up" than to dress "down"; so if you can't discover what is appropriate, take the better dress option. At the least, this conveys respect for the organization that you are visiting.

Once there, be very courteous and considerate of the person whom you're observing. Be on the lookout for areas of his work that might be confidential and offer to excuse yourself from the room if you think he could use some privacy for a meeting or phone conversation.

Whenever you're introduced to anyone, give a firm handshake, say your name, and express enthusiasm for being there. It's helpful to ask for the business cards of everyone you meet, so that you can contact them in the future.

Whom to Contact If You Need Help Getting Into the School of Your Choice

If you're a high school student applying to college, or a college student applying to graduate school, you might need more assistance than your school's guidance counselor has the time or resources to provide. If so, you can contact the Independent Educational Consultant's Association (IECA) at 703-591-4850 (Tel,) or 703-591-4860 (fax) for a referral to an experienced consultant in your area. They can't wave a magic wand to get you into the school of your dreams, but they can be valuable members of your network. Educational consultants provide top-notch advice and support as you go through the school selection and application process.

Prepare specific questions to ask on your shadowing day. Some of these you'll ask outright, and others you'll just keep to yourself and find answers to through observation. These questions are similar to the objectives for a fact-finding mission (as discussed in chapter 7). You're there for a reality check to find out if this type of workplace fits with who you are and what you want out of a career. The shadowing experience may also be one long strategy session if you already know you want to enter that field and just need to figure out how to do so. (See chapter 8 for a description of strategy sessions.) In that case, too, go with questions that you want to have answered.

Like all networking encounters, following up with a thank-you note is important when someone has been willing to squire you around a workplace, instead of just granting a brief phone call or face-to-face meeting. Also be sure to thank all the people you met in addition to your main "shadowee." (That's another reason for collecting business cards throughout the day.) It doesn't hurt to follow up with anyone involved in coordinating your shadowing day as well, both at your school and in the workplace (someone in the organization's human resources department, for example, might have arranged for you to shadow someone else in the company). Doing so not only is considerate, but also helps you create allies in your network for the future, rather than just one-time contacts.

9. **Be an intern.** Holding internships while in school has become a necessity in order to keep up with your competition when it comes time to look for a job. A resume without internships (or paid, part-time jobs) won't get you nearly as far as one with work experience, even if your academic record is stellar.

   Aside from the direct job hunting benefits, however, internships are also valuable networking opportunities. Whether you're interning for a few weeks over winter break or for several months during the academic year, internships expose you to many people who could become important members of your network. Since you're actually doing work as an intern and not just observing or interviewing, the people with whom you work have a chance to get to know you as a professional. This situation is fertile ground for cultivating the relationships that are the key to a strong network. So, while interning, be sure to make an extra effort to introduce yourself to people at the workplace beyond your immediate supervisor and coworkers. Also be open to projects or duties that would team you up with a wide variety of people.

10. **Help out in your community.** Like shadowing and internships, community service lets you test career fields that you're considering. It's also a way to gain valuable experience that can open doors which might otherwise be closed to you. Of course, true community service can also be done purely because you want to help in some way. There's no denying, however, that it can also be an excellent way to meet people who could be valuable strategists, targets, allied forces, role models, or supporters in your networking efforts. (See chapter 3 if you need a reminder of the STARS concept of networking.)

11. **Go on fact-finding missions.** As a student, FFMs are a particularly important feature of your networking efforts. You should be conducting lots of FFMs to get information about the career fields you're considering and to establish relationships with people in "the real world." Remember, there's much more to the work world than what you learn in class, so look for ways you can talk with people who can give you a needed reality check. For a full description of FFMs and how to handle them, see chapter 7.

12. **Conduct strategy sessions.** As with FFMs, strategy sessions are essential for bridging the gap between what you know as a student and what you need to know to transition into a career. They help you get your job search "tools" in order (resumes, letters, interviewing techniques), and they help you map out an effective strategy for getting a job. They also have an added benefit in that during the process of having a strategy session, you are developing a valuable contact. You are not only getting useful advice, but also giving someone the chance to get to know you, see how you think, and observe you "at work" in a sense. Strategy sessions are therefore one of the most important parts of your networking as a student. (For further information refer to chapter 8 for ideas of how strategy sessions fit into the job search process.)

13. **Broaden your horizons.** When you graduate from high school, college, or graduate school, you'll be entering a world that is likely to

be filled with a broad range of people from diverse backgrounds. To learn to appreciate all types of people and to learn to deal appropriately and respectfully with them, consider ways to broaden your horizons. If you tend to hang around in one clique of friends, why not make an effort to get to know someone with whom you wouldn't naturally associate? Also think about organizations you could join or social events you could attend to introduce you to a wider circle. If studying abroad is an option (or even being an exchange student at another school or college within the U.S.), that too is a great way to expand your horizons and learn valuable networking skills.

14. **Diversify.** Similar to the last point, broadening your horizons within your own scope of activities, not just people, is important as well. In other words, look for ways to make yourself a well-rounded person. As you saw in the examples at the start of this chapter, just doing your school work is not sufficient as a foundation on which to build a career. Having a diverse range of interests and experiences will not only help you get a job or get into your next academic program, but also, like Tip #13, teach you important skills for dealing with a complex world.

Why It's Important to Be Well-Rounded

When you get out of college or graduate school and try to enter the job market, you may be surprised at how much importance prospective employers place on your being well-rounded. Of course, their main concern is that you have the knowledge and experience necessary to do the job you're being hired for. But they also want to know that they are hiring people who are made up of more than grade-point-averages and summer jobs listed on a resume. When prospective employers see that you have been on sports teams, belonged to academic clubs, enjoyed art and music, and volunteered in your community, they know they're dealing with someone who is adaptable, flexible, naturally curious, and simply an interesting person. And, just as importantly, you've learned how to get along with a wide range of types of people—an essential skill for the networking you'll be doing later in your career. To be well-rounded, you don't have to be a dabbler, getting involved on a superficial level in anything and everything. Just make sure that you venture into a few arenas that expand your horizons.

15. **Start a job search club.** In addition to relying on your campus career counselors and other professionals for help, consider starting a job search club with your friends and classmates. You don't need to be experts in job search strategy to do so. Just the process of getting together with peers to discuss the ups and downs of your searches and to share leads and resources is a good start. You can also use a book like *The Very Quick Job Search* (see Appendix D for this and other resources) to guide your discussions.

16. **Don't hesitate to enlist the assistance of relatives.** You might be reluctant to let Aunt Gladys get you a job, but remember that as a student, relatives likely make up the majority of your network. You probable haven't had much of a chance to cultivate professional contacts yet. While you shouldn't expect family members to hand you a job, it is OK to let a relative pave the way. Remember that once you do get the job, it's up to you to keep it and to grow in it. Your relative can only help you get started, but after that, it's you who earns your keep. Having the assistance of a relative is nothing to be ashamed of, although you may take some heat from those who are jealous of your connections.

17. **Use the Internet.** With more and more campuses making Internet access easier, if not required, you are likely to find plenty of opportunities as a student to start networking online. If you don't have such access, check with your local public library to see if they offer access to the Internet. Suffice it to say that networking online is key for students because the Internet is "The Great Equalizer." It doesn't matter if you're a high school sophomore or president of a large company; everyone has equal access to the same people and places on the information superhighway. (For a more-detailed description of how to network electronically, refer to chapter 10.)

18. **Have a resume on hand whether you think you need it or not.** If you're not actively looking for a job, or if you're young and don't have much work experience, it's easy to assume that you don't need to have a resume. Ah, but you do! A resume is a snapshot of who you are, so even if you don't have a lot to put on it, it's helpful to have one on hand as a way of introducing yourself. Having one also shows

that you take a professional, organized approach to things. Several good books on resumes are listed in the bibliography in Appendix D.

19. **Have a business card.** If you thought a resume wasn't necessary to have, you probably think that having a business card is an even sillier idea. It's not, though. Think of it as a calling card (which is what they used to be called). What do you do when someone asks for your name and number? It's time-consuming and unprofessional to have to fish for a scrap of paper and write down the information. Wouldn't it be much easier to pull out a card that has your name, address, and phone number on it (fax number and e-mail address too if you have them)? You don't need to put a job title or company name since you're not employed full-time; just your basic contact information will do. Doing this can really set you apart from other students.

Where to Get Business Cards

Having business or calling cards made up need not be expensive. Check with an office supply or stationery store to have some nice, but reasonably priced, cards made up for you. If you're handy on the computer, you can also create your own with software templates and perforated card sheets for laser printers. These are available from mail-order catalogs and online sources. The best of these are Paper Direct at (800) 272-7377 and www.paperdirect.com as well as Paper Access at (800) PAPER-01 and www.paperaccess.com. The do-it-yourself version is especially useful if your address is likely to change often (not unusual for a student). You can print up a small number of cards at one time and then print a new batch when you need to change the information on them. (You can also print both your current address and your permanent home address on the cards as well. Doing so ensures that people can get in touch with you even after long periods of no contact.)

20. **Find role models.** As discussed in chapter 3, role models are an important component of any network, but they are particularly valuable for students. As a student, whether you're 18 or 48, you're likely to feel that you're starting at "square one" when it comes to a career. Having people who can guide you along the way and provide

a good example for you is all the more important for you as a student. Be on the lookout for people who can fill this role and start developing relationships with them.

21. **Take advantage of public speaking opportunities.** You don't have to start your own cable TV show like Wayne and Garth or go on a worldwide speaking tour, but you can look for less ambitious ways to get in front of groups to say a few words. Some classes will require this if oral reports are part of your assignments. If not, look for opportunities to speak before groups, such as introducing speakers at an assembly, giving a speech to campaign for a classmate running for student government, or accompanying a professor to present a paper at a conference. Whatever the occasion, public speaking is an important skill to acquire. It is also a great way to gain visibility, which can lead to opportunities down the road. If the thought of all this terrifies you, consult some of the books on public speaking that are listed in Appendix D.

22. **Publish an article.** As with public speaking, gaining visibility and establishing yourself as a professional can also be accomplished by getting something you have written published. If you're in high school or college, a published article might simply be a piece in your school newspaper or a letter to the editor of your local paper. In college and graduate school, however, you might also have the opportunity to publish an essay or research report in a professional journal, particularly if you collaborate with a professor on a project. However you do it, published writing is a great way to get a strong portfolio started. (See Tip #25 for a discussion of portfolios.)

Getting Your Name in Print

If you have a knack for writing, don't assume that your publishing opportunities are limited only to the school newspaper. Keisha, now a journalism major at a large university, had applied to college with an impressive portfolio of writing samples. During high school she was a staff writer for her school paper, but she also frequently wrote letters-to-the-editor of her city's daily newspaper as well. An editor there began to notice that her perspective as a student and a teenager would be a nice addition to his paper. So, he invited her to contribute occasional editorials on issues that were particularly relevant to her generation. When it came time to apply to colleges with competitive journalism departments, these published articles helped to distinguish Keisha's application from all the other students who had only high school publications in their portfolios.

23. **Learn and practice good time management habits.** As you may have gathered from the rest of this book, networking can be time-consuming. That's why it's important to start acquiring good habits regarding time and organization early in your networking life. Now is the time to learn how to get to appointments promptly, schedule assignments and meetings in an appointment book, and keep neat and tidy files of information you collect.

24. **Get in the habit of writing thank-you notes.** Another good habit is that of writing notes to let people know you appreciated something they've done for you. It's usually obvious that you should write a thank-you note after a fact-finding mission or an interview, but did you think of writing notes to people you worked with during an internship? How about to a professor for a great class? (Write the note *after* you get the grade so it doesn't look as if you're just kissing up for an A!) Acknowledging people who do you a favor, provide an opportunity, or inspire you not only is a nice thing to do, but also keeps them as active members of your network.

25. **Start a portfolio.** As described in chapter 5, portfolios are folders or notebooks that contain information which documents your accomplishments and provides evidence of your skills. Portfolios usually include letters of recommendation, writing samples, and other documents that show relevant work you've done. The portfolio is something you take to interviews, internships, or educational programs to which you're applying. Your portfolio is a supplement to your resume and other self-promotion materials. While it's not a requirement that you have a portfolio, portfolios are becoming more common. In order to keep up with your competition, consider creating and maintaining your own portfolio while you're still in school.

If you're an artist or designer of some sort, a portfolio contains samples of your work and takes on a whole new meaning. Instructors and people who work in the arts can advise you on how to assemble an art-based portfolio.

Quick Summary

It's never too early to begin to network. In today's world, a degree alone won't get you a good job. You have to start developing contacts early, both to help you explore your career options and to get leads to employment opportunities.

Use the 25 ideas presented in this chapter to help you begin networking while you are still a student.

Doing unto Others—
The Art and Science of Giving Back

Thanksgiving comes before Christmas.

—PETER KREEFT

"Could I have a few minutes of your time?"

"Would you mind giving me the names of other people I should talk to?"

"Do you have any suggestions for how I can improve my resume?"

"Can you advise me how I might expand my business?"

Networking can appear to be a very self-centered activity. It sometimes seems to be summed up best in the phrase "How can you help ME?" but, in fact, it is *not all* about you. The needs of the people who help you should be as much on your mind as your own needs. People in your network deserve your thanks, and they might need some assistance themselves. After all, they have careers and businesses, too.

It's important, therefore, not only to show your appreciation through thank-you notes or small gifts, but also to return a favor when the opportunity arises. The "Ways to Show Appreciation" section of this chapter discusses specific methods of thanking and giving back to people in your network.

Always remember that networking is based on cultivating and nurturing relationships, not on on one-time interactions, so consider small (or sometimes large) ways that you can do nice things for people in your network—often for no particular reason. The "Performing Random Acts of Kindness" section of this chapter gives you some ideas of ways to do so. Such acts might include calling someone when you come across an article that would be of interest to that individual or volunteering to help out at the person's favorite charity. These not only are nice things to do, but also have indirect benefits to you in that they strengthen relationships and keep you visible.

The final aspect of giving discussed in this chapter is that of developing other people. Whether you are well established in your career or just getting started, it's likely that you have something to offer someone else. Serving as a mentor or just giving occasional advice is an important responsibility that we all have. Chances are that you wouldn't be where you are without the help of others, so why not give something back by helping out someone who's a few steps behind you in his or her career or business?

In the remainder of this chapter, we take a look at the art and science of giving back in detail.

Ways to Show Your Appreciation

Thanking people who give you advice, leads, or any kind of assistance is not just a nice thing to do, it's an absolute necessity. When people take time out of their busy schedules or go out on a limb for you, the least you can do is take a few minutes to write a quick note or call to say thanks. Perhaps you can even spend a few dollars on a small gift.

There are many ways to show your appreciation, depending on the size of the favor done for you, the nature of your relationship with the person you're thanking, and your budget. The following are typical ways of giving thanks, with tips on how to know which networking situations each is appropriate for.

Thank-You Letters

Thank-you notes should be sent promptly after every fact-finding mission, strategy session, referral meeting, job interview, phone conversation, or other encounter in which you receive advice, guidance, support, or leads. Showing appreciation by a thank-you note is not only a common courtesy but also an opportunity to remind someone of your career goals and objectives or, if self-employed, your services and products. Because this piece of correspondence should contain more than just thanks, it's helpful to be familiar with the following six components of a networking thank-you letter.

⇒ **Thank the person.** Your letters should, of course, thank the recipients for their time, sharing of expertise, and anything else given. Thanks are usually given in the first sentence or two to make it clear that the purpose of the letter is to show appreciation. You might say, for example, "Dear Bob, You were more than generous with your time on the phone yesterday, and I truly appreciate it." Or, "Dear Harriette, I want to thank you for meeting with me on Monday. Knowing how busy your schedule is, I particularly appreciated your fitting me in on short notice and taking the time to share your wisdom with a newcomer to the world of entrepreneurship."

⟶ **Acknowledge what was helpful**. In addition to thanking someone for help, it is important to acknowledge which specific information or assistance was particularly useful and why. For example, the letter begun to Harriette in #1 could continue with, "I particularly found your comments on the marketing strategy portion of my business plan useful. As I told you, I had been concerned about how best to survey the competition without giving away the unique ideas for my business, but your suggestions can solve that problem."

⟶ **State how you'll follow through on suggestions**. People who give advice like to know that you'll follow through on at least some of what they suggest. Otherwise, what was the point of sharing experience, knowledge, and insight with you? It is considerate to let people know that you took what they said seriously and plan to follow through (or have already followed through). The Harriette letter could go on to say, "I have started researching those Web sites you suggested and can already see that they will be very useful while I develop my marketing plan.

⟶ **Promote yourself.** A thank-you note can also be a place to remind the recipient of your career or business goals and why you deserve to reach those goals. Remember that every networking interaction offers the chance to promote yourself subtly, but effectively, so that others see you as a worthy candidate for the assistance and opportunities you seek. The letter to Harriette could also express the writer's enthusiasm for the ideas and confidence that the business will be successful.

⟶ **Remind the reader of his or her offer for further assistance**. If the recipient offered to act further on your behalf in some way, such as forwarding your resume to colleagues or recommending other people you should talk to and providing their names and numbers, now is the time to gently remind them of their promise. (Here's where you can take a first step in preventing the problem of the "false promisers" as discussed in the difficult people section of chapter 11.)

For example, a job seeker might say, "I appreciated your offer to pass my resume along to the director of your company's research and development department and to your friend in R & D at Acme Consumer Products Corp."

After a strategy session, you might write, "Thanks also for offering to look over a revised draft of my resume. I expect to finish it over the weekend and will fax a copy to you early next week."

By couching these reminders in statements of appreciation, they are subtle, but by clearly restating the complete promise for further action, you gently nudge the reader to take action.

➡ **Include a closing and statement of follow-up plans.** In addition to reiterating your appreciation as mentioned early in the letter, the closing is the place to clarify the next steps in your networking relationship. Here is where you offer to keep the reader apprised of your plans and progress or ask for permission to stay in touch. After a fact-finding mission for help with a career decision, a closing might go something like this: "Thank you again for your time and valuable input. I will let you know which direction I decide to head." Other letters might close with, "While you certainly answered most of my questions during our meeting, I will probably take you up on your offer to call if I have others. In any case, I thank you again for your time and will keep you posted on my progress."

Not every letter will need to include all six components, so adapt these guidelines to your own situations, being sure to keep your letter to less than one page.

What Your Letter Should Look Like

The overall presentation of a thank-you letter is almost as important as its content. The way a letter looks reflects your professionalism, attention to detail, and the amount of effort you put into it. Be sure that your letter has no typos or messy corrections and is centered on the page with adequate margins (or neatly spaced and legible if handwritten).

The main decision to make regarding format is whether to handwrite or type the note. While most professional correspondence should be typed, there are times when a handwritten thank-you note is acceptable or even preferable. These include:

➠ When writing to an established member of your network (that is, a colleague whom you know well) with an informal thank-you for a favor or referral.

➠ When writing to someone you know personally, but have dealt with in a professional capacity. A typical example of this is a family friend who gave you some career advice in an informal setting like your home. (Even with personal acquaintances or relatives, though, a typed letter is often more appropriate if you need to reinforce the professional nature of this particular interaction—for example, getting Uncle Joe to take you seriously since he thinks of you as the little girl in pigtails even though you're forty.)

➠ When writing to someone who would probably appreciate the lost art of an elegantly handwritten letter or card.

Most other situations call for a letter typed in appropriate business format. (Examples of business correspondence formats are provided in chapter 6.) This is particularly true for most communication in a job search. Letters following fact-finding missions, strategy sessions, and job interviews should almost always be typed. The rule of thumb is that the more formal the situation, and the less well you know the recipient, the more likely you should type the letter.

Choosing Paper

For a traditional business letter, choose a paper of substantial weight (24 to 32 pound) in a conservative color—white, ivory, or pale gray. If, however, the person or the organization you're writing to is very informal or creative, you can possibly take some liberties with the color and texture of the paper. Recycled selections with bits of "debris" or subtle patterns have an interesting texture and can jazz up the look of your letter, while still sticking to traditional colors. If you're tempted to go for wilder colors or styles of paper, get a second opinion from someone who knows the intended recipient's field before getting too far out.

For a handwritten note, use either the same type of paper or a smaller sheet of stationery (usually called Monarch size), or write on a nice note card. Choose a stiff card or fold-over note card. Stationery and office supply stores usually have a good selection of plain note cards in nice, subtle colors or ones with a simple design, such as a border. Be sure not to get the ones that say "Thank You" on the outside. You should be able to express that sentiment clearly enough on the inside! Sometimes, greeting cards are appropriate, particularly the kind that are blank with no message on the inside and some kind of appealing (and relevant to the reader) scene on the front—maybe flowers, a work of art, a city or nature scene—whatever fits the situation and the recipient.

Sending Your Letter

Most of the advice up to this point has been for a regular letter or note card sent through the mail—called "snail mail" in today's jargon. There may be times, however, when a more expedient method is appropriate, such as faxing, e-mailing, or express mailing. Sending a thank-you note by overnight or second-day air is the least desirable method and should be used only if faxing and e-mailing are not available options. Why? Because it makes the letter seem like too much of an ordeal. A thank-you note should seem effortless and natural, not something done just to satisfy some rigid rule of etiquette. Sometimes it is important that your letter be received right away, perhaps because you'll be speaking to the person again within a day or two or you need to remind the individual of action to be taken very soon. In those cases, consider faxing or e-mailing your note. It's a less formal way to show appreciation and makes for a less polished presentation, but is a suitable method when time is of the essence.

The following samples will give you an idea of how thank-you letters and notes should read.

Sample Thank-You Letter

Here's an example of a detailed follow-up letter written after a strategy session in which the recipient had advised Ana about how to make a career transition from law to finance.

> Ana Hernandez
> 75 Allstate Road, Apt. 7
> Chicago, IL 11111
>
> Ms. Mary M. Seibert
> CHS Economic Group
> 1111 40th Avenue, Ste. 2500
> Chicago, IL 11111
>
> December 1, 1997
>
> Dear Mary,
>
> I really appreciated your taking the time to meet with me last week. I hope that you had a nice Thanksgiving since we spoke.
>
> I took advantage of the holiday weekend to begin acting on some of the useful suggestions you provided. Your ideas for revising my resume to make it more finance-oriented and less specific to the practice of law were right on target. I've rewritten some of the job descriptions, added a profile statement, and can already see that it is now a much stronger marketing tool.
>
> The books that you recommended to get me up to speed on finance sound most useful, and I've ordered most of them from an online bookstore. I am looking forward to receiving them this week.
>
> In addition to the valuable advice and resources, I want to thank you also for being supportive of my plans to make this transition. I am confident that I bring a valuable combination of skills and experience with my five years of bankruptcy law practice as well as my prior work in economics as an undergrad. It was encouraging to hear your enthusiasm for the marketability of my background.
>
> I look forward to staying in touch with you and will probably take you up on your offer to critique my revised resume. I should have something ready to fax to you in the next couple of days and will call to see when you might have a few minutes to discuss it by phone. Thank you again for all your assistance.
>
> Best Regards,
>
> *Ana Hernandez*
>
> Ana Hernandez

Sample Handwritten Thank-You Note

The following note is an example of a typical note a self-employed person might write to a network contact who has referred business to him. In this case, a real estate agent has referred a prospective client to a landscape designer. The designer is writing a short note to acknowledge that the prospective client has called to inquire about his services. If the inquiry were to turn into an actual contract, the landscape designer should type up a more formal thank-you letter or perhaps send a gift to the real estate agent. (Gift-giving is discussed later in this chapter.)

ELSON LANDSCAPES, INC.

Dear Harry,

Just a quick note to let you know that I got a call from Allyson Epstein of Maplewood Properties to discuss the possibility of my doing the landscaping for their new development in Watertown. She said you had raved about the quality of my work, so I really appreciate the referral and the glowing recommendation. I'll keep you posted.

When we both get some breathing room, let's get together for breakfast again. Thanks so much for your support!

Regards,

Jim Elson

Thank-You Calls

Putting your appreciation in writing is usually the best way to thank someone since it shows that you put more effort into the thank-you, and it is a bit more professional than other ways. There are times, however, when a phone call will suffice or might even be more effective. The rule of thumb is to ask yourself two questions:

➠ How well do I know this person?

➠ Could I benefit by having a two-way communication over the phone rather than the one-sided communication of a letter?

If you know the person well, a letter or note might be an overly formal, and somewhat impersonal, way to show your appreciation. Just as you're more likely to pick up the phone and call a friend in personal situations rather than write a letter, professional situations with people you know well or fairly well often dictate a phone call rather than written communication. This is also true if you have frequent contact with someone. With people you find yourself thanking frequently, writing letters can become somewhat repetitive. If you have people who are helping you continually, you might prefer to call them each time you need to thank them, instead of writing the same kind of note over and over.

Another benefit to calling someone (and actually having a conversation, not just leaving a message) is that you might have a chance to exchange valuable information. Sending a letter is one-sided and kind of passive. You say what you have to say, stick it in the mail or fax it, and the communication is over. With a phone call, however, you have an opportunity to gain further visibility; remind the other person of your career goals or business objectives; and, most importantly, get feedback and strengthen the rapport with that contact.

I can't count the number of times I have come close to writing thank-you notes to people who referred clients to me, but decided to call instead. I sometimes found that they said something like, "I'm so glad you called. I need more copies of your brochure, but keep forgetting to ask you." Or, "I'm so glad you called, I think I have another client for you but wasn't sure if you offer what this person needs. Let me tell you about him and see if he'd be right for you."

For the self-employed, phone calls often serve as valuable memory joggers for the people you call, giving you the chance to answer questions they've had about you, provide information and resources, and just generally keep you fresh in their mind. That doesn't always happen with a letter that gets read quickly and filed or tossed.

Also, for those not self-employed who are networking for career planning or advancement purposes, a phone call can have the same benefits. It reminds people of who you are and what you're looking for. One note of caution, however: Most traditional job search meetings, such as strategy sessions and job interviews, call for a formal thank-you letter rather than a phone call. A call can be viewed as somewhat intrusive and as breaking the traditional job search "rules."

Gift Giving to Show Appreciation

A gift can be a thoughtful way to say thank you to someone in your network who has been particularly helpful, but it can be also a major faux pas. Knowing when to send gifts, what to choose, and how much to spend is an essential skill for any savvy networker. You don't want to send a box of steaks to a vegetarian, a case of wine to a teetotaler, or a cheap paperweight to a heavyweight business executive. Many of the books listed in the Business Etiquette and Protocol section of Appendix D give excellent advice on the issues of professional gift giving. In addition to those sources, following are some tips on the subject.

When a Gift Is Appropriate

In some industries and career fields, gift giving is the norm, so you might already be aware of when it is appropriate and what to choose. If you're not sure, though, it's helpful to ask for advice from someone in your network who knows the field you're dealing with. Some companies actually have policies prohibiting their employees from receiving gifts from anyone who does (or would like to) do business with them. These rules evolve from ethical concerns over preferential treatment and obligations that inevitably come with receiving a present. In other words, no one wants to look as if they're accepting a bribe.

For most networkers, however, gift giving is a perfectly acceptable, innocent activity. If someone has been particularly helpful with your career plans or job search, there is no harm in sending a small token of your thanks.

A Gift-Giving Faux Pas

Never, ever give a gift to a government employee in anything other than a personal relationship.

This is also true for self-employed people who want to thank those who have supported their businesses in a significant way. As a self-employed career counselor, for example, every December I usually send holiday gifts to the individuals or organizations who have sent me the most client referrals. I might also send a small gift to someone who referred a client to me for the first time as a sort of "introductory" show of appreciation and to encourage future referrals. I also receive gifts at the end of the year from fellow career counselors and other professionals to whom I have referred clients. It is important, however, that most gifts exchanged not be extravagant, lest it look like you're putting undue influence on the recipient. Business should be earned by the quality of your work, not by the size or frequency of the gifts you send.

What to Give

Like any kind of gift giving, choosing a present in professional networking is easiest when you know the recipient well. If that's the case, choose something that the person is likely to enjoy and appreciate, not just something that *you* like. If you don't know much about the recipient's personal tastes and interests—which is usually the case—then it's best to select something fairly neutral that most anyone would like.

The following are popular, and usually appropriate, business gifts:

➠ Flowers and plants

➠ Food items such as fruit or baked goods

➠ Champagne or wine (if you are sure that the recipient won't be offended by receiving alcohol)

➠ Gift baskets

➠ Gourmet tea or coffee

➠ Ties or scarves

➠ Desk items like letter openers, attractive paperweights, and so on.

➡ Books and magazine subscriptions

➡ Gift certificates to a day spa, store, or restaurant

➡ Stationery or nice writing instruments

It is generally best to stay away from overly personal items unless you know the person well. In addition to stores in your neighborhood that might be good sources of gifts, be sure to check mail-order catalogs and shopping sites on the Web for convenient ways to order and ship gifts. Some department stores and other businesses have handy personal shopping services that can help you select professional gifts and arrange for wrapping and delivery.

Some of the Best Mail-Order Companies for Professional Gifts

Calyx & Corolla (800) 800-7788

Elegant, fresh flower arrangements with prompt delivery.

Harry & David (800) 547-3033

Delicious fruits and baked goods with friendly service.

Tiffany (800) 526-0649

The epitome of taste and understated elegance for silver and crystal items and other personal and houseware gifts.

Ross-Simons (800) 556-7376

Top-quality silver, crystal, and housewares at discount prices.

Omaha Steaks (800) 228-9055

Known for quality, succulent steaks, but also have other great foods for the non-carnivores on your list.

Levenger (800) 544-0880

Calling their products "Tools for Serious Readers," Levenger offers elegant items like leather portfolios and notepads, fountain pens, wood desk items, and other nice business gifts.

The Popcorn Factory (800) 323-2676

Colorful tins of flavored and plain popcorn make for fun gifts, particularly for a whole office. The Popcorn Factory even has a helpful corporate gift department.

Horchow (800) 456-7000

A sophisticated selection of office and household decorative and practical items at a range of prices.

Lillian Vernon (800) 285-5555

A classic in the mail-order world. Offers a wide range of useful office, personal, and household items at reasonable prices.

Terra Verde Trading Co. (212) 925-4533

A purveyor of beautiful, earth-friendly "lifestyle" products. Their gift boxes have satisfied the likes of Oprah Winfrey and Martha Stewart.

Wishes Under Wraps (212) 628-4962 and (718) 544-2922

Elegant gift baskets for all occasions shipped nationwide.

More Tips for Gift Giving

DO

Make sure the recipient is in town and that someone is at the office (or home) to receive your gift when sending a perishable item like food or flowers.

Make sure your full name and address are clearly visible to the recipient so the gift is not a mystery.

Enclose a note or gift card so the recipient knows the purpose of the present.

DON'T

Go overboard on what you spend.

Send something that requires assembly, is extremely large, or would in some other way be troublesome for the recipient.

Expect a response. Most people will and should acknowledge a gift so you can rest assured it was received, but since your gift was a thank-you to them, they won't necessarily see the need to perpetuate the thanking cycle by sending you a formal reply.

Performing Random Acts of Kindness

Another way to give back to people in your network is through simple, considerate actions that are not necessarily a response to something they've done for you. In other words, you don't have to wait until it's time to thank someone to do something nice. Since networking is based on relationships that are cultivated over time, random acts of kindness should be a natural part of that process. Sometimes just picking up the phone to say hello (and not to ask for anything!) is all you need to do to brighten someone's day. Let's look at the many ways you can be considerate and show appreciation on an ongoing basis:

⟹ **Birthdays and Holidays.** Try to keep track of the birth dates of people in your database and send a card (or a gift if you know the person well) to acknowledge them. Also consider sending cards for holidays other than Christmas and Hanukah. Thanksgiving, New Year's, and Independence Day are among some of the "safe" holidays that most Americans celebrate regardless of their religious affiliation. If you do know of people who celebrate certain religious holidays, it can be nice to send acknowledgments of those, but just be sure you know they do participate in a particular holiday and don't make assumptions about their religious or ethnic background based on incomplete information.

➠ **Doing Favors.** It's nice to get in the habit of asking people if you can do anything for them. Remember that networking is a two-way street. It's not all about you; other people have needs, too. The following are typical ways to give of your time or resources for people in your network:

> ➤ Speak on a panel that someone is coordinating.

> ➤ Volunteer for, or contribute money to, a charity they're involved with.

> ➤ Send clippings from magazines or newspapers that would be of interest.

> ➤ Notify them of events they might want to attend.

> ➤ Share your discovery of valuable resources, such as a new book.

> ➤ Give a professional courtesy discount, offering your products or services at a reduced rate or no charge.

> ➤ If you're not sure how you could help someone, ask!

A Special Note for Students and Beginning Networkers

You might feel that you have little to offer someone who is older or more advanced in a career than you, but that's not necessarily true. As a student or recent graduate, you have access to valuable resources that are often out of reach of more experienced people. Is there something you've learned in a class, or an interesting book you've come across, that could be informative for someone who's been away from academia for a while? Are you friendly with a professor who could be a good contact for someone you've met? Also, if you're involved in an entry-level job search, you might come across interesting information as you research industries, career fields, and companies. People with busy jobs don't often have time to do online research, go to the library, or keep up with magazine and journal reading as you can during a search.

⟱ **Give Acknowledgments**. Acknowledging and congratulating people are not only ways for you to stay visible, but are also just nice things to do. If you hear that someone has been promoted, completed a big project, received an award, started a business, or achieved some other accomplishment, consider giving that individual a call or sending a congratulatory note.

It's gratifying to know that one's accomplishments are recognized. This can also be a great way to expand your network since you can write to people who are visible and whose work you admire but whom you've never met. If someone has written a book or article you enjoyed or found helpful or was profiled for particular work, let that person know what you think.

Developing Others

Another important way to give back is to help others develop in their jobs and professional lives. As with "random acts of kindness," developing others is not always directed at those who have done something nice for you. You can have a positive effect on the professional life of someone who is not an active member of your network and who is not in a position to repay the favor, at least not directly.

Most people realize that the accomplishments in their careers can be traced in part to the help of other considerate people.

Maybe you landed a job with the assistance of a particularly helpful strategist who gave advice and leads, or you reached a high level in your field because of the guidance of a role model. While you can repay these debts directly to the strategists and the role models by thanking them and doing whatever favors they might need, chances are you feel as if you can never repay them fully. Because you have been fortunate, one way to satisfy your need to repay is to give of yourself to help develop the careers of people who are where you once were. It's not a direct gift to the people who helped you get your start or grow, but it's a valid and valued way to give back. It's the idea of what goes around comes around. As I discussed in chapter 1, networking isn't just made up of direct give and take between two people. That proverbial straight line between two points might take a few detours and pick up some other people along the way.

The following are specific ways you can develop others:

⟹ Look for people in your workplace to mentor formally or advise informally.

⟹ Hire an intern or volunteer whom you can teach.

⟹ Take part in a community-based program like Big Brothers/Big Sisters.

⟹ See if your professional association has a mentoring program in which you can take part. Many do.

⟹ Offer shadowing opportunities and grant fact-finding missions to students or others exploring your field.

Service Organizations That Let You Do Good *and* Network

Kiwanis Int'l (800) KIWANIS or (317) 875-8755

Lions Club (708) 571-5466

Optimists Int'l (314) 371-6000

Rotary Int'l (708) 866-3000

⟹ Speak at career days or on panels at schools and colleges to inform students about opportunities and career paths in your field.

The "New Career": A More Altruistic Endeavor

In *The Career is Dead* (San Francisco: Jossey-Bass Publishers, 1996), Douglas Hall writes: "...in the new career, notions of caregiving, mentoring, caring and respect, connection, and colearning (that is, learning through relationship with others), especially colearning with others whom one regards as different, provide clues to growth and success." (page 4)

Quick Summary

Networking can start to seem like a very self-centered activity. It's important to remember that other people have needs that you may be able to help with.

It's also important to show your appreciation to people who help you, and to do so in appropriate ways.

The following are ways to show your appreciation:

⟹ Thank-you notes and letters

⟹ Thank-you calls

⟹ Gifts

⟹ "Random acts of kindness"

⟹ Developing others

In addition to thanking and giving back to the immediate people in your network, it is also a good idea to assist others who might not be in a position to help you directly. Developing others by serving as a mentor, hiring an intern, granting fact-finding missions or strategy sessions, and other methods are great ways to perpetuate the concept of "what goes around comes around."

Your Action Plan—
The Key to Networking Success

They are able who think they are able.

—Virgil

So, it's taken fourteen chapters to get to this point—not exactly rushing you into action, am I? As you've probably surmised by now, I don't advocate taking action until you're really ready to do so. Before taking action, you should set career or business goals, learn and practice the best communication techniques, prepare top-notch written materials, organize your contacts, learn how to conduct one-to-one meetings, figure out how to make yourself visible at big gatherings, and master the art of showing appreciation. When you have done all that (or at least most of those things), you are ready to tackle actual networking. Whew!

Every networking encounter is precious because it has the potential to get you one step closer to your goals. If you blow it, you could be one step further from your goals and could lose a valuable ally. It would be a shame to have your efforts lead to dead ends only because of some minor problems that could have been avoided. Because a poorly written resume, sloppy brochure, monotone voice, or outdated contact database may be all that's standing between you and successful networking, it makes sense to take the time to prepare thoroughly before entering the fray.

That said, there comes a time when you have to say enough is enough. "I've prepared, planned, primped, and planted seeds long enough. Now it's time to get on with it." If you're at that point, then this chapter is for you. The following pages will guide you through establishing and executing an action plan—one that not only gets you started but also helps you make networking an ongoing part of your life.

The rationale behind getting your action steps down on paper is that even the best laid plans of mice and men can go awry—especially if they're just vague ideas floating around in your head. An action plan needs to be specific; doable; and, most importantly, *on paper* (or in your computer). If you've read this book from cover to cover, you might have occasionally said to yourself, "Oh, that's a useful idea. I'll have to try it." (At least, I hope you said that!) It's easy, though, for those ideas to be forgotten when it comes time to take action, so the worksheets and checklists on the following pages summarize points made throughout the book to help you keep sight of your objectives.

The other main point of this chapter is to have you create an action plan that is specific. It's not enough to say things like, "Well, my plan is to meet more people," or "I'm going to network more." As you learned in chapter 2, goals need to be broken down into concrete objectives, and those objectives into specific action steps. As a student, for example, you might choose five activities from the 25 Tips for Students list as priorities for the coming semester. As an entrepreneur, you might have a plan that includes a commitment to making ten calls a day to potential clients and attending one event per week. Whatever your situation, taking action is more likely to pay off if the action is part of a well-thought-out plan that includes clear objectives. In the following sections, you'll have the opportunity to revise or reiterate the goals and objectives you set in chapter 2 in light of what you have learned since then.

Goal Setting

To plan the actions that will lead to networking success, use the following sections to help you identify the questions that you need to answer.

Define General Goals

In order to define a plan, you need to start with goals. Do you want to:

➡ Make a satisfying career choice?

➡ Find a job?

➡ Manage your career more effectively?

➡ Start or expand a business?

Establish Your Priorities

If you identified more than one goal, which area is your first priority? List it first, followed by the other goals if applicable. Make an actual list, something like the following:

First priority: _____Make a satisfying career choice_____

Second priority: _____Find a job_____

Third priority: _____

Fourth priority: _____

Define Objectives

Now it's time to develop your specific objectives, which involves taking the goals you identified previously and breaking them down into specific milestones that you can identify and accomplish. Create a table (on paper or in your computer) containing two columns: one column for the overall goals, and one for the objectives that lead to those goals. *Example*: Someone who has a goal in career management might have specific goals of negotiating a raise within the next six months; improving a relationship with a particular coworker; and managing time more effectively. Their table might look like the following:

What Makes a Goal Achievable?

It's specific—not vague.

It's based on what you want—not what others want for you.

It is consistent with your values.

It's a dream, not a fantasy. Dreams are more realistic.

Goals	Objectives
Being more successful in my career.	Negotiate a raise within the next six months
	Improve working relationship with Joe Coworker
	Manage time more effectively; specifically, stop missing deadlines; spend more time on priority projects and less on busy work.

Designing an Action Plan

Throughout this book, I have suggested many specific things you can do to meet your objectives and reach your career or business goals. To increase the likelihood that you will actually act on some of these suggestions, I've put together the following chart. You'll see that this chart lists many of the specific activities that may or may not be relevant to your own needs and goals. To create your action plan, I suggest that you consider the extent to which each of these activities will help you build a stronger network of contacts and be more effective and efficient in your networking efforts. Mark each activity as a high, medium, or low priority or as not applicable to your goals and objectives.

Activity	High Priority	Medium Priority	Low Priority	N/A
Assemble or expand a portfolio				
Assess my personality style as related to networking				
Assess my strengths and skills				
Attend conferences				
Be more open to the serendipity factor				
Be more positive				
Consult a voice coach				
Consult an image consultant				
Contact former teachers, professors, and advisors				
Contact people I've known through classes or seminars				
Contact people to whom I haven't spoken in a long time				
Develop relationships with executive recruiters				
Do more research at the library				
Do volunteer work				
Expand my network				
Find and use relevant Web sites				
Find more role models				
Find more strategists				
Find more supporters				

Activity	High Priority	Medium Priority	Low Priority	N/A
Find more targets				
Find out about career and job fairs				
Find someone to mentor				
Get a listing of alumni from my school(s)				
Get connected to and learn to use the Internet				
Get more involved in a religious organization				
Get more involved in associations to which I already belong				
Get more involved in community and civic activities				
Get more involved in group sports				
Get on mailing lists of places that are sources of good business gifts				
Get out more socially				
Get public speaking training				
Get to know my neighbors				
Hire an intern				
Hold fact-finding missions				
Hold strategy sessions				
Improve my speaking voice and style				
Improve my writing skills				
Intern at a business or organization in which I am interested				
Join a gym (or go more often to the one to which I belong)				
Join a networking group or lead club				
Join Internet newsgroups				
Join professional or trade associations				
Keep in touch with my network more regularly				
Look for potential contacts in magazines, newspapers, and books				
Look up distant or "forgotten" relatives				
Look up former bosses, coworkers, and clients				

Activity	High Priority	Medium Priority	Low Priority	N/A
Make more friends				
Make my thank-you and follow-up notes more powerful				
Meet with a business strategy advisor				
Meet with a career counselor				
Meet with an executive coach				
Obtain and read books listed in the bibliography of this book				
Offer a shadowing opportunity to someone				
Order business cards				
Perform more random acts of kindness				
Polish my image (wardrobe, appearance, etc.)				
Prepare or revise my bio				
Prepare or revise my business promotional materials				
Prepare or revise my resume				
Reorganize or update an existing database				
Set up a contact database				
Set up more breakfast, lunch, and dinner meetings				
Shadow someone in a career that interests me				
Sign up with an employment agency				
Take a continuing education course				
Take an inventory of my network STARS				
Try new methods of dealing with difficult people				
Try new methods of dealing with difficult situations				
Work on my interpersonal skills				
Write overdue thank-you notes (or make calls or send gifts)				

Doing First Things First

Now look back over the chart and find the items that you identified as high priority. Choose the four most pressing activities and list them here:

1. _____

2. _____

3. _____

4. _____

When Is First?

Don't write the answer to this question here! Go to your appointment book, calendar, or other time management system and schedule specific times (or at least indicate blocks of time or particular days) when you'll get to work on these top-priority tasks.

Identify the Secondary Objectives

Which activities will you get to after the first four are under way? (Review your remaining high-priority items from the objectives worksheet or go to the medium priority ones if necessary.) It's OK if you don't identify a large number of additional tasks, but you do need to make sure that you have a number of tasks ongoing to help you reach your goals. Don't just focus on the top-tier objectives.

Turn to your appointment book or other time management system again and schedule these secondary-priority tasks. If you can't give something a specific day or time slot, at least indicate the week (or even month) you'll take care of it.

Make a Back Burner List

Make a list of any remaining activities that don't have to be done any time soon. Keep the list handy to refer to whenever your schedule lightens up and you can get to the back burner projects. Whether your schedule loosens up or not, check the list periodically (maybe once or twice a month) to see if you can move anything off the list and into your appointment book. (See chapter 4 for ideas of organizational systems that can help you keep track of back burner projects.)

Making Networking an Ongoing Part of Your Life

All through this book, I've said that networking needs to be incorporated into your daily life as a regular activity—in fact, not even an activity, but rather as a way of life. As you live the networking lifestyle, you may find that you have some questions about how to network to the best of your abilities. In the following sections, I answer some questions people typically ask about maintaining their networking efforts.

How Much Follow-Through with Contacts Is Too Much, and How Much Is Not Enough?

As a general rule, you need to keep in touch with your contacts more than you probably think you need to. People have surprisingly short memories, especially when they're busy—and who isn't busy? There have been many times when I have had aspiring career counselors hold a fact-finding mission with me to learn about the profession, inquire about possible internships, or ask about available jobs in career counseling. I may listen to them with rapt attention, be very impressed, and even receive a thank-you note a few days later. But, what happens a month later when I hear that a colleague is looking for an assistant? I might not be able to think of anyone who fits the bill. Is this because the person who met with me wasn't a good referral? No, it's more likely that I just don't remember that person. If people are out of sight, they're likely to be out of mind as well. So, whether you want people to keep you in mind for jobs, referrals, or other business, it is crucial to stay in touch so that your contacts will think of you when such opportunities arise.

That said, you might worry that you'll become a pest if you keep in touch too much. If done with courtesy and purpose, keeping in touch with contacts is typically not bothersome to them. It is possible, though, to become a pest if you push too hard. Stay alert to subtle (or not so subtle!) cues that someone really doesn't want you to be part of their active network. Their reasons often have nothing to do with you as a person— your contact just might not feel that the two of you share enough in common to make it worth while to stay in touch.

A colleague of mine, for example, once complained to me that she had been receiving calls once a month (like clockwork) from someone she had met about a year prior at a conference. She had had lunch with this person a couple of times after the conference. The two of them were in totally different businesses, which ordinarily would be great since knowing people in other arenas can expand your own network significantly. In this case, however, it was clear to her that the chances of them being useful to each other were fairly remote. My friend wouldn't have minded keeping up with this person through an occasional phone call, mailings about her business, or even lunch from time to time. But, she was so turned off by the frequency with which the person kept calling to ask that they get together for lunch, that she no longer wanted to deal with her at all. My friend got the feeling that this persistent networker had a list of people to call once a month and that she was just a name to be checked off that list.

Remember that professional relationships are like any other relationship you may have. You have to establish a basis of mutual respect, under-standing, and shared interests and needs before moving to a level at which you spend time with each other regularly. Some busy people have trouble finding the time to have lunch with even their closest friends regularly, so they aren't much interested in devoting one precious lunch a month, every month, to a distant professional acquaintance.

So, when determining how much to follow up with a newly established contact or how often to stay in touch with an existing one, use some common sense. Make sure that you establish a solid, mutually beneficial relationship before expecting to occupy too much of someone's time. On the other hand, though, don't go to the opposite extreme and let people forget that you exist. As you saw in the example of my forgetting about people I meet once briefly in fact-finding missions, it is important to stay fresh in people's minds. An occasional phone call, note, or e-mail may be all it takes to do so.

As I Know People in My Network in More Depth, Won't I Cross the Boundary Between a Professional Relationship and a Personal Friendship?

Not necessarily. Most people find that they can develop long-term professional relationships without crossing over into the realm of personal relationships. If you're an active networker with a busy career, you might sometimes feel that you spend more time with certain professional colleagues than with your own family or close friends, but that doesn't mean your professional relationships have become personal ones. It is really a question of type of contact rather than frequency or duration.

You don't have to invite these professional acquaintances to your son's bar mitzvah, your sister's wedding, or to dinner every Friday night. A sort of unspoken code of behavior in the professional world is that people can become very close to each other in their work lives while respecting the privacy of each other's personal lives.

This doesn't mean that you can't inquire about the general well-being of the other person's family or talk about how much fun your latest vacation was. It's common courtesy to show a certain, reserved level of interest in professional colleagues' personal lives after you get to know them well. It is also normal to want to talk about events in your own life, especially significant ones like a marriage, the birth of a child, or purchasing a home. Strong professional relationships are friendships of a sort.

Remember, we're all human beings, and just because we're interacting in a professional arena doesn't mean that we lose our humanity.

Occasionally, a professional relationship does cross over the line and becomes a true personal friendship. There's nothing wrong with that if the feelings are mutual. Just be careful not to push it. Simply because you have lunch with someone on Wednesday and seem to click, doesn't mean she wants to double-date with you and your boyfriend on Friday.

Managing Cross-Cultural Networking Relationships

There are major cultural differences around the world regarding the issue of how personal you can get in business interactions. In some cultures, for example, it is considered extremely rude to ask a businessman about his wife, while in others it's impolite *not* to inquire about someone's family. Some of the books listed in the Cross-Cultural Networking section of Appendix D can help you learn what's appropriate where.

How Can I Keep Expanding My Network of Contacts?

It is important to keep your network growing. Doing so ensures that you'll never get that uncomfortable feeling of "overusing" your contacts. You want to have enough people to turn to for advice, leads, or support so that you don't have to worry that you're relying too heavily on any one person. Expanding your circle also infuses your network with fresh ideas, strategies, and insights. It also brings new adventures to keep you interested and motivated, making it more likely that networking will remain an ongoing part of your life. The following are some ways to expand your contacts:

➠ **Identify some new STARS.** Review the description of the STARS categories in chapter 3 and think about where your network is lacking. Could you use more strategists to help with new issues that have arisen in your career? Are you worried that you're becoming a burden on the people who have been providing emotional support and could use some professional help from the Allied Forces category? Should you think of more friends who could be in the Supporter role? Be sure that the people in your network are well distributed across the

➤ **Go back to the basic sources of contacts.** To make sure you're covering all bases, have a look at chapter 3 again to be certain you've cultivated contacts from all possible sources—personal, work-related, educational, professional groups, and multimedia. Which sources remain untapped? Go after them.

➤ **Rediscover your interests.** Make sure you've thought of all your personal and professional interests and the activities or groups that those could lead you to. When you first begin networking, it's tempting to say, "Sure, I have an interest in *x*, but I don't have time now to attend lectures on it. I need to do the kind of networking that has more immediate benefits." After you've been networking a while, though, those more remote activities might be just the thing you need to revive and expand your network.

➤ **Get more involved.** Among those professional associations or networking groups to which you already belong, take an honest look at how involved you've been. A common trap is to say, "I belonged to three professional groups this year, and they haven't done anything for me." Well, have you attended meetings regularly? Did you go to any national or regional conferences? Did you volunteer for a committee or some other leadership role? Just reading the monthly newsletter and listing the affiliation on your resume won't necessarily get your phone ringing with offers, leads, and ideas.

How Do I Keep a Positive Attitude Toward Networking?

As you saw in chapter 11 and elsewhere throughout this book, networking inevitably brings some challenge. People who are difficult to deal with, situations that you maybe didn't handle so well, and goals that seem unattainable can easily foster a negative attitude. To keep a positive outlook on networking, some advice I have offered before bears repeating here. That is to use positive reinforcements. Each time you make positive strides toward your networking goals, take the time to reflect on your accomplishments. It's easy to get caught up in the process and not stop to see how far you've come. So, give yourself a pat on the back and maybe even a treat of some sort.

When I was a child, my mother used to take me to the toy store after every trip to the pediatrician and buy a toy car for my Matchbox car collection. As a mature professional or student, you might not need to baby yourself with a trip to the toy store every time you make a cold call, but don't forget to reward yourself with some kind of grown-up toy when you successfully stretch past your comfort zone or achieve some sort of networking coup.

What Can I Do When Networking Seems to Be Too Overwhelming?

Take a break occasionally. Just as you need to reward yourself from time to time, it can also be helpful and rejuvenating to take an occasional break from your networking efforts. If you're doing intense networking (particularly the networking associated with a job search or launching a business), the process can become quite wearing on you. Although you might not have the luxury of sparing days or weeks from your networking efforts, try to take at least a brief break, whether that's a day off here and there or just an afternoon. Doing so can bring new vitality to your search or business development.

If your networking is a more gradual, ongoing process—perhaps as part of managing your career or maintaining an existing business—your break can probably be a little longer. If you're a freelancer or consultant, for example, you might feel that you spend all your time looking for the next assignment or project. It's easy to get burned out in that process, so consider taking "cyclical breaks."

Every business has cycles dictated by various factors. There might, for example, be times of the year when the professional associations or individuals you typically deal with are less active. This often occurs during the summer, but your own slow time might be some other part of the year. Whenever it occurs, avoid being so in the habit of networking that you forget you can take a time-out. Every business owner, consultant, or freelancer—as well as those who are not self-employed—needs a break occasionally—that time of year when a person can fall out of touch with people, maybe for a few weeks or a month or two. These breaks are an excellent time to focus on your actual work, such as improving your products or services or on reorganizing your office or business procedures.

Some Final Tips

I've covered a lot of ground in this book, so I now want to highlight for you what I consider to be the most salient points from among all these pages. My intention is for these final tips to serve as a quick, handy reference to which you can turn to guide your action, both now and in the future.

20 Common Networking Mistakes to Avoid

As you execute your networking plan, make sure to avoid the following common pitfalls:

1. Networking nonstrategically—that is, without clearly defined objectives.

2. Losing sight of your ultimate goals.

3. Relying on networking as the only means of reaching your goals.

4. Having a hidden agenda—not being up-front and honest with others.

5. Being too clingy, needy, or pessimistic. Nobody likes a whiner!

6. Expecting too much of others. Ultimately, only you can help you.

7. Being impatient. Results can come when you least expect them, and they usually take time to come to you.

8. Mixing business and pleasure too overtly.

9. Being insensitive to cultural differences.

10. Not following through when you're given leads.

11. Contacting people only when you need something.

12. Not showing your appreciation in a timely and appropriate manner.

13. Being passive.

14. Going for quantity over quality in your relationships.

15. Having poor quality self-marketing materials (resumes, letters, promotional literature, etc.).

16. Trying to do too much and getting spread too thin.

17. Not keeping up with people regularly.

18. Having poor oral or written communication skills.

19. Trying to network in a way that doesn't fit your personality style.

20. Not doing it at all!

20 Quick Tips for Successful Networking

Now that you have seen what *not* to do, the following list tells you what you should do:

1. Always be specific about what you need.

2. Know your strengths.

3. Network even when you think you don't need to.

4. Don't wait for people to come to you. Be proactive.

5. Be more persistent than you think you need to be.

6. Don't internalize rejection.

7. Don't speak negatively about anyone.

8. Be friendly and down-to-earth.

9. Be helpful to others even if there's no obvious direct benefit to you.

10. Stay in touch with people regularly.

11. Never leave home without business cards (or resumes).

12. Occasionally call people just to say hello.

13. Get known as an information clearinghouse, and thus a valuable resource for others.

14. Sit next to strangers at events, not alone or just with people you know.

15. Focus on names when you meet people.

16. Learn and follow basic rules of business and social etiquette.

17. Don't be afraid to ask others for help.

18. Keep your goals in sight.

19. Take a break occasionally—don't get overexposed.

20. Keep a positive attitude.

Keeping It All in Perspective

Having made it this far in *Networking for Everyone*, you may feel relieved that you've already been doing most of what this book recommends—or you may be overwhelmed at all the things you *should* be doing. Well, if you're relieved that you're on the right track, then keep up the good work.

If you're like many people, however, you worry that you're not doing enough networking and can't imagine how you'll ever catch up. Don't despair. Keep it all in perspective. You don't have to become a manic networker, following every single suggestion in this book to the letter. Even though networking is becoming more and more essential to professional success and security, there is something to be said for simply doing your job and doing it well. As long as you supplement that good work with at least some of the strategies recommended here and don't become complacent, you'll do just fine.

Networking should not be a chore. Yes, it takes effort, persistence, and a positive attitude in the face of occasional rejection and frustration, but it should also be fun and rewarding. If you lay a solid foundation for your networking efforts through the preparation and strategy techniques offered throughout this book, you've done the hard part. Networking at that point should be integrated into your daily life in a way that makes it an almost routine, effortless activity rather than a burden.

Keeping your expectations realistic also helps keep networking from being a chore. Don't expect miracles overnight. Networking is a learned skill that takes time to master. I'm still working on it myself! Even when you do feel you've mastered it, patience is still needed. Relationships take time to develop, and it can sometimes take weeks, months, or even years for results to come from seeds you plant.

So, keep your goals clearly in sight and be persistent, positive, and patient. If you do that, and if you take other people along on the journey with you, you'll be on the short road to your dreams. You *can* reach your goals! As an old Saudi Arabian proverb says:

If the camel once gets his nose in a tent, his body will soon follow.

The No Excuses List—You *Can* Track Down Anyone in Any Field!

If you need to contact someone in a given field, but don't know anyone in that field, it's tempting to say, "I don't know anyone to talk to about this field." I have good news and bad news for you. The bad news is you have no more excuses; the good news is that you're probably connected to more people than you might think. The following table covers more than 100 career fields, industries, and interest areas and gives you examples of the types of people who might know someone in different fields. This list will help you brainstorm when you are searching for contacts in a given field. You can add your own ideas to this list and tailor it to your specific interests.

If you need contacts in...	Track them down through...
Accounting	Auditors, bookkeepers, insurance agents, tax attorneys, estate planners, personal financial planners, stockbrokers, mortgage brokers, corporate finance executives, management consultants
Acting	Agents, talent scouts, directors, producers, publicists, singers, musicians, theater workers, voice coaches
Actuarial Science	Accountants, auditors, insurance agents, tax attorneys, estate planners, personal financial planners, stockbrokers, mortgage brokers, corporate finance executives, computer programmers, mathematicians, statisticians, bankers, insurance underwriters, management consultants, risk management experts
Advertising	Public relations specialists, corporate communications departments, freelance writers and artists, graphic designers, media executives, photographers, market researchers, corporate marketing executives, fashion stylists, magazine personnel, songwriters
Aerospace	Engineers, biologists, chemists, physicists, other scientists, government officials, astronauts, computer technicians
Animal-Related Fields	Veterinarians, veterinarian's aides, breeders, trainers, blacksmiths, kennels, show judges, groomers, pet sitters, zoo keepers, zoologists, farmers
Animation	Computer programmers, software designers, producers, voice-over specialists, artists, graphic designers, actors
Anthropology	Archaeologists, geologists, environmental scientists, linguists, translators, writers, editors, sociologists, urban planners, museum curators and administrators, demographers, professors, graduate students

Antiques and Collectibles	Interior decorators/designers, art historians, historic preservationists, auction house employees, furniture restorers, lighting designers and restorers, art dealers, rare book/manuscript experts, coin and stamp dealers, upholsterers
Archaeology	Anthropologists, geographers, geologists, architects, environmental scientists, linguists, translators, writers, editors, social scientists, urban planners, museum curators and administrators, classicists, theologians, chemists, historians, historic preservationists, graduate students, professors
Architecture	Engineers, draftsmen, interior designers, interior decorators, space planners, historic preservationists, construction workers, contractors, real estate agents, developers, landscape architects, landscapers and lawn maintenance workers, painters, wallpaper hangers, lighting designers, handymen/women, urban planners, landlords, property managers
Art Dealing and Consulting	Fine artists, photographers, gallery owners, museum curators and administrators, art critics, art historians, corporate purchasing, facilities management departments, interior decorators and designers, architects, event planners, set designers, art appraisers
Arts Administration	Performing artists, fine artists, photographers, fundraising consultants, producers, other nonprofit organizations
Auditing	Accountants, insurance agents, tax attorneys, estate planners, personal financial planners, stockbrokers, mortgage brokers, corporate finance executives, bookkeepers, state and federal government officials, management consultants

Aviation	Pilots, air traffic controllers, FAA officials, flight attendants, military personnel
Benefits	Human resources personnel, compensation analysts, benefits and pension consultants, actuaries
Bioethics	Hospital and HMO administrators, physicians, lawyers, social workers, genetic counselors, nurses
Biology	Chemists, environmental scientists, ecologists, Research and Development departments in manufacturing companies, statisticians, professors
Biotechnology	Patent attorneys, biologists, medical professionals, professors, laboratory scientists, corporate R and D departments, biotech firms
Buying	Inventory control workers, manufacturers reps, market researchers, retail salespeople and managers, anyone who works in department stores, purchasing departments, facilities managers, operations departments, office administrators, fashion designers
Career Counseling	Psychologists, psychotherapists, educational consultants, outplacement specialists, school guidance counselors, executive search recruiters, employment agencies, resume writers, job search coaches, executive coaches, corporate trainers, human resources personnel
Carpentry	Architects, construction managers, interior designers and decorators, plumbers, electricians, historic preservationists, contractors, real estate developers, property managers, real estate agents, landlords
Catering	Restaurateurs, waiters, food service suppliers, gourmet market personnel, event planners, chefs, cooks
Commercial Art	Graphic designers, advertising executives, industrial designers, product and package designers, curators, art professors, agents

Culinary Arts	Restaurant owners, managers, staff, sommeliers; food service suppliers; caterers; hotel, resort, club, and corporate dining service managers
Chemistry	Professors, other scientists, engineers, pharmaceutical personnel, lab technicians, physicians
Child Care	Teachers, social workers, child psychologists, nurses, pediatricians, dietitians, nannies, child care agencies
Civil Engineering	Architects, computer specialists, technicians and technologists, electricians, government officials, contractors, construction workers, electrical engineers, urban planners
Comedy	Agents, club managers and personnel, producers, publicists, writers, cartoonists, actors
Commercial Banking	Accountants, attorneys, auditors, loan officers
Commodities Brokerage	Financial analysts, stock brokers, personal financial planners, investment bankers, agriculture specialists
Computer Programming	Computer engineers, systems analysts, compute operators, software developers, telecommunications specialists, computer salespeople, computer consultants
Contracting and Construction	Architects, carpenters, construction workers, suppliers, real estate developers, interior designers, electricians
Corporate Communications	Writers, graphic designers and artists, desktop publishers, printers, public relations, marketing, advertising personnel
Corporate Finance	Investment bankers, corporate attorneys, financial analysts, accountants, business school faculty, other corporate executives
Court Reporting	Attorneys, judges, transcribers, translators, court clerks, paralegals
Criminology	Lawyers, federal agents, law enforcement officials, pathologists, sociologists, professors

Curators	Art historians, archaeologists, anthropologists, historic preservationists, art galleries, art dealers, antique dealers, professors, librarians, historical societies
Dentistry	Dental lab technicians, oral surgeons, orthodontists, physicians, medical supply salespeople, hygienists, dental assistants
Directing (film, TV, theater)	Actors, agents, editors, producers, photographers, cinematographers, production assistants, script readers
Ecology	Biologists, environmentalists, scientists, waste management experts, botanists, horticulturists, urban and regional planners
Economics	Bankers, policy analysts, statisticians, professors, government officials
Editing (Books)	Literary agents, writers, reviewers, printers, publicists, proofreaders
Editing (Film)	Producers, actors, production assistants, technicians, cinematographers, photographers
Editing (Magazines)	Literary agents, writers, reviewers, printers, publicists, proofreaders
Editing (Journals)	Literary agents, writers, reviewers, printers, publicists, proofreaders, professors, professional association personnel
Educational Advising	Admissions reps, financial aid officers, independent educational consultants, guidance counselors, teachers, psychologists, career counselors (school and colleges)
Electrical Engineering	Computer programmers, technicians and technologists, electricians, architects, other engineers
Electricians	Construction workers, plumbers, carpenters, property managers, landlords, telecommunication specialists

Employee Assistance

EAP counselors and managers in hospitals and large corporations, substance abuse counselors, social workers, psychologists, physicians

Event Planning

Conference and meeting planners, party planners, restaurant and hotel banquet managers, caterers, travel agents, hotel employees, airline ticket agents, public relations and promotions executives, invitation and party favor designers and printers, calligraphers, tour guides

Environmental Science

Biologists, ecologists, scientists, waste management experts, botany, horticulturists, lobbyists, energy conservation specialists, soil scientists, oceanographers

Fashion Design

Textile designers and manufacturers, buyers, advertising executives, production managers, models, photographers, retail managers and salespeople, milliners, tailors

Fine Arts

Art dealers, agents, gallery owners and employees, museum curators, photographers, professors, publishers, editors, art supply store managers and salespeople

Firefighting

Paramedics, police officers, safety inspectors, government officials, arson investigators

Floral Design

Florists, horticulturists, botanists, artists, photo stylists, photographers, interior decorators

Food and Wine

Sommeliers, restaurant owners and managers and staff, chefs and cooks, vintners, cookbook writers and editors, food service suppliers, wine importers, people who eat out a lot, food and wine magazine editors and writers, pastry chefs, bakers, bartenders, food stylists for photo shoots, cooking equipment reps, menu designers and consultants

Foreign Service

Policy analysts in government agencies and think-tanks, government officials, politicians, tourism boards, translators, political science, economics, international affairs professors, international business people

Forestry	Park rangers, tourism boards, fish and wildlife officials, fishing guides, botanists, horticulturists, environmental planners, paper industry executives, soil scientists
Fund-Raising and Development	Nonprofit organization personnel; school, college, and university administrators; foundation executives; event planners; corporate giving department executives; estate planners
Genetics	Medical research centers, clinics, hospitals, neuroscientists, oncologists, obstetricians, midwives, social workers
Geology	Geophysicists, land developers, petroleum engineers, surveyors, professors
Gerontology	Attorneys specializing in elder law, managers of residential retirement communities, physicians, nurses, social workers estate planners
Graphic Design	Advertising executives, artists, market researchers, product managers
Guidance Counseling	Teachers, professors, university administrators, career counselors, students, independent educational consultants
Health Care Administration	Insurance agents, physicians, nurses, medical personnel
Holistic Health	Acupuncturists, yoga instructors, herbalists, nutritionists, movement specialists, fitness trainers, psychotherapists, midwives, natural food purveyors, macrobiotic chefs, massage therapists, naturopathic physicians, art therapists
Hotel Management	Event and meeting planners, party planners, food service workers, food service suppliers, travel agents, housekeepers
Human Resources	Anyone in a large corporation or nonprofit organization, employment agencies, executive search firms, management consultants, training consultants

Import-Export	Customs brokers, art dealers, antique dealers, lawyers, manufacturers, shippers, couriers
Industrial and Organizational Psychology	Human resources personnel, training consultants or in-house corporate trainers, management consultants, productivity experts, clinical psychologists, business school faculty
Information Systems	Computer engineers, computer programmers, systems analysts, financial analysts, production managers, librarians, researchers, telecommunications specialists, database managers, employee records administrators, security consultants
Insurance	Actuaries, attorneys, bankers, policy holders, employee benefits specialists, pension fund reps, underwriters
Interior Decoration and Design	Architects, carpenters, contractors, decorative arts suppliers, antique dealers, design magazine editors and writers, art historians, museum curators, historic preservationists, furniture manufacturer's reps, fabric and textile manufacturers and salespeople, homeowners
International Affairs	Translators, diplomats, ambassadors, international business people, reporters, editors, government officials, linguists, political scientists, economists, not-for-profit organization staff
Investment Banking	Commercial bankers, accountants, researchers, stockbrokers, attorneys, real estate developers
Jewelry Design	Jewelry store personnel, jewelry appraisers, gemologists, artists
Journalism	Editors, reporters, photographers, publishers, researchers, media specialists, broadcasters, publicists
Labor Relations	Attorneys, human resources personnel, mediators, conflict resolution specialists, social workers, union reps, arbitrators

Law	Paralegals, legal secretaries, accountants, other attorneys, bankers, judges, law professors. Depending on the specialty area within law, might also be tracked down by social workers, investment bankers, commercial bankers, realtors, corporate executives, medical professionals, etc.
Law Enforcement	Criminologists, lawyers, federal agents, paramedics, chemists, pathologists, private investigators
Lobbying	Politicians, political aides, political campaign workers, corporate government relations or public affairs reps, corporate human resources personnel, nonprofit organizations, union reps
Literary Agencies	Producers, directors, publishers, editors, writers, lawyers, market researchers
Management Consulting	Business people, including strategic planners, managers, financial analysts, scientists, economists, accountants, organizational development specialists, industrial and organizational psychologists, training and development consultants and specialists
Market Research	Marketing executives, advertising executives, statisticians, computer programmers, communications experts, public relations executives, demographers
Marketing	Advertising executives, market researchers, media specialists, public relations executives, anyone in a large corporation
Mathematicians	Actuaries, computer programmers, electrical engineers, statisticians, professors, financial analysts, economists
Medicine	Nurses, social workers, therapists and psychologists, nursing home administrators, child care centers, hospital administrators

Multimedia	Computer programmers, software developers, educators, publishers, computer magazine writers, reporters, editors, graphic designers, musicians, artists
Mortgage Brokers	Bankers, loan officers, real estate brokers, lawyers, accountants, personal financial planners
Musicians	Club managers, promoters, publicists, songwriters, talent agents, arts organization administrators
Nursing	Physicians, medical technicians, patients, pharmacists
Nutrition	Chefs and cooks, restaurateurs, teachers, school and college administrators, psychologists, physicians, eating disorder specialists, dietitians, natural food suppliers and stores, herbalists, fitness trainers, health club personnel
Package Design	Graphic artists, marketing executives, art design directors, advertising executives, production managers
Pharmaceuticals	Physicians, nurses, medical office managers, hospital and HMO administrators, pharmacists, chemists, biochemists
Pharmacoeconomics	Economists, management consultants, hospital administrators, government officials, insurance companies, HMOs, pharmaceutical companies
Physical and Occupational Therapy	Physicians, nurses, sports medicine specialists, vocational therapy and rehabilitation counselors, social workers, speech pathologists, audiologists, nursing home administrators, hospital administrators, health care agencies, dance and movement therapists, chiropractors
Photography	Advertising executives, art directors, party planners, graphic designers, reporters, magazine art directors, darkroom and lab technicians

Politics	Campaign workers, political aides, political researchers, policy analysts in think tanks and government, corporate government relations executives, lobbyists, speech writers, pollsters
Printing	Graphic designers, public relations specialists, publishers, editors, party and event planners
Private Investigation	Credit bureaus, police officers, government record clerks
Promotions and Publicity	Marketing executives, public relations specialists, advertising executives, market researchers, publicists, agents, corporate communications specialists, media, music, film, journalists, editors, event planners
Psychology	Physical and occupational therapists, psychiatrists, social workers, college and university administrators, school administrators, teachers, independent educational consultants
Public Health	Epidemiologists, physicians, not-for-profit organizations, sociologists, anthropologists, demographers, biostatisticians, economists, government officials, health care administrators.
Public Relations	Advertising and marketing executives, anyone in a business that uses a PR firm, media personnel, writers, journalists
Publishing	Bookstore reps and managers, writers, freelance editors, illustrators, intellectual property lawyers

Appendix B

A Sampling of Professional and Trade Associations

Trade and professional associations offer a wealth of networking opportunities. To encourage you to make use of these valuable resources, this appendix lists over 400 associations representing more than 50 career fields and industries. Since there are literally tens of thousands of trade and professional associations in this country, this is by no means an exhaustive list—it contains just some of the more significant and useful associations within each field.

This list should serve simply as a starting point for you. To be really thorough, I suggest you do a search of the association directories that can be found in your local library (see Appendix D). You can also consult the American Society of Associations on the Web at www.asaenet.org.

Internet addresses are listed for organizations that had Web sites up and running as of press time, but others may have developed sites by the time you read this. I have also made an effort to provide accurate snail mail addresses and phone numbers for all groups.

Accounting

Accountants for the Public Interest

(202) 347-1668
1625 I Street NW, Suite 717
Washington, DC 20006
www.accountingnet.com

American Accounting Association

(941) 921-7747
5717 Bessie Drive
Sarasota, FL 33423
www.rutgers.edu/accounting/raw/aaa/aaa.html

American Association of Hispanic Certified
Public Accountants

(718) 823-6144
P.O. Box 871
Bronx, NY 10465
www.hispanic-org.com

American Society of Women Accountants

(901) 680-0470
1255 Lynnfield Road., Ste 257
Memphis, TN 38119
www.aswa.org

Institute of Internal Auditors

(407) 830-7600
249 Maitland Avenue
Altamonte Springs, FL 32701
www.theiia.org

National Association of Black Accountants

(301) 474-6222
7249A Hanover Parkway
Greenbelt, MD 20770

Actuaries

American Academy of Actuaries

(202) 223-8196
1100 17th Street NW, 7th flr
Washington, DC 20036
www.actuary.org

Advertising

American Advertising Federation

(202) 898-0089
1101 Vermont Avenue, Ste 500
Washington, DC 20005
www.aaf.org

American Association of Advertising Agencies

(212) 682-2500
666 Third Avenue, 13th flr
New York, NY 10017
www.commercepart.com/AAAA

International Advertising Association

(212) 557-1133
342 Madison Avenue, Ste 2000
New York, NY 10017
www.iaaglobal.org

The Advertising Council

(212) 922-1500
261 Madison Avenue
New York, NY 10016
www.adcouncil.org

Archaeology

Archaeological Institute of America

(617) 353-9361
656 Beacon Street
Boston, MA 02215
csaws.brynmawr.edu:443/AIA.HTML

Center for American Archaeology

(618) 653-4316
P.O. Box 366
Kampsville, IL 62053

Society of American Archaeology

(202) 789-8200
900 2nd Street NE, Ste 12
Washington, DC 20002
www.saa.org

Architecture

American Institute of Architects

(202) 626-7300
1735 New York Avenue NW
Washington, DC 20006
www.aia.org

Associated Landscape Contractors of America

(703) 620-6363
12200 Sunrise Valley Drive, Ste 150
Reston, VA 22091
www.alca.org

American Society of Landscape Architects

(202) 898-2444
4401 Connecticut Avenue NW
Washington, DC 20008
www.asla.org

Arts

American Association of Museums

(202) 289-1818
1225 I Street NW
Washington, DC 20005
www.aam-us.org

Americans for the Arts

(212) 223-2787
1 East 53rd Street
New York, NY 10022

American Crafts Council

(212) 274-0630
72 Spring Street
New York, NY 10012

Art Dealers Association of America

(212) 940-8590
575 Madison Ave.
New York, NY 10022
www.artdealers.org

Association for Hispanic Arts

(212) 860-5445
173 East 116th Street, 2nd flr
New York, NY 10029

National Antique and Art Dealers

(212) 826-9707
Association of America
12 East 56th Street
New York, NY 10022
www.dir-dd.com/naadaa.html

National Association of Artists' Organizations

(202) 347-6350
918 F Street NW
Washington, DC 20004
www.artswire.org/artswire/naao

Professional Art Management Institute

(212) 579-2039
110 Riverside Drive, Ste 4E
New York, NY 10024

Professional Photographers of America

(800) 786-6277
57 Forsyth Street NW
Atlanta, GA 30303
www.ppa-world.org

Society of Illustrators

(212) 838-2560
128 East 63rd Street
New York, NY 10021

Aviation/Airlines

Airline Employees Association

(708) 563-9999
6520 Cicero Avenue
Bedford Park, IL 60638

Association of Flight Attendants

(202) 328-5400
1625 Massachusetts Avenue NW
Washington, DC 20036

Banking

American Bankers Association

> (202) 663-5000
> 1120 Connecticut Avenue NW
> Washington, DC 20036
> www.aba.com\aba

Mortgage Bankers Association of America

> (202) 861-6500
> 1125 15th Street NW
> Washington, DC 20005
> www.mbaa.org

National Bankers Association

> (202) 588-5432
> 1802 T Street
> Washington, DC 20009
> www.nationalbanker.org

Savings and Community Bankers Association

> (202) 857-3100
> 900 19th Street NW, Ste 400
> Washington, DC 20006
> acbankers.org

Woman's World Banking—USA

> (212) 768-8513
> 8 W. 40th Street
> New York, NY 10018
> www.wwb.@igc.apc.org

Clerical/Administrative

American Society of Corporate Secretaries

> (212) 681-2000
> 521 Fifth Avenue
> New York, NY 10175
> www.ascs.org

National Association of Executive Secretaries

> (703) 237-8616
> 900 South Washington Street
> Falls Church, VA 22046

Professional Secretaries International

> (816) 891-6600
> 10502 NW Ambassador Drive
> P.O. Box 20404
> Kansas Cty, MO 64195
> www.gvi.net/psi

Computers/Information Technology/Library Science

American Library Association

> (312) 944-6780
> 50 East Huron Street
> Chicago, IL 60611
> www.ala.org

American Society for Information Science

> (301) 495-0900
> 8720 Georgia Avenue, Ste 501
> Silver Springs, MD 20910
> www.asis.org

Association for Computer Educators

> (405) 744-8632
> College of Business Admin. OSU
> Stillwater, OK 74078

Association for Women in Computing

> (415) 905-4663
> 41 Sutter Street, Ste 1006
> San Fransisco, CA 94104
> www.awc@acm.org

Association of Personal Computer User Groups

> (914) 876-6678
> 1730 M Street NW
> Washington, DC 20036
> www.apcug.org

Independent Computer Consultants Association

> (314) 892-1675
> 1131 S. Towne Square, Ste F
> St. Louis, MO 63123
> www.icca.org

Information & Technology Association of America

(703) 522-5055
1616 North Fort Myer Drive, Ste 1300
Arlington, VA 22209
www.itaa.org

Information Industry Association

(202) 986-0280
1625 Massachusetts Avenue NW, Ste 700
Washington, DC 20036
www.infoindustry.org

Society for Information Management

(312) 644-6610
401 N. Michigan Avenue
Chicago, IL 60611
www.simnet.org

Special Libraries Association

(202) 234-4700
1700 18th Street NW
Washington, DC 20009
www.sla.org

Consulting

American Consultants League

(941) 952-9290
1290 Palm Avenue
Sarasota, FL 34236

Association of Management Consulting Firms

(212) 697-9693
521 Fifth Avenue
New York, NY 10175
www.acmeworld.org

Professional and Technical Consultants Association

(415) 903-8305
P.O. Box 4143
Mountain View, CA 94040
www.patca.org/patca

Culinary/Food & Wine

American Bakers Association

(202) 789-0300
1350 I Street NW
Washington, DC 20005
www.sosland.com/aba

American Culinary Federation

(904) 824-4468
10 San Bartola Road
P.O. Box 3466
St. Augustine, FL 32085
www.acfchefs.org

National Restaurant Association

(202) 331-5900
1200 17th Street NW
Washington, DC 20036
www.restaurant.org

Sommelier Society of America

(212) 679-4190
201 East 25th Street
New York, NY 10159

Dentistry

American Association of Dental Assistants

(312) 541-1550
203 North LaSalle Street
Chicago, IL 60601
www.members.aol.com/adaa1/index.html

American Dental Association

(312) 440-2736
211 East Chicago Avenue, Ste 1804
Chicago, IL 60611
www.ada.org

American Dental Hygienists Association

(312) 440-8900
444 North Michigan Avenue, Ste 3400
Chicago, IL 60611
www.adha.org

Design

American Design and Drafting Association

> (301) 460-6875
> P.O. Box 799
> Rockville, MD 20848
> www.adda.org

American Society of Interior Designers

> (202) 546-3480
> 608 Massachusetts Avenue NE
> Washington, DC 20002
> www.asid.org

American Society of Furniture Designers

> (910) 884-4074
> P.O. Box 2688
> High Point, NC 27261

American Textile Manufacturers Institute

> (202) 862-0500
> 1801 K Street NW, Ste 900
> Washington, DC 20006
> www.atmi.org

Association of Professional Landscape Designers

> (312) 201-0101
> 11 S. LaSalle Street, No. 1400
> Chicago, IL 60603
> 74733.1624@compuserve.com (e-mail address)

Council of Fashion Designers of America

> (212) 302-1821
> 1412 Broadway, Ste 2006
> New York, NY 10018
> www.seventhonsixth.com

Industrial Designers Society of America

> (703) 759-0100
> 1142-E Walker Road
> Great Falls, VA 22066
> www.idsa.org

International Association of Clothing Designers

> (212) 685-6602
> 475 Park Avenue South, 17th flr
> New York, NY 10016

International Association of Lighting Designers

> (212) 206-1281
> 1133 Broadway, Ste 520
> New York, NY 10010
> www.aecnet.com/iald/IALD.html

Society of American Florists

> (703) 836-8700
> 1601 Duke Street
> Alexandria, VA 22314
> consumer website pending

Surface Design Association

> (707) 829-3110
> P.O. Box 20799
> Oakland, CA 94620
> www.uidaho.edu/~art/sda/index.html

Economics

American Economic Association

> (615) 322-2595
> 2014 Broadway, Ste 305
> Nashville, TN 37203
> www.vanderbilt.edu/AEA

National Association of Business Economists

> (202) 463-6223
> 1233 20th Street NW, Ste 505
> Washington, DC 20036
> www.nabe.com

Education

American Association for Adult and Continuing Education

> (202) 429-5131
> 1200 19th Street NW, Ste 300
> Washington, DC 20036

American Association for Higher Education

> (202)293-6440
> 1 Dupont Circle, Ste 360
> Washington, DC 20036
> www.aahe.org

American Association of School Administrators

> (703) 528-0700
> 1801 North Moore Street
> Arlington, VA 22209
> www.aasa.org

American Association of University Administrators

> (205) 463-2682
> P.O. Box 2183
> Tuscaloosa, AL 35403
> www.tusc.net/~aaua/

American Association of University Professors

> (202) 737-5900
> 1012 14th Street NW
> Washington, DC 20005
> www.igc.apc.org/aaup/

American Association of University Women

> (202) 785-7700
> 1111 16th Street NW
> Washington, DC 20036
> www.aauw.org

American Federation of Teachers

> (202) 879-4400
> 555 New Jersey Avenue NW
> Washington, DC 20001
> www.aft.org

Independent Educational Consultants Association

> (703) 591-4850
> 4085 Chain Bridge Road, Ste 401
> Fairfax, VA 22030
> www.educationalconsulting.org

Institute of International Education

> (212) 883-8200
> 809 United Nations Plaza
> New York, NY 10017
> www.iie.org

Modern Language Association

> (212) 475-9500
> 10 Astor Place
> New York, NY 10003
> www.mla.org

National Association of Student Personnel Administrators

> (202)265-7500
> 1875 Connecticut Avenue NW, Ste 418
> Washington, DC 20009
> www.naspa.org

National Education Association

> (202) 833-4000
> 1201 16th Street NW
> Washington, DC 20036
> www.nea.org

Women in Higher Education

> (608) 251-3232
> 1934 Monroe Street
> Madison, WI 53711
> www.itis.com/wihe

Energy

American Gas Association

> (703) 841-8600
> 1515 Wilson Blvd.
> Arlington, VA 22009
> www.aga.org

American Petroleum Institute

> (202) 682-8000
> 1220 L Street NW, Ste 900
> Washington, DC 20005
> www.api.org

National Coal Association

> (202) 463-2625
> 1130 17th Street NW, Ste 900
> Washington, DC 20005
> www.nma.org

National Petroleum Council

> (202) 393-6100
> 1625 K St. NW
> Washington, DC 20006
> www.npc.org

Engineering

American Association of Engineering Societies

> (202) 296-2237
> 1111 19th Street NW, Ste 608
> Washington, DC 20036
> www.aaes.org/aaes/ewc

American Institute of Chemical Engineers

> 212-705-7338
> 345 East 47th Street
> New York, NY 10017
> www.aiche.org

American Society of Civil Engineers

> (202) 789-2200
> 1015 15th Street NW, Ste 600
> Washington, DC 20005
> www.asce.org

American Society of Mechanical Engineers

> (212) 705-7722
> 345 East 47th Street
> New York, NY 10017
> www.asme.org

Institute of Electrical and Electronics Engineers

> (212) 705-7900
> 345 East 47th Street
> New York, NY 10017
> www.ieee.org

Institute of Industrial Engineers

> (770) 449-0460
> 25 Technology Park
> Norcross, GA 30092
> www.iie.org

Junior Engineering Technical Society

> (703) 548-JETS
> 1420 King Street, Ste 405
> Alexandria, VA 22314
> www.ase.org/jets

Environment

Ecological Society of America

> (202) 833-8773
> 2010 Massachusetts Avenue NW, Ste 400
> Washington, DC 20036
> www.edsc.edu/~esa/esa

Environmental Protection Agency

> (202) 260-2090
> 401 Main Street, SW, Room 3634
> Washington, DC 20460
> www.epa.gov

Student Conservation Association

> (603) 543-1700
> P.O. Box 550
> Charlestown, NH 03603
> www.sca-inc.org

Water Environment Federation

> (703) 684-2400
> 601 Wythe Street
> Alexandria, VA 22314
> www.wef.org

Film/TV/Music/Radio

American Federation of Television and Radio Artists

> (212) 532-0800
> 260 Madison Avenue
> New York, NY 10016

American Film Institute J.F. Kennedy Center for the Performing Arts

> (202) 828-4000
> New Hampshire Avenue at Rock Creek Pkwy.
> Washington, DC 20566
> www.afionline.org

American Women in Radio and Television

> (703) 506-3290
> 1650 Tysons Blvd., Ste 200
> McLean, VA 22101
> www.awrt.org

Independent Feature Project

> (212) 465-8200
> 104 West 29th Street
> New York, NY 10001
> www.ifp.org

Motion Picture Association of America

> (202) 293-1966
> 1600 Eye Street NW
> Washington, DC 20006
> www.mpaa.org

National Academy of Television Arts and Sciences

> (212) 586-8424
> 111 West 57th Street
> New York, NY 10019
> www.emmyonline.org

National Association of Black-Owned Broadcasters

> (202) 463-8970
> 1730 M Street NW
> Washington, DC 20036
> www.bin.com.assocorg/nabob/nabobcnf.htm

National Association of Broadcasters

> (202) 429-5300
> 1771 N Street NW
> Washington, DC 20036
> www.nab.org

National Cable Television Association

> (202) 775-3550
> 1724 Massachusetts Avenue NW
> Washington, DC 20036
> www,ncta.com

Producers Guild of America

> (310) 557-0807
> 400 South Beverly Drive, Ste 211
> Beverly Hills, CA 90212
> www.producersguild.com

Radio-Television News Directors Association

> (202) 659-6510
> 1717 K Street NW, Ste 615
> Washington, DC 20006
> www.rtnda.org/rtnda

Recording Industry Association of America

> (202) 775-0101
> 1020 19th Street NW, Ste 200
> Washington, DC 20036
> www.riaa.com

Songwriters Guild of America

> (201) 867-7603
> 1500 Harbor Blvd.
> Weehawken, NJ 07087
> www.songwriters.org

Finance

American Finance Association

> (212) 998-0370
> Stern, 44 West 4th Street, Ste 9-190
> New York, NY 10012
> www.cob.ohio-state.edu/~fin/journal/
> afaabout.htm

American Financial Services Association

> (202) 296-5544
> 919 18th Street NW
> Washington, DC 20016
> www.americanfinsvcs.com

Association for Investment Management and
Research

(800) 247-8132
5 Boar's Head Lane, P.O. Box 3668
Charlottesville, VA 22903
www.aimr.com

Financial Analysts Federation

(804) 977-8977
P.O. Box 3726
Charlottesville, VA 22903

Financial Women's Association of New York

(212) 533-2141
215 Park Avenue South, Ste 2010
New York, NY 10003
www.fwa.org

Financial Women International

(703) 807-2007
200 North Glebe Road, Ste 1430
Arlington, VA 22203
www.fwi.org

Institute of Certified Financial Planners

(303) 759-4900
3801 East Florida Avenue, Ste 708
Denver, CO 80231
www.icsp.org

Institute of Chartered Financial Analysts

(804) 977-6600
P.O. Box 3668, University of Virginia
Charlottesville, VA 22901

Investment Council Association of America

(212) 344-0999
1050 17th Street NW, Ste 725
Washington, DC 20036
www.ica.word

National Association of Corporate Treasurers

(703) 318-4227
11250 Roger Bacon Drive, Ste 8
Reston, VA 22090
www.nact.org/treasurers/

National Association of Credit Management

(410) 740-5560
8815 Centr Park Drive
Columbia, MD 21045
www.nacm.org

National Association of Securities Dealers

(202) 728-8000
1735 K Street NW
Washington, DC 20006
www.nasdaq.com & www.nasdr.com

Security Traders Association

(212) 524-0484
World Trade Center, Ste 4511
New York, NY 10048

Graphic Design/Arts

American Institute of Graphic Arts

(212) 807-1990
164 Fifth Avenue
New York, NY 10021
www.aiga.org

Graphic Artists Guild

(212) 791-3400
90 John Street, Ste 403
New York, NY 10038
www.gag.org

National Computer Graphics Association

(703) 698-9600
2722 Merrilee Drive
Reston, VA 22031

Health Care/Medicine

American Academy of Physician Assistants

(703) 836-2272
950 North Washington Street
Alexandria, VA 22314
www.aapa.org/

American Association for Respiratory Care

> (214) 243-2272
> 11030 Ables Lane
> Dallas, TX 75229
> www.aarc.org

American Association of Colleges of Pharmacy

> (703) 739-2330
> 1426 Price Street
> Alexandria, VA 22314
> www.aacp.org

American Association of Colleges of Podiatric Medicine

> (301) 990-7400
> 1350 Piccard Drive, Ste 322
> Rockville, MD 20850
> www.aacpm.org

American Association of Medical Assistants

> (312) 899-1500
> 20 North Wacker Drive, Ste 1575
> Chicago, IL 60606
> www.aama.org

American College of Nurse Midwives

> (202) 728-9860
> 1522 K Street NW, Ste 1000
> Washington, DC 20005
> www.acnm.org

American Medical Association

> (312) 464-5000
> 535 Dearborn Street
> Chicago, IL 60610
> www.ama-assn.org

American Nurses Association

> (202) 651-7000
> 600 Maryland Avenue SW, Ste 100
> Washington, DC 20024
> www.nursingworld.org

American Occupational Therapy Association

> (301) 652-2682
> 4720 Montgomery Lane
> P.O. Box, 31220
> Bethesda, MD 20824
> www.aota.org

American Optometric Association

> (314) 991-4100
> 243 North Lindbergh Blvd.
> St. Louis, MO 63141
> www.aoa.org

American Physical Therapy Association

> (800) 999-2782
> 1111 North Fairfax Street
> Alexandria, VA 22314
> www.apta.org

American Psychiatric Association

> (202) 682-6000
> 1400 K Street NW
> Washington, DC 20005
> www.psych.org

American Society of Radiologic Technologists

> (505) 298-4500
> 15000 Central Avenue SE
> Albuquerque, NM 87123
> www.asrt.org

American Speech-Language-Hearing Association

> (301) 897-5700
> 10801 Rockville Pike
> Rockville, MD 20852
> www.asha.org/asha/

Gerentological Society of America

> (202) 842-1275
> 1275 K Street NW, Ste 350
> Washington, DC 20005
> www.geron.org

International Chiropractors Association

(703) 528-5000
1110 North Glebe Road, Ste 1000
Arlington, VA 22201
www.ica.org

National Association for Home Care

(202) 547-7424
519 C Street NE,
Washington, DC 20002
www.nahc.org

National Association of Emergency Medical
Technicians

(800) 346-2368
601-924-7744
102 West Leake Street
Clinton, MS 39056
www.naemt.org

National Society of Genetic Counselors

(610) 872-7608
233 Canterbury Drive
Wallingford, PA 19086
www.kumc.edu/GEC/prof/nsqc.html

National League for Nursing

(212) 989-9393
350 Hudson Street
New York, NY 10014
nlninform@nln.org

Society of Diagnostic Medical Sonographers

(214) 239-7367
12770 Coit Road, Ste 508
Dallas, TX 75251
www.sdms.org

The Society of Nuclear Medicine

(703) 708-9000
1850 Samuel Morse Drive
Reston, VA 22090
www.snm.org

Health Administration/Public Health

American Association of Healthcare Consultants

(703) 691-AAHC
11208 Waples Mill Road, Ste 109
Fairfax, VA 22030
www.mcninet.com/aahc/

American College of Healthcare Executives

(312) 424-2800
1 North Franklin Streer, Ste 1700
Chicago, IL 60606
www.ache.org

American College of Hospital Administrators

(312) 424-2800
840 North Lake Shore Drive
Chicago, IL 60611
www.acha.org

American Health Care Association

(202) 842-4444
1201 L Street NW
Washington, DC 20004
www.acha.org

American Health Infomation Management
Association

(312) 787-2672
919 North Michigan Avenue, Ste 1400
Chicago, IL 60611
www.ahima.org

American Hospital Association

(312) 422-3000
1 North Franklin
Chicago, IL 60606
www.amhpi.com

American Public Health Association

(202) 789-5600
1015 15th Street NW
Washington, DC 20005
www.alpha.org

National Association for Hospital Development

> (703) 532-6243
> 112B East Broad Street
> Falls Church, VA 22046
> www.go-ahp.org

National Health Council

> (202) 785-3910
> 1730 M Street NW, Ste 500
> Washington, DC 20036
> www.healthanswers.com

National Health Lawyers Association

> (202) 833-1100
> 522 21st Street NW, #120
> Washington, DC 20006
> www.nhla.org/nhla

History

American Association for State and Local History

> (615) 255-2971
> 1400 Eighth Avenue South
> Nashville, TN 37203
> www.nashville.net/~aaslh

American Folklore Society

> (703) 528-1902
> c/o American Anthropological Association
> 4350 North Fairfax Drive, Ste 640
> Arlington, VA 22203
> www.amercanthassn.org

National Trust for Historic Preservation

> (202) 588-6000
> 1785 Massachusetts Avenue NW
> Washington, DC 20036
> www.nthp.org

Society of American Archivists

> (312) 922-0140
> 600 South Federal, Ste 504
> Chicago, IL 60605
> www.archivists.org

Hospitality

American Hotel and Motel Association

> (202) 289-3100
> 1201 New York Avenue NW, Ste 600
> Washington, DC 20005
> www.ahma.com

Club Managers Association of America

> (703) 739-9500
> 1733 King Street
> Alexandria, VA 22314
> www.cmaa.org

Council on Hotel, Restaurant and Institutional Education

> (202) 331-5990
> 1200 17th Street NW
> Washington, DC 20036
> www.access.digex.net/~alliance

Independent Innkeepers Association

> (616) 789-0393
> P.O. Box 150
> Marshall, MI 49068
> www.innbook.com

National Restaurant Association

> (202) 331-5900
> 1200 17th Street NW
> Washington, DC 20036
> www.access.digex.net/~alliance

Human Resources/Training/ Labor Relations

American Arbitration Association

> (212) 484-4000
> 140 West 51st Street
> New York, NY 10020
> www.adr.org/

American Compensation Association

(602) 951-9191
14040 Northsight Blvd.
Scottsdale, AZ 85260
www.ahrm.org/aca/aca.htm

American Society for Training and Development

(703) 683-8100
1640 King Street
P.O. Box 1443
Alexandria, VA 22313
www.astd.org

International Personnel Management
Association
(703) 549-7100
1617 Duke Street
Alexandria, VA 22314
www.ipma-hr.org

Society for Human Resource Management

(703) 548-3440
606 North Washington Street
Alexandria, VA 22314
www.shrm.org

Insurance

American Insurance Services Group

(212) 669-0400
85 John Street
New York, NY 10038
www.aisq.org

Insurance Information Institute

(212) 669-9200
110 William Street
New York, NY 10038
www.iii.org

Reinsurance Association of America

(202) 638-3690
1301 Pennsylvania Avenue NW, Ste 900
Washington, DC 20036
www.raanet.org

International

American Association of Exporters and Importers

(212) 944-2230
11 West 42nd Street
New York, NY 10036

American Translators Association

(703) 683-6100
1800 Diagonal Road, Ste 220
Alexandria, VA 22314
www.humanities.byu.edu/trq/ata/
atahome.htm

International Trade Council

(703) 548-1234
1900 Mount Vernon Avenue
P.O. Box 2478
Alexandria, VA 22301
www.itctrade.erols.com

Law

American Bar Association

(312) 988-5000/(800) 621-6159
750 North Lake Shore Drive
Chicago, IL 60611
www.abanet.org

National Association of Legal Assistants

(918) 587-6828
1516 South Boston, Ste 200
Tulsa, OK 74119
www.nala,org

National Court Reporters Association

(703) 556-6272
8224 Old Courthouse Road
Vienna, VA 22182
www.ncraonline.org

National Federation of Paralegal Associations

(816) 941-4000
P.O. Box 33108
Kansas City, MI 64114
www.paralegals.org

National Legal Center for the Public Interest

(202) 296-1683
1101 17th Street NW
Washington, DC 20036
www.nlcpi.org

Law Enforcement/Corrections/ Investigation

American Correctional Association

(301) 918-1800
8025 Laurel Lakes Court
Laurel, MD 20707
www.corrections.com/aca

American Federation of Police

(305) 573-0070
3801 Biscayne Blvd.
Miami, FL 33137
www.aphf.org

American Jail Association

(301) 790-3930
P.O. Box 2158
Hagerstown, MD 21742
www.corrections.com/aja

American Probation and Parole Association

(606) 244-8203
P.O. Box 11910
Lexington, KY 40578
www.csq.org/appa/appa.html

American Society of Criminology

(612) 292-9207
1314 Kinnear, Ste 214
Columbus, OH 43212
www.bsos.umd.edu/asc/

National Association of Investigative Specialists

(512) 719-3595
P.O. Box 33244
Austin, TX 78764
www.pimall.com/nais

World Association of Detectives

(410) 544-0119
P.O. Box 1049
Severna Park, MD 21146

Management

American Management Association

(212) 586-8100
135 West 50th Street
New York, NY 10020
www.ama.org

American Society for Public Administration

(202) 393-7878
1120 G Street NW, Ste 500
Washington, DC 20005
www.aspanet.org

American Society of Association Executives

(202) 626-2723
1575 I Street NW
Washington, DC 20005
www.asaenet.org

Institute of Management Consultants

(212) 697-8262
521 Fifth Avenue, 35th flr
New York, NY 10175
www.imcusa.org

National Association for Female Executives

(212) 477-2200
127 West 24th Street
New York, NY 10011
www.nafe.com

National Federation of Business & Professional Women of the USA

(202) 293-1100
2012 Massachusetts Avenue NW
Washington, DC 20036

Women in Management

(312) 263-3636
Two North Riverside Plaza, Ste 2400
Chicago, IL 60606

Manufacturing

National Association of Manufacturers

(202) 637-3000
1331 Pennsylvania Avenue NW, Ste 1500
Washington, DC 20004
www.nam.org

Marketing

American Marketing Association

(312) 648-0536
250 South Wacker Drive, Ste 200
Chicago, IL 60606
www.ama.org

Direct Marketing Association

(212) 768-7277
1120 Avenue of the Americas
New York, NY 10036
www.the-dma.org

Marketing Research Association

(860) 257-4008
P.O. Box 230
Rocky Hill, CT 06067
www.mranet.org

Mathematics

Mathematical Association of America

(202) 387-5200
1529 18th Street NW
Washington, DC 20036
www.maa.org

Society for Industrial and Applied Mathematics

(215) 382-9800
117 South 17th Street
Philadelphia, PA 19103
www.siam.org/index/htm

Meeting/Event/Party Planning

Association of Bridal Consultants

(860) 355-0464
200 Chestnutland Road
New Milford, CT 06776
www.infopost.com/ypages/weddings/
brideconsult/index.html

Meeting Professionals International

(972) 702-3000
4455 LBJ Freeway, Ste 1200
Dallas, TX 75244
www.mpiweb.org

Multimedia

Interactive Multimedia Association

(401) 626-1380
48 Maryland Avenue, Ste 202
Annapolis, MD 21401
www.ima.org; e-mail info@ima.org

The HTML Writers Guild

www.hwg.org
(Accessible only by the Internet)

Also consult the Multimedia Wire site at
www.mmwire.com:80/directory/
association.html.

This site lists trade organizations dedicated to
promoting the interactive/new media industry.

Not-for-Profit/Public Sector/ Social Service

American Society for Public Administration

(202) 393-7878
1120 G Street NW, Ste 500
Washington, DC 20005
www.aspanet.org

Association for Community-Based Education

(202) 462-6333
1805 Florida Avenue NW
Washington, DC 20009

Center for Community Change

(202) 342- 0519
1000 Wisconsin Avenue NW
Washington, DC 20007

Council on Foundations

(202) 466-6512
1828 L Street NW
Washington, DC 20036
www.cof.org

National Congress for Community Economic Development

(202) 234-5009
2025 I Street NW, Ste 901
Washington, DC 20006

National Network of Grantmakers

(619) 231-1348
1717 Kettner Blvd., Ste 100
San Diego, CA 92101

National Society of Fund Raising Executives

(703) 684-0410
1101 King Street, Ste 700
Alexandria, VA 22314
www.nsfre.org

Social Service Association

(201) 444-2980
6 Station Plaza
Ridgewood, NJ 07450

Society for Nonprofit Organizations

(608) 274-9777
6314 Odana Road, Ste 1
Madison, WI 53719
www.damnet.icip.org/snpo

Nutrition

American Dietetic Association

(312) 899-0040
216 West Jackson Blvd., Ste 800
Chicago, IL 60606
www.eatright.org

American Society for Clinical Nutrition

(301) 530-7110
09650 Rockville Pike, Room L-2310
Bethesda, MD 20814
www.faseb.org/ascn

Operations/Production/ Facilities Management

American Production and Inventory Control Society

(703) 237-8344
500 West Anandale Road
Falls Church, VA 22046
www.apics.org

American Society for Quality Control

(414) 272-8575
310 West Wisconsin Avenue
Milwaukee, WI 53203
www.asqc.org

Council of Logistics Management

(708) 574-0985
2803 Butterfield Road, Ste 380
Oak Brook, IL 60521
www.clm1.org

International Facility Management Association

(713) 623-IFMA
1 Greenway Plaza, 11th flr
Houston, TX 77046
www.ifma.org

Operations Research Society of America

(410) 850-0300
Mount Royal & Guildford Avenues
Baltimore, MD 21202
www.informs.org

Performing Arts

Actors' Equity Association

(212) 869-8530
1560 Broadway
New York, NY 10036

American Dance Guild

> (212) 932-2789
> 31 West 21st Street, 3rd flr
> New York, NY 10010

American Federation of Musicians

> (212) 869-1330
> 1501 Broadway, Ste 600
> New York, NY 10036
> www.afm.org

American Guild of Musical Artists

> (212) 265-3687
> 1727 Broadway
> New York, NY 10019

Associated Actors and Artists of America

> (212) 869-0358
> 165 West 46th Street
> New York, NY 10036

International Society of Performing Arts
Administrators

> (616) 364-3000
> 2920 Fuller Avenue NE, Ste 205
> Grand Rapids, MI 49505
> www.ispa-online.org

League of Historic American Theaters

> (440) 659-9533
> 34 Market Place, Ste 320
> Baltimore, MD 21202

Screen Actors Guild

> (213) 549-6400
> 5757 Wilshire Blvd.
> Los Angeles, CA 90036

Theater Communications Group

> (212) 697-5230
> 355 Lexington Avenue
> New York, NY 10017
> www.tcg.org

Pharmaceuticals

American Pharmaceutical Association

> (202) 628-4410
> 2215 Constitution Avenue NW
> Washington, DC 22037
> www.aphanet.org

Pharmaceutical Manufacturers Association

> (202) 835-3400
> 1100 15th Street NW
> Washington, DC 20005
> www.phrma.org

Psychology/Counseling

American Counseling Association

> (703) 823-9800
> 5999 Stevenson Avenue
> Alexandria, VA 22304
> www.counseling.org

American Psychological Association

> (202) 336-5500
> 750 First Street NE
> Washington, DC 20002
> www.apa.org

American School Counseling Association

> (703) 683-2722
> 801 North Farifax Street, Ste 301
> Alexandria, VA 22314
> www.edge.net/asca/

Public Relations/Promotions

International Communication Association

> (512) 454-8299
> Balcones Research Center
> 10100 Burnet Road
> Austin, TX 78758
> www.io.com/~icahdg/ica/ica.html

Promotion Marketing Association of America

(212) 420-1100
257 Park Avenue South, 11th flr
New York, NY 10010
www.pmaalink.org

Public Relations Society of America

(212) 995-2230
33 Irving Place, 3rd flr
New York, NY 10003
www.prsa.org

Public Relations Student Society of America

(212) 460-1474
33 Irving Place, 3rd flr
New York, NY 10003
www.prssa.org

The Council of Sales Promotion Agencies

(203) 325-3911
750 Summer Street, 2nd flr
Stamford, CT 06901
www.atmaw.org

Publishing/Journalism/Writing/ Communications

American Society of Journalists and Authors

(212) 997-0947
1501 Broadway, Ste 302
New York, NY 10036
www.asja.org

American Society of Magazine Editors

(212) 872-3700
919 Third Avenue
New York, NY 10022
www.magazine.org

Association of American Publishers

(212) 255-0200
71 Fifth Avenue
New York, NY 10003
www.publishers.org

Magazine Publishers Association

(212) 872-3700
919 Third Avenue
New York, NY 10022
www.magazine.org

National Newspaper Association

(703) 907-7900
1525 Wilson Blvd., Ste 550
Arlington, VA 22209
www.oweb.com/nna

National Writers Union

(212) 254-0279
113 University Place, 6th flr
New York, NY 10003
www.iqc.apc.org

Society for Technical Communication

(703) 522-4114
901 N. Stuart Street, Ste 304
Arlington, VA 22203
www.stc-va.org

The Association for Women in Communications

(410) 544-7442
1244 Ritchie Highway, Ste 6
Arnold, MD 21012
www.womcom.org

The Newspaper Guild

(301) 585-2990
8611 Second Avenue
Silver Spring, MD 20910
www.newsguild.org

Writers Guild of America

(212) 767-7800
555 West 57th Street
New York, NY 10019
www.wgaeast.org

Purchasing

National Association of Purchasing Management

(602) 752-6276
2055 East Centennial Circle
P.O. Box 22160
Tempe, AZ 85282
www.napm.org

National Association of State Purchasing Officials

(606) 231-1877
P.O. Box 11910
Lexington, KY 40578
www.naspo.org

Real Estate

Institute of Real Estate Management

(312) 661-1930
430 North Michigan Avenue
Chicago, IL 60611
www.irem.org

National Association of Real Estate Brokers

(202) 785-4477
1629 K Street NW, No. 2, Ste 605
Washington, DC 20006
www.nareb.org

National Association of Realtors

(312) 329-8449
430 North Michigan Avenue
Chicago, IL 60611
www.realtor.com

Retailing

American Retail Federation

(202) 783-7971
325 7th Street NW, Ste 1000
Washington, DC 20004
www.nrf.com

Sales

American Telemarketing Association

(818) 766-5324
5000 Van Nuys Blvd., No. 400
Sherman Oaks, CA 91403
www.ata.aw3s.com

Association of Industry Manufacturers Representatives

(312) 464-0092
222 Merchandise Mart Plaza, Ste 1360
Chicago, IL 60654
www.asa.net

National Association of Sales Professionals

(602) 951-4311
8300 N. Hayden Road, Ste 207
Scottsdale, AZ 85258
www.nasp.com

National Association of Wholesaler-Distributors

(202) 872-0885
1725 K Street NW
Washington, DC 20006

Science (Including Social Sciences)

Academy of Political Science

(212) 870-2500
475 Riverside Dr, Ste 1274
New York, NY 10015
www.epn.org/psq.html

Botanical Society of America

(614) 292-3519
1735 Neil Avenue
Columbus, OH 43210
www.botany.org/bsa

American Academy of Political and Social Science

(215) 386-4594
3937 Chestnut Street
Philadelphia, PA 19104

American Anthropological Association

(703) 528-1902
4350 N. Fairfax Drive, Ste 640
Arlington, VA 22203
www.ameranthassn.org

American Astronomical Society

(202) 328-2010
200 Florida Avenue NW, Ste 400
Washington, DC 20009
www.aas.org

American Chemical Society

(202) 872-4600
(800) 227-5558
1155 16th Street NW
Washington, DC 20036
www.acs.org

American Geological Institute

(703) 379-2480
4220 King Street
Alexandria, VA 22302
www.Agiweb.org

American Institute of Biological Sciences

(202) 628-1500
730 11th Street NW
Washington, DC 20001
www.aibs.org

American Meteorological Society

(617) 227-2425
45 Beacon Street
Boston, MA 02108
www.ametsoc.org/AMS

American Physical Society

(301) 209-3235
1 Physics Ellipse
College Park, MD 20740
www.aps.org

American Physiological Society

(301) 530-7164
9650 Rockville Pike
Bethesda, MD 20814
www.fased.org/aps

American Political Science Association

(202) 483-2512
1527 New Hampshire Avenue NW
Washington, DC 20036
www.apsanet.org

American Society for Microbiology

(202) 737-3600
1325 Massachusetts Avenue NW
Washington, DC 20005
www.asmusa.org

American Sociological Association

(202) 833-3410
1722 N Street NW
Washington, DC 20036
www.asanet.org

Genetics Society of America

(301) 571-1825
9650 Rockville Pike
Bethesda, MD 20814
www.faseb.org/genetics

Marine Technology Society

(202) 775-5966
1825 K Street NW, Ste 218
Washington, DC 20006
email: mtspubs@aol.com

National Science Foundation

(703) 306-1070
4201 Wilson Blvd.
Arlington, VA 22230
www.nsf.gov

Skilled Trades/Technicians

American Welding Society

(305) 443-9353
550 NW LeJeune Road
Miami, FL 33126
www.amweld.org

Associated General Contractors of America

(202) 393-2040
1957 E Street NW
Washington, DC 20006
www.agc.org

Association of Manufacturing Technicians

(703) 893-2900
7901 Westpark Drive
McLean, VA 22102
www.mfgtech.org

Automotive Service Association

(817) 283-6205
520 Central Parkway East, Ste 114
Plato, TX 75074
www.asashop.org

Electronics Technicians Association Int'l

(765) 653-8262
602 North Jackson Street
Greencastle, IN 46135
www.eta-sda.com

Independent Electrical Contractors

(703) 549-7351
P.O. Box 10379
Alexandria, VA 22310
www.ieci.org

National Association of Women in Construction

(800) 552-3506
327 S. Adams Street
Ft. Worth, TX 76104
www.nawic.org

National Electrical Contractors Association

(301) 657-3110
7315 Wisconsin Avenue
Bethesda, MD 20814
www.necanet.org

Small Business/Entrepreneurs/ Franchising

American Association of Black Women Entrepreneurs

(301) 585-8051
P.O. Box 13858
Silver Spring, MD 20911

American Home Business Association

(800) 664-2422
4505 South Wasatch Blvd.
Salt Lake City, UT 84124
www.homebusiness.com

American Women's Economic Development Corp.

(212) 692-9100
71 Vanderbilt Avenue, 3rd flr
New York, NY 10169

Center for Entrepreneurial Management

(212) 633-0060
180 Varick Street
New York, NY 10014
www.ceo-clubs.org

Chamber of Commerce of the United States

(202) 659-6000
1615 H Street NW
Washington, DC 20006
www.uschamber.org

International Franchise Association

(202) 628-8000
1025 Connecticut Avenue NW
Washington, DC 20036
www.franchise.org

National Association for the Self-Employed

> (800) 232-NASE
> P.O. Box 612067
> Dallas, TX 75261
> www.nase.org

U.S. Small Business Administration

> (800) 827-5722
> 1441 L Street NW, Washington, DC 20416
> www.sba.gov

Young Entrepreneur's Organization

> (800) 804-3688
> 1321 Duke Street, Ste 300
> Alexandria, VA 22314

Social Work

National Association of Social Workers

> (202) 408-8600
> 750 First Street NE, Ste 700
> Washington, DC 20002
> www.naswdc.org

Telecommunications

Cable Telecommunications Association

> (703) 691-8875
> P.O. Box 1005
> Fairfax, VA 22030
> www.catanet.org

Cellular Telecommunications Industry Association

> (202) 785-0081
> 1250 Connecticut Avenue NW, Ste 200
> Washington, DC 20036
> www.wow-com.com

National Association of Telecommunications Officers and Advisors

> (703) 506-3275
> 1650 Tysons Blvd., Ste 200
> McLean, VA 22102
> www.natoa.org

Society of Telecommunications Consultants

> (408) 659-0110
> 13766 Center Street, No. 212
> Carmel Valley, CA 93924
> www.stcconsultants.org

Travel

Adventure Travel Society

> (303) 649-9016
> 6551 South Revere Parkway, Ste 160
> Englewood, CO 80111
> www.adventuretravel.com/ats

American Society of Travel Agents

> (703) 739-2782
> 1101 King Street
> Alexandria, VA 22134
> www.astanet.com

Cruise Lines International Association

> (212) 921-0066
> 500 Fifth Avenue, Ste 1407
> New York, NY 10110
> www.cruising.org

Institute of Certified Travel Agents

> (617) 237-0280
> 148 Lindon Street
> P.O. Box 56
> Wellesley, MA 02181
> www.icta.com

Society of American Travel Writers

> (919) 787-5181
> 4101 Lake Boone Trail, Ste 201
> Raleigh, NC 27607
> www.writersmarketplace.com

Urban/Regional Planning

American Planning Association

> (312) 431-9100
> 1313 East 60th Street
> Chicago, IL 60603
> www.planning.org

International Downtown Association

> (202) 783-4963
> 915 15th Street NW, Ste 600
> Washington, DC 20005
> www.ida-downtown.org

National Policy Association

> (202) 265-7685
> 1424 16th St NW, Ste 700
> Washington, DC 20036
> www.npa1.org

Veterinary Medicine/Animals

American Association of Zookeepers

> (913) 273-1980
> 635 Gage Blvd.
> Topeka, KS 66606
> http://aazk.ind.net/

American Association of Zoological Parks & Aquariums

> (304) 242-2160
> Olgebay Park, Rte 88
> Wheeling, WV 26003
> www.aza.org

American Society of Zoologists

> (312) 527-6697
> 401 North Michigan Avenue
> Chicago, IL 60611
> www.sicb.org

American Veterinary Medical Association

> (847) 925-8070
> 930 North Meacham Road
> Schaumburg, IL 60196
> www.avma.org

The Humane Society of the United States

> (202) 452-1100
> 2100 L Street NW
> Washington, DC 20037
> www.hsus.org

Waste Management

Air and Waste Management Association

> (412) 232-3444
> P.O. Box 2861
> Pittsburgh, PA 15230
> www.awma.org

National Solid Wastes Management Association

> (202) 244-4700
> 4301 Connecticut Avenue NW, Ste 300
> Washington, DC 20008
> www.envasns.org

Potpourri

Just when you thought you'd seen everything, here are a few examples of some of the more specialized associations that exist. If you have an interest that's a bit offbeat, you might want to consult Organized Obsessions, a directory of unusual and not-so-unusual associations (*see* Appendix D for the complete reference).

American Association of Small Ruminant Practitioners

American Beekeeping Federation

American Shetland Pony Club

Association of Tongue Depressors

Clowns of America International

Embroiders' Guild of America, Inc.

Green Olive Trade Association

Guild of American Luthiers

Ice Skating Institute of America

International Cake, Candy, and Party Supply Association

International Sprout Growers Association

International Staple, Nail, and Tool Association

Appendix C

Where to Find Experts to Help with Your Networking

Chapter 3 introduced you to the concept of "allied forces" as an essential part of your network. These are the "behind the scenes" experts who make sure that all your networking encounters are up to par. They help you look good, sound professional, write well, plan effective strategies, make the right choices, and stay healthy and relaxed, among other things.

This appendix is designed to help you track down many of the professionals who can support your networking efforts. It is arranged according to categories of professional expertise, and within each category, you will find contact information for professional associations, referral organizations, individuals, service businesses, and Web sites. These resources can provide the services you need or can refer you to someone who can.

Business Strategy Consulting

Small Business Administration (SBA)

SBA Answer Desk: (800) 827-5722; www.sba.gov

The SBA offers a wide range of services for small businesses and has offices across the country.

SCORE—The Service Corps of Retired Executives

Contact the Small Business Administration for referral to a SCORE office near you. The retired executives who volunteer for SCORE use their many years of business experience to advise you about your small business or one you're thinking of starting.

American Women's Economic Development Corporation (AWED)

71 Vanderbilt Avenue, Suite 320, New York, NY 10169, (212) 692-9100

AWED is a national organization that offers individual counseling, mentoring, workshops, seminars, conferences, publications, and other resources to established and new businesses owned by women.

Center for Entrepreneurial Management

180 Varick Street, PH, New York, NY 10014, (212) 633-0060

A national, not-for-profit organization that offers a variety of services including networking opportunities for entrepreneurs.

The Business Strategy Seminar (BSS)

120 East 34th Street, #14B, New York, NY 10016, (212) 481-7075 tel; (212) 481-7690 fax; GroBiz@aol.com

BSS provides ongoing strategy and support to small business owners and self-employed individu-als from all industries. BSS operates 10-week support groups for business owners at all levels of development. BSS also offers individual consulting in areas of marketing, sales, goal setting, career direction, and personal development.

Web Sites Related to Small Business

www.workingsolo.com

www.ideacafe.com

www.edgeonline.com (*Entrepreneurial* magazine online)

www.fastcompany.com (*Fast Company* magazine online)

www.inc.com (*Inc.* magazine online)

www.successmagazine.com

For more referral sources, see the Small Business, Entrepreneurs, and Franchising section of the professional association listings in Appendix B.

Career Counseling

Career Planning and Adult Development Network

4965 Sierra Road, San Jose, CA 95132, (408) 559-4946 tel; (408) 559-8211 fax

This international network consists of approximately 1,000 career development professionals, many of whom are in private practice or work in organizations that serve the general public. The main office in San Jose can tell you how to get in touch with the Network contact person in your area (there's at least one in most U.S. states and in several other countries). Your local contact can then refer you to a career counselor.

Appendix of What Color Is Your Parachute?

The appendix of the popular job search guide, *What Color Is Your Parachute?* (by Richard Bolles and published annually by Ten Speed Press) has a listing of career counselors by state and in several foreign countries.

Academic and Community-Based Career Centers

If you're in college or graduate school, be sure to take advantage of your campus career counseling services. And, as an alum, you may still have access to career counseling, job listings, and other resources at your alma mater. Contact your schools to see what they have to offer locally and long-distance. Many career counseling services (individual advising and workshops) are also available to the general public in such settings as nonprofit agencies, churches and other religious institutions, adult education centers such as The Learning Annex, and the continuing education or adult learning division of universities.

Career Counseling on the World Wide Web

There are many sites on the Web that post useful advice on career choice, career management, and job search topics, as well as career seminars in online auditoriums and information exchanges on bulletin boards and in chat rooms. Some sites also offer actual counseling online in "real time" sessions or link you to a counselor who can work with you by phone. Most career-related Web sites focus on job listings or resume posting rather than straight advice (and many of these are listed in the "Job Search Coaching" section of this appendix), but some sites offer good general career information, resources, and counseling. Some of these are described in the following sections.

JIST Works, Inc.

www.jist.com/jist

This site provides information on JIST's many career planning, job search, educational, and life skills products.

AboutWork

www.aboutwork.com

This is an interesting site from the company iVillage, Inc., which puts together some of the Web's most information-packed and graphically pleasing spots. It posts lots of lively career advice on a variety of topics and also includes a live chat room.

America's Employers: The Job Seeker's "Home"

www.americasemployers.com

This is a major career "hub" with a directory of 50,000 companies that can be searched by industry, lists of headhunters arranged by specialty areas, interactive discussion groups and chat rooms, and career advising. This is a well-designed, significant site.

The Black Collegian Online

www.black-collegian.com

The online version of *The Black Collegian* magazine, this site is a great place for African-Americans to network. It includes career advice, lots of resources, and job listings.

Career Action Center

www.careeraction.org

This site is distinguished by the seriousness and professional nature of its career advice. Staffed by actual career counselors, this site offers valuable information on career management issues.

Career Center for Workforce Diversity

www.eop.com

This site comes from the people who publish *Careers for the Disabled, Minority Engineer, Women Engineer, and Equal Opportunity* magazines, which circulate primarily on college campuses. It includes top-notch articles on career development and job search topics.

Career Crafting

www.well.com/user/careerc/

This site focuses solely on career advice rather than on jobs. Career information is posted at the site, and free career counseling is available if you call a posted 800 number.

Career Magazine

www.careermag.hub

This is a major site that is especially useful for networking purposes in that it contains an index of over 100 newsgroups searchable by career fields. Its magazine format offers articles on various career and job search topics.

Career Mosaic

www.careermosaic.com

This major site was one of the first career sites on the Web. Its employer profiles and links to company home pages are helpful for networking research, and career advice is provided through articles.

Career Resource Center

www.CareerResource.com

The Career Resource Center provides an extensive index of career resources on the Web with links to over 7,500 sites.

Career Toolbox

www.careertoolbox.com

Produced by a somewhat unlikely purveyor of career advice—the liquor company Seagram's Chivas Regal—this site, with very snazzy graphics, provides on-target career and job search advice from experienced career counselors. Of course, this is not an entirely unbiased critique, as yours truly contributed sample cover letters to the CD-ROM version of this site.

EOP

www.eop.com

This is an excellent networking resource for women, Hispanics, African-Americans, and the disabled. It provides information about conferences, job fairs, employment opportunities, and career advice, all with an eye toward diversity issues.

Getting Past Go: A Survival Guide for College

www.lattanze.loyola.edu:80/mongen/home.html

This is a major site for college students and recent grads with advice on many topics including finances, relocating geographically, careers, and jobs. It also provides good advice on managing your career as a newcomer to the work world.

JobWeb

www.jobweb.org

The site of the National Association of Colleges and Employers (NACE), this is an outstanding source of resources, links to useful sites including professional associations, and lots of excellent advice from career management experts.

Latino Web

www.catalog.com/favison/latnoweb

This site is full of resources, information, and links to other sites of interest to Latinos.

The Riley Guide

www.jobtrak.com/jobguide/

Margaret Riley is known in the career counseling and job coaching world as something of a guru on

Internet job searching. Her site is an excellent starting point for networking and job searching online. It includes an annotated index of job sites and links to most of the sites where you can apply for jobs.

StudentCenter

www.studentcenter.com

This is a strong site for people in entry-level positions. It provides good advice and company profiles for students and recent graduates entering the job market.

Women's Professional Directory

www.womensdirectory.com

This is a true networking site offering opportunities to find mentors, resources, and advice to help women manage and advance in their careers.

Executive Coaching

International Association of Career Management Professionals (IACMP)

P.O. Box 1484, Pacifica, CA 94044, www.iacmp.org

IACMP's members work in outplacement firms, corporate career development and human resources departments, consulting firms, and other settings in which they assist individuals and groups in developing and managing their careers. Many members maintain full-time or part-time private practices that often include executive coaching services along with career management and job search coaching. Others may provide executive coaching through the outplacement or career management firms for which they work. For the current IACMP regional rep in your area, consult the IACMP home page at the indicated Web address.

National Association for Female Executives (NAFE)

30 Irving Place, New York, NY 10003, (800) 634-NAFE; (212) 477-2200 tel.; (212) 477-8215 fax; www.nafe.com

NAFE offers conferences, training programs, and other resources to promote success among female executives.

Executive Recruiters/Employment Agencies

The best way to find a good career search firm or employment agency is through word of mouth, by asking friends and colleagues for referrals to anyone who has placed them in a job in the past. In addition, many recruiters can be found through the jobs they list in the help wanted section of newspapers. You can also consult the following sources:

- *Directory of Executive Search Firms,* Kennedy Publications

- *1997 Guide to Executive Recruiters,* McGraw-Hill

- *The Directory of Executive Temporary Placement Firms,* John Wiley & Sons

- *The Job Seekers Guide to Executive Recruiters,* Kennedy Publications

Image Consulting

Association of Image Consultants International

1000 Connecticut Avenue NW, Ste 9, Washington, DC 20036, (800) 383-8831; (301) 371-9021 tel; (301) 371-8847 fax

This organization can refer you to a consultant in your area who has professional member status with AICI. To find additional names (or ones who might charge less than those endorsed by AICI, but are nonetheless well qualified), consult your local *Yellow Pages*.

Color Me Beautiful

(800) COLORME

Call this 800 number for a referral to an independent consultant who is certified to do a color analysis according to the Color Me Beautiful system.

Job Search Coaching

Some of the organizations and Web sites listed in the Career Counseling section of this appendix are also sources of job search advice. In addition to those sources, there are a number of people and places whose primary (or sole) function is to help people find jobs. They include the following sources.

The Five O'Clock Club

300 East 40th Street, #6L, New York, NY 10016, (212) 286-4500

Headquartered in Manhattan with affiliates across the U.S. and abroad, The Five O'Clock Club offers coaching and networking opportunities in small groups for job hunters and those who want to change careers. The organization's director, Kate Wendleton, is the author of several excellent job search books (see Appendix D). You may contact the New York office to find out if there is a Five O'Clock Club near you.

Forty Plus Clubs

Forty Plus Club of New York, 15 Park Row, New York, NY 10038, (212) 233-6086

For job seekers forty years old or older, these nationwide clubs offer great networking opportunities and job search guidance. You can contact the New York club for information on a location near you.

Job Search Advice and Job Listings on the World Wide Web

There are many Web sites with job listings, resume posting services, and links to employers. Of the sites listed in the Career Counseling section of this appendix, those which provide both career advice and job opportunities are repeated here, along with additional sites whose sole or primary focus is on locating available jobs.

America's Job Bank

www.ajb.dni.us:80/

The Black Collegian Online

www.black-collegian.com

Career America

www.careeramerica.com

Career Center for Workforce Diversity

www.eop.com

Career City

www.careercity.com

Career Magazine

www.careermag.com

Career Mosaic

www.careermosaic.com

Career Path

www.careerpath.com

CAREERXROADS

www.careerxroads.com

Drake Beam Morin

www.dbm.com/candidate

Eagleview

www.eagleview.com

Entry-Level Job Seeker Assistant

members.aol.com/Dylander/jobhome.html

E-Span

www.espan.com

Help Wanted-USA

iccweb.com/employ.html

I-Search

www.isearch.com

JobWeb

www.jobweb.org/

Latino Web

www.catalog.com/favison/latnoweb

The Monster Board

www.monster.com

The Riley Guide

www.jobtrak.com/jobguide/

Professional Organizers

National Association of Professional Organizers

Walter Schatz, Executive Director, 1604 N. Country Club Road., Tucson, AZ 85716, (602) 322-9753

NAPO is a nonprofit association that can refer you to a professional organizer in your area. These are people who can help you get organized and manage your time more effectively.

CareerTrack

3085 Center Green Drive, Boulder, CO 80301, (800) 334-1018 tel; (800) 832-9489 fax

Among many other topics, CareerTrack offers nationwide seminars on setting priorities, meeting deadlines, and other time management and organizational issues in the workplace.

CROSS IT OFF YOUR LIST

404 Park Avenue South, Ste 1201, New York, NY 10016, (212) 725-0122 tel; (212) 779-4349 fax; xofflist@aol.com

This professional organizing and concierge service has a national and international clientele and "Does What You Don't Have Time to Do." They provide a vast array of services to get and keep you organized and to free up your time at work and home.

Psychotherapy/Mental Health/ Wellness

The following professional associations can refer you to members who are qualified psychologists or psychotherapists.

American Psychological Association

Public Affairs, 750 First Street NE, Washington, DC 20002, (800) 374-2721

National Association of Social Workers

750 First Street NE, Ste 700, Washington, DC 20002, (202) 408-8600

National Institute of Mental Health

(800) 969-6642

The remaining organizations in this section offer referrals to professionals who can address your mental (and physical) health from other perspectives.

American Holistic Health Association

P.O. Box 17400, Anaheim, CA 92817, (714) 779-6152

This association can refer you to wellness and holistic health professionals to keep you healthy, centered, and relaxed as you network.

American Association of Professional Hypnotherapists

William S. Brink, P.O. Box 29, Boones Mill, VA 24065

This organization can refer you to clinical social workers, therapists, psychologists, and others with training in hypnosis therapy. Hypnosis might come in handy for anyone who gets exceptionally nervous when networking!

IDEA: The Association for Fitness Professionals

6190 Cornerstone Court East, Ste 204, San Diego, CA 92121, (619) 535-8979 tel; (619) 535-8234 fax

IDEA has a membership of more than 25,000 professionals in the areas of dance, exercise, and fitness training. They can refer you to a personal trainer or movement specialist to help with your personal presentation.

Public Speaking

The following organizations offer seminars and workshops in public speaking and other business communication skills. Some offer individual sessions as well.

Dale Carnegie Courses

(800) 342-7787

Fred Pryor Seminars

(800) 255-6139; (913) 722-8580 fax

The Executive Speaker

(561) 664-5256

The Executive Technique

(312) 266-0001

Publicity/Public Relations

One of the best ways to find a freelance publicist to help with your self-promotion or marketing is simply to ask someone who seems to be getting lots of good publicity! In addition to a word-of-mouth referral, though, you can also find someone through many of the professional groups listed in the Business Strategy Consulting section of this Appendix and through the following organizations.

Public Relations Society of America (PRSA)

33 Irving Place, New York, NY 10003, (212) 995-2230; www.prsa.org

PRSA has a placement service for public relations professionals seeking temporary project work. If you need to hire a freelance publicist, you can list your project as a job with this service.

Voice Coaching/Speech Therapy

American Speech-Language-Hearing Association

10801 Rockville Pike, Rockville, MD 20852, (301) 897-5700; (800) 638-8255

This is the principal professional association for speech pathologists and speech therapists who treat serious speech disorders, as well as help those who simply need to improve their speaking style or voice. This organization can refer you to an appropriate specialist in your area.

Also see listings under Public Speaking for organizations that provide voice coaching.

Written Communication Consulting

Association of Professional Writing Consultants

3924 S. Troost, Tulsa, OK 74105, (918) 743-4793.

This organization offers a referral service to consultants and trainers who can assist you with all types of written communication.

Editing-by-Fax Service

Marcia Yudkin, P.O. Box 1310, Boston, MA 02117, (617) 266-1613 tel; marcia@yudkin.com

This author and writing consultant can critique and edit your written business materials by fax with a quick turnaround time. Call for rates and services.

Books and Software to Enhance Your Networking

During the process of networking, you are likely to be dealing with a lot of complicated issues, such as making career decisions, conducting a job search, trying to advance in your career, or dealing with the ups and downs of running your own business. You might also find that as you practice the networking techniques advocated in this book, you need to work on related personal issues, such as your speaking voice or professional wardrobe. That's why this bibliography includes books and other resources on these and other topics. You'll also find resources for readers with special interests, such as networking in other countries or with special populations.

The information in this appendix is just a brief survey of what's available. The books, directories, and software listed here are the ones I consider to be the best of the bunch. My assessment is largely based on what clients have told me about how well these resources have worked for them.

I am sure, however, that there are lots of other good resources that aren't listed here. If you do find useful resources that I haven't included, or if you want to comment on any that are included, feel free to e-mail me at CareerDr@aol.com.

Resources to Help with Your Career or Job Search

Job Search and Career Books Published by JIST

Career Guide to America's Top Industries, J. Michael Farr, 1995.

Career Satisfaction and Success, Bernard Haldane, 1995.

Complete Guide for Occupational Exploration (CGOE), J. Michael Farr, 1993.

Dare to Change Your Job and Your Life, Carole Kanchier, 1995.

Gallery of Best Resumes: A Collection of Quality Resumes by Professional Resume Writers, David F. Noble, 1994.

Job Savvy—How to Be a Success at Work, LaVerne Ludden, 1997.

The Quick Interview & Salary Negotiation Book—Dramatically Improve Your Interviewing Skills in Just a Few Hours, J. Michael Farr, 1995.

The Quick Resume & Cover Letter Book—Write and Use an Effective Resume in Only One Day, J. Michael Farr, 1994.

Using the Internet and the World Wide Web in Your Job Search, Fred Jandt and Mary Nemnich, 1997.

The Very Quick Job Search, J. Michael Farr, 1995.

Other Good Books on Choosing or Changing Careers

Do What You Are, Paul Tieger and Barbara Barron-Tieger, New York: Little, Brown, 1995.

I Could Do Anything if Only I Knew What it Was, Barbara Sher, New York: Bantam Doubleday Dell, 1995.

Wishcraft: How to Get What You Really Want, Barbara Sher, New York: Ballantine Books, 1986.

Zen and the Art Making a Living, Laurence Boldt, New York: Penguin USA, 1993.

Other Good Books and Directories for Job Searching

Best Jobs for the 1990s and into the 21st Century, Ronald Krannich and Caryl Krannich, Manassas Park, VA: Impact, 1993.

Career Smarts: Jobs with a Future, Martin Yate, New York: Ballantine Books, 1997.

Complete Job Search Handbook, Howard Figler, New York: Henry Holt, 1988 (revised and updated).

Directory of Executive Recruiters, Kennedy Publications, 1997 (annual).

Directory of Outplacement Firms, Kennedy Publications, 1997 (annual).

Job Smart, Michelle Tullier, Tim Haft, Margaret Heenehan, and Marci Taub, New York: Princeton Review/Random House, 1997.

Job Strategies for People with Disabilities, Melanie Astaire Witt, Princeton, New Jersey: Peterson's, 1992.

Portfolio Power, Martin Kimeldorf, Princeton, New Jersey: Peterson's, 1997.

Professional's Job Finder 1997-2000, Daniel Lauber, River Forest, Illinois: Planning/ Communications, 1997.

Targeting the Job You Want, Kate Wendleton, New York: Five O'Clock Books, 1997.

Through the Brick Wall, Kate Wendleton, New York: Villard/Random House, 1992.

Trashproof Resumes, Tim Haft, New York: Princeton Review/Random House, 1995.

What Color Is Your Parachute? Richard Bolles, Berkeley, California: Ten Speed Press (annual).

Books on the Changing World of Work

The Career Is Dead: Long Live the Career, Douglas T. Hall and Associates, San Francisco: Jossey-Bass, 1996.

The Changing Nature of Work, Ann Howard, San Francisco: Jossey-Bass, 1995.

The End of Work, Jeremy Rifkin, New York: Tarcher/Putnam, 1995.

We Are All Self-Employed, Cliff Hakim, San Francisco: Berrett-Koehler, 1995.

Work in the New Economy, Robert Wegmann, Robert Chapman, and Miriam Johnson, Indianapolis, Indiana: JIST, 1989.

Other Good Books for Networking

The African-American Network: Get Connected to More than 5,000 Prominent People and Organizations in the African-American Community, Crawford Bunkley, New York: Plume, 1996.

Asian American Information Directory, K. Backus & J. C. Furtaw, Gale Research, Inc. (annual).

Big Book of Minority Opportunities, Chicago: Ferguson Publ., 1997.

Big Book of Opportunities for Women, Chicago: Ferguson Publ., 1997.

Endless Referrals: Network Your Everyday Contacts into Sales, Bob Burg, New York: McGraw-Hill, 1993.

Keeping Customers for Life, Cannie and Caplin, New York: AMACOM Books, 1992.

Minority Organizations: A National Directory, Chicago: Ferguson Publ., 1997.

Native American Connections, Published annually by the Native American Connection.

Networking at Writer's Conferences: From Contacts to Contracts, Steven Spratt and Lee Spratt, New York: John Wiley & Sons, 1995.

Networking in the Music Business, Dan Kimpel, Cincinnati, Ohio: Writer's Digest Books, 1993.

Success Runs in Our Race: The Complete Guide to Effective Networking in the African-American Community, George Fraser, New York: William Morrow & Co., 1994.

Books Related to Networking OnLine

The African American Resource Guide to the Internet & Online Services, Stafford Battle

& Rey Harris, New York: Computing McGraw-Hill, 1996.

CAREERXROADS, Gerry Crispin and Mark Mehler, Kendall Park, New Jersey: MMC Group, 1997.

Culture of the Internet, Sara Kiesler, Mahwah, New Jersey: Lawrence Erlbaum Associates, 1997.

How to Grow Your Business on the Internet, Vince Emery, Scottsdale, Arizona: Coriolis Book Group, 1996.

netjobs, Michael Wolff, New York: Michael Wolff & Co., 1997.

Publicity on the Internet, Steve O'Keefe, New York: John Wiley & Sons, 1996.

Using the Internet and the World Wide Web in Your Job Search, Fred Jandt and Mary Nemnich, Indianapolis, Indiana: JIST, 1997.

The Virtual Community: Homesteading the Electronic Frontier, Howard Rheingold: New York: Harper Perennial Library, 1994.

What's on the Internet: The Definitive Guide to the Internet's User Newsgroups, Eric Gagnon, Berkeley, California: Peachpit Press/Internet Media, 1996.

What's on the Web 1997, Eric Gagnon, Berkeley, California: Peachpit Press/Internet Media (published twice yearly).

Women's Wire Web Directory, Ellen Pack, Indianapolis, Indiana: Lycos Press/Que Corp., 1997.

World Wide Web Yellow Pages, Indianapolis, Indiana: New Riders Publishing/Que Corp. (annual).

Books for Cross-Cultural Networking

Different Games, Different Rules: Why Americans and Japanese Misunderstand Each Other, Haru Yamada, New York: Oxford University Press, 1997.

Doing Business in Latin America and the Caribbean, Lawrence Tuller, New York: AMACOM Books, 1993.

Do's and Taboos Around the World, Roger Axtell, New York: John Wiley & Sons, 1993.

Do's and Taboos Around the World for Women in Business, Roger Axtell, New York: John Wiley & Sons, 1997.

International Business Culture Series, Peggy Kenna and Sondra Lacy, Lincolnwood, Illinois: NTC Publishing Group. This series includes guides to doing business in many countries including France, Germany, Mexico, China, Japan, and others. Sample title: *Business China: A Practical Guide to Understanding Chinese Business Culture,* 1994.

Kiss, Bow, or Shake Hands: How to Do Business in Sixty Countries, Terri Morrison, Holbrook, Massachusetts: Bob Adams, Inc., 1994.

Passport to the World Series, World Trade Press. This series includes books on business etiquette, customs, and culture for many countries including Thailand, the Phillipines, India, Germany, and Italy. Sample title: *Passport India: Your Pocket Guide to Indian Business, Customs & Etiquette,* 1997.

World Chamber of Commerce Directory, Published by World Chamber of Commerce Directory, annual.

Resources for Developing or Expanding Your Network

Professional and Trade Association Directories

Encyclopedia of Associations, Gale Research Company, Gale Research (annual). This is the most comprehensive of all association directories, listing over 22,000 professional and trade associations and other nonprofit organizations in the United States. This encyclopedia is organized in three volumes, with one entire volume as a keyword/subject index. It is an essential networking resource.

NTPA: National Trade and Professional Associations of the United States, Columbia Books (annual). This is not as comprehensive as the *Encyclopedia of Associations,* but it is less cumbersome to use, as everything is in one volume. It includes most major associations for any field. Also useful is Columbia Books' *SRA: State and Regional Associations.*

Organized Obsessions: 1,001 Offbeat Associations, Fan Clubs, and Microsocieties You Can Join, Deborah Burek, Martin Connors, and Christa Brelin, Detroit, Michigan: Visible Ink Press, 1992.

Books and Directories Listing Companies

There are so many resources for identifying corporations which might become part of your networking efforts that a full listing is beyond the scope of this book. Your best bet is to consult a business librarian and search the Internet. Also, to find a directory of just about anything, consult *Directories in Print* published by Gale Research. It has 3,500 subject headings and lists over 15,000 directories.

In this section, I have listed the resources that are typically considered the most popular and helpful. Many of these are also available on CD-ROM or online. (Note that most of these directories are published annually, so publication dates have not been listed.)

The 100 Best Companies for Gay Men and Lesbians, Ed Mickens, New York: Pocket Books/Simon & Schuster, 1994.

Directory of Management Consultants, Kennedy Publications.

Dun & Bradstreet Million Dollar Directory, Dun & Bradstreet Information Services.

Hidden Job Market: a Guide to America's 2000 Little-Known Fastest Growing High-Tech Companies, Peterson's.

Hoover's Directory of Human Resources Executives, Reference Press, Inc.

Hoover's Handbook of American Businesses, Reference Press, Inc.

Hoover's Handbook of Emerging Companies, Reference Press, Inc.

Hoover's Masterlist of Major U.S. Companies, Reference Press, Inc.

The Job Bank Series, Bob Adams, Inc.

The Job Seeker's Guide to Socially Responsible Companies, Katherine Jankowski, Gale Research, Inc.

National Business Telephone Directory, Gale Research, Inc.

National Directory of Minority-Owned Business Firms, Gale Research, Inc.

National Directory of Women-Owned Business Firms, Gale Research, Inc.

Owners and Officers of Private Companies, Taft Group.

Peterson's Business and Management Jobs, Peterson's.

Polk's Directories, R. L. Polk & Co.

Standard & Poor's Register of Corporations, Directors and Executives, Standard & Poor's Corporation.

Standard Directory of Advertising Agencies, Reed Elsevier Publ.

Try Us 97: National Minority Business Directory, Try Us Resources, Inc.

Ward's Business Directory of U.S. Private and Public Companies, Gale Research, Inc.

Books and Directories for Nonprofit/Public Sector Careers

Community Jobs: ACCESS, Networking in the Public Interest—(212) 475-1001. This is a monthly newspaper with articles, organization profiles, and job listings for organizations in the nonprofit sector.

Good Works: A Guide to Careers in Social Change, Donna Colvin and Ralph Nader, New York: Barricade Books, 1994.

Fourth of July Guide to Careers, Internships, and Volunteer Opportunities in the Nonprofit Sector, Devon Cottrell Smith and Garrett Park, Maryland: Garrett Park Press, 1990.

Government Job Finder, Daniel Lauber, River Forest, Illinois: Planning/Communications, 1997.

Resources for Keeping Track of Your Network

Books

Clutter Control, Jeff Campbell, New York: Dell Publishing, 1992.

If You Haven't Got the Time to Do it Right, When Will You Find the Time to Do It Over? Jeffrey Mayer, New York: Simon & Schuster, 1991.

Organizing for the Creative Person, Dorothy Lehmkuhl and Dolores Cotter Lamping, New York: Crown Publishing, 1994.

The Original Internet Address Book, The Mesa Group, Englewood Cliffs, New Jersey: Prentice Hall, 1996 (Not a list of Internet addresses, but a blank book with spaces for you to write in your favorite Web sites, e-mail addresses, and other Internet information.)

Ready, Set, Organize! Pipi Campbell Peterson, Indianapolis, Indiana: JIST, 1996.

The Seven Habits of Highly Effective People, Steven Covey, New York: Simon & Schuster, 1989.

Computer Software

The following software packages contain contact management and organizing systems.

ClarisWorks

Corel Office Professional 8

Lotus SmartSuite

Microsoft Office

There are also individual programs that will assist you in networking (publishers are in parentheses; numbers indicating versions have been omitted since that information is highly subject to change).

1st Act (Symantec)

ACT! (Symantec)

Address Book for Windows (Parsons Technology)

Day-Timer Organizer (Day Timer)

ECCO PRO (Net Manage)

Filemaker Pro (Claris)

Lotus Organizer (Lotus)

Sidekick (Starfish Software)

There are also lots of programs that are designed primarily for salespeople or anyone keeping track of customers or clients. Two of these are the following:

Maximizer (Maximizer Technologies)

Turn Your Contacts into Gold (Goldmine)

Resources for Understanding Your "Networking Personality"

Beyond Shyness: How to Conquer Social Anxieties, Jonathan Berent and Amy Lemley, New York: Fireside/Simon & Schuster, 1994.

The Hidden Face of Shyness: Understanding and Overcoming Social Anxiety, Franklin Schneier and Lawrence Welkowitz, New York: Avon Books, 1996.

Myers-Briggs Type Indicator (MBTI), Consulting Psychologists Press.

The MBTI is the world's most widely used measure ("test") of personality style. Based on Jung's theories of personality and grounded in solid test construction methods and decades of research, the MBTI is a useful tool for understanding why you do the things you do in the way that you do them. The MBTI can be administered only by qualified specialists (typically career counselors, human resources specialists, management

consultants, training specialists, and psychotherapists, among others) and should be accompanied by a thorough explanation of your results and adequate counseling to apply the results to your career and personal goals. Taking the MBTI can help you understand how your personality type affects your networking style.

Shyness: What It Is, What to Do About It, Philip Zimbardo, Reading, Massachusetts: Addison-Wesley, 1990.

There are several good books that discuss personality type or the MBTI specifically. They include the following:

Do What You Are, Paul Tieger and Barbara Barron-Tieger, New York: Little, Brown, 1995.

Gifts Differing, Isabel Briggs Myers and Peter Myers, Palo Alto, California: Consulting Psychologists Press, 1995.

Please Understand Me, David Keirsey and Marilyn Bates, Del Mar, California: Prometheus Nemesis Book Co., 1984.

Type Talk at Work, Otto Kroeger and Janet Thuesen, New York: Dell Publishing, 1994.

Books on Business Etiquette and Protocol

At Ease Professionally: An Etiquette Guide for the Business Arena, Hilka Klinkenberg, Chicago: Bonus Books, 1992.

Business and Social Etiquette with Disabled People: A Guide to Getting Along with Persons Who Have Impairments of Mobility, Vision, Hearing or Speech, Chalda Maloff and Susan MacDuff Wood, Springfield, Illinois: Charles C. Thomas Publ. Ltd., 1988.

Business Etiquette in Brief, Anne Marie Sabath,

Holbrook, Massachusetts: Bob Adams, Inc., 1993.

Complete Business Etiquette Handbook, Barbara Pachter, Marjorie Brody, and Betsy Anderson, Englewood Cliffs, New Jersey: Prentice Hall, 1994.

Don't Slurp Your Soup: A Basic Guide to Business Etiquette, Elizabeth Craig and Betty Craig, St. Paul, Minnesota: Brighton Publications, 1996.

Letitia Baldrige's New Complete Guide to Executive Manners, Letitia Baldrige, New York: Scribner, 1993.

The Polished Professional, Elizabeth Haas Fountain, Hawthorne, New Jersey: Career Press, 1994.

Books on Image, Attire, and Self-Presentation

110 Mistakes Working Women Make and How to Avoid Them: Dressing Smart in the '90s, Joanna Nicholson, Manassas Park, Virginia: Impact Publications, 1994.

Cindy Crawford's Basic Face: A Makeup Workbook, Cindy Crawford. New York: Broadway Books, 1996.

Color Me Beautiful's Looking Your Best: Color, Makeup, and Style, Mary Spillane and Christine Sherlock, Lanham, Maryland: Madison Books, 1995.

Fabulous You! Unlock Your Perfect Personal Style, Tori Hartman, New York: Berkley Publishing Group, 1995

Getting What You Want by Being Who You Are: You Are the Message, Roger Ailes, New York: Doubleday, 1995.

John T. Molloy's New Dress for Success, John T. Molloy, New York: Warner Books, 1995.

Mistakes Men Make That Women Hate: 101 Image Tips for Men, Kenneth Karpinski, Park, Virginia: Impact Publications, 1994.

The New Professional Image: From Corporate Casual to the Ultimate Power Look, Susan Bixler and Nancy Nix-Rice, Holbrook, Massachusetts: Adams Media, 1997.

New Women's Dress for Success, John T. Molloy, New York: Warner Books, 1996.

Women of Color: The Multicultural Guide to Fashion and Beauty, Darlene Mathis, New York: Ballantine Books, 1994.

Work Clothes: Casual Dress for Serious Work, Kim Johnson Gross, New York: Knopf, 1996.

Books on Voice, Speech, and Making Conversation

The Articulate Executive: Learn to Look, Act, and Sound Like a Leader, Granville N. Toogood, New York: McGraw-Hill, 1997.

Basics of Oral Communication: Skills for Career and Personal Growth, Paul R. Timm, Cincinnati, Ohio: South-Western Pub., 1992.

Do's and Taboos of Public Speaking: How to Get Those Butterflies Flying in Formation, Roger Axtell and Mike Fornwald, New York: John Wiley & Sons, 1992.

High Impact Public Speaking for Business and the Professions, Regis O'Connor, Lincolnwood, Illinois: NTC Publishing Group, 1997.

How to Give a Terrific Presentation, Karen Kalish, New York: AMACOM, 1997.

How to Say It Best: Choice Words, Phrases, and Model Speeches for Every Occasion, Jack Griffin, Englewood Cliffs, New Jersey: Prentice Hall, 1994.

Managing Your Mouth, Robert Genua, New York: AMACOM, 1993.

Speak Now or Forever Fall to Pieces, Thomas K. Mira, New York: Princeton Review/ Random House, 1995.

Telephone Skills from A to Z, Nancy J. Friedman, Menlo Park, California: Crisp Publications, 1995.

Using the Telephone More Effectively, Madeline Bodin, Hauppage, New York: Barrons Educational Series, 1997.

What Do I Say Now? Talking Your Way to Business and Social Success, Susan Roane, New York: Warner Books, 1997.

Winning Telephone Tips: 30 Fast and Profitable Tips for Making the Best Use of Your Phone, Paul R. Timm, Hawthorne, New Jersey: Career Press, 1997.

Books on Written Communication

The 100 Most Difficult Business Letters You'll Ever Have to Write, Fax, or E-Mail, Bernard Heller, New York: HarperCollins, 1994.

Better Business Writing: Techniques for Improving Correspondence, Susan Brock, Menlo Park, California: Crisp Publications, 1991.

Business Letters for Busy People, Jim Dugger, Hawthorne, New Jersey: Career Press, 1995.

Cover Letters (Job Notes Series), Michelle Tullier, New York: Princeton Review/ Random House, 1997.

How to Write Better Business Letters, Andrea Geffner, Hauppage, New York: Barrons Educational Series, 1995.

The Perfect Memo!, Patricia Westheimer, Indianapolis, Indiana: JIST, 1995.

Vest Pocket Guide to Business Writing, Deborah Dumaine, Englewood Cliffs, New Jersey: Prentice Hall, 1997.

Resources for Entrepreneurs, Consultants, etc.

Books

The Complete Guide to Being an Independent Contractor, Herman Holtz, Chicago: Upstart Publishing, 1995.

The Do-It-Yourself Business Promotions Kit, Jack Griffin, Englewood Cliffs, New Jersey: Prentice-Hall, 1995.

The Frugal Entrepreneur: Creative Ways to Save Time, Energy & Money in Your Business, Terri Lonier. New Paltz, New York: Portico Press, 1996.

Going Indie, Kathi Elster and Katherine Crowley, New York: Kaplan, 1997.

Guerilla Marketing for the Home-Based Business, Jay Conrad Levinson, New York: Houghton Mifflin, 1995.

How to Succeed on Your Own, Karin Abarbanel, New York: Henry Holt & Co., 1994.

How to Think Like an Entrepreneur, Michael Shane, New York: Brett Publishing, 1994.

Mind Your Own Business, LaVerne Ludden, Indianapolis, Indiana: JIST, 1994.

Successfully Self-Employed, Gregory Brennan, Chicago: Upstart Publishing, 1996.

Working from Home, Paul & Sarah Edwards, New York: Putnam Publishing, 1994.

Working Solo, Terri Lonier, New Paltz, New York: Portico Press, 1994.

Working Solo Sourcebook, Terri Lonier, New Paltz, New York: Portico Press, 1995.

Interesting Books for Networkers with a Scholarly Bent

Composing a Life, Mary Catherine Bateson, New York: Plume/Penguin, 1989.

Conflict & The Web of Group Affiliations, Georg Simmel, New York: Macmillan, 1955.

The Cult of Information, Theodore Roszak, Berkeley, California: University of California Press, 1994.

The Great Good Place: Cafes, Coffee Shops, Community Centers, Beauty Parlors, General Stores, Bars, Hangouts & How They Get You Through the Day, Ray Oldenburg, New York: Marlowe & Co., 1997.

A New Outline of Social Psychology, Martin Gold, Washington, DC: American Psychological Association, 1997.

Our Kind: Who We Are, Where We Came From, and Where We Are Going—The Evolution of Human Life and Culture, Marvin Harris, New York: Harperperennial, 1989.

The Pursuit of Loneliness, Philip Slater, Boston: Beacon Press, 1976.

The Roots of Coincidence, Arthur Koestler, New York: Random House, 1974.

The Social Animal, Elliot Aronson, Salt Lake City, Utah: W. H. Freeman & Co., 1994.

Where to Find These Resources and More

Bookstores. Most of the books listed in this appendix can be found in the career, business, or how-to/self-help section of any bookstore.

Libraries. Most directories that list companies, professional associations, and other organizations are not readily available in bookstores. They can be found in the reference or business section of most public and university libraries, as well as on CD-ROM and the World Wide Web in many cases. (Even if they were in bookstores, you would probably not want to purchase them because they can cost as much as several hundred dollars.)

Some branches of the pubic library have extensive career resource collections containing books on career planning, job search, and occupational information, among other resources.

If you are currently a college or graduate student or an alum with access to your alma mater, find out if your campus career counseling or placement office has a career resource library.

Catalogs. One of the best-kept secrets career counselors have is the catalogs we receive that list books, software, and videos on career, job search, and personal growth topics. Most of these companies are happy to sell their products to people outside the career development profession, so you might want to get on their mailing lists. Here's a sampling of catalogs from companies that sell books of many different publishers.

The Whole Work Catalog. Available from The New Careers Center.
>   (800) 634-9024 tel
>   (303) 447-8684 fax

Career Development Resources. Available from Career Research & Testing, Inc.
>   (800) 888-4945 tel
>   (408) 559-4945 tel
>   (408) 559-8211 fax

Garrett Park Press. Available from Garrett Park Press.
>   (301) 946-2553 tel

Jobs and Careers for the 1990s. Available from Impact Publications.
>   (703) 361-7300 tel
>   (703) 335-9486 fax

JIST 1997 Resource Directory. Available from JIST Works, Inc.
>   (800) 648-5478 tel
>   (800) 547-8329 fax

Online. Those who love books will find it hard to tear themselves away from the computer once they discover the Web site billed as "Earth's Biggest Bookstore"—Amazon.com books. Located at www.amazon.com, this online bookstore lists over 2.5 million titles in its catalog. You can search by author, title, subject, or ISBN number to find any type of book you're looking for, often with a synopsis of the book, reviews by other readers, and information on the author. If it exists, Amazon probably has it! Amazon has an easy ordering system and provides great customer service.

Computer Stores. Most of the software listed in this bibliography is available in any of the computer product and office supply superstores like CompUSA, ComputerLand, Staples, and many others, as well as in some bookstores.

Index

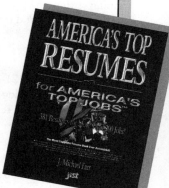